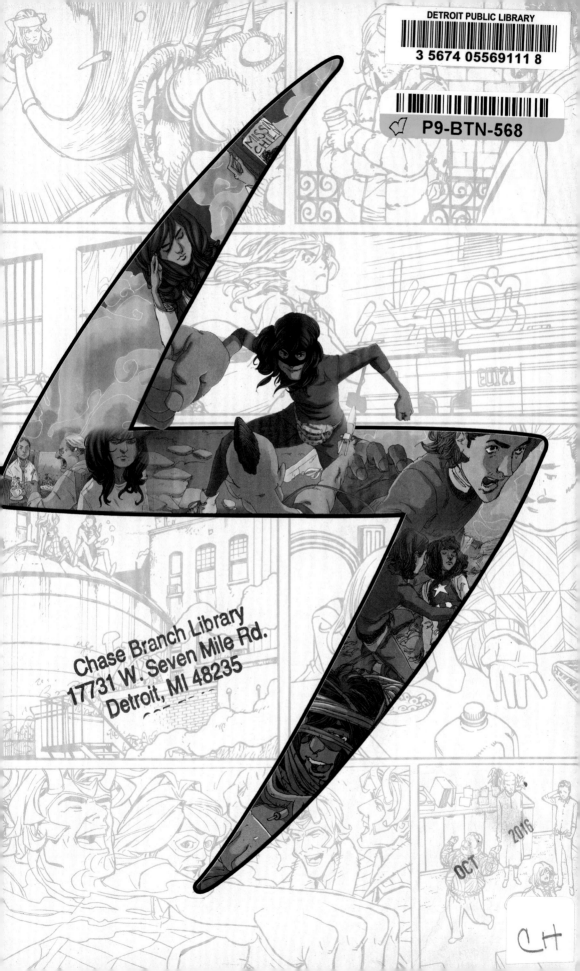

MS. MARVEL VOL. 3: CRUSHED. Contains material originally published in magazine form as MS. MARVEL #12-15 and S.H.I.E.L.D. #2. First printing 2015. ISBN# 978-0-7851-9227-5. Published by MARVEL WORLDWIDE, INC., a subsidiary of MARVEL ENTERTAINMENT, LLC. OFFICE OF PUBLICATION: 135 West 50th Street, New York, NY 10020. Copyright © 2015 MARVEL No similarity between any of the names, characters, persons, and/or institutions in this magazine with those of any living or dead person or institution is intended, and any such similarity which may exist is purely coincidental. **Printed in Canada.** ALAN FINE, President, Marvel Entertainment; DAN BUCKLEY, President, TV, Publishing and Brand Management; JOE QUESADA, Chief Creative Officer; TOM BREVOORT, SVP of Publishing; DAVID BOGART, SVP of Operations & Procurement, Publishing; C.B. CEBULSKI, VP of International Development & Brand Management; DAVID GABRIEL, SVP Print, Sales & Marketing; JIM O'KEEFE, VP of Operations & Logistics; DAN CARR, Executive Director of Publishing Technology; SUSAN CRESPI, Editorial Operations Manager; ALEX MORALES, Publishing Operations Manager; STAN LEE, Chairman Emeritus. For information regarding advertising in Marvel Comics or on Marvel.com, please contact Jonathan Rheingold, VP of Custom Solutions & Ad Sales, at jrheingold@marvel.com. For Marvel subscription inquiries, please call 800-217-9158. **Manufactured between 4/17/2015 and 5/25/2015 by SOLISCO PRINTERS, SCOTT, QC, CANADA.**

10 9 8 7 6 5 4 3 2 1

MS. MARVEL

writer
G. WILLOW WILSON

artists
ELMO BONDOC (#12) &
TAKESHI MIYAZAWA (#13-15)

color artist
IAN HERRING WITH IRMA KNIIVILA (#13)

letterer
VC'S JOE CARAMAGNA

cover art
KRIS ANKA (#12 & #15), **MARGUERITE SAUVAGE** (#13)
& JAKE WYATT (#14)

assistant editors
CHARLES BEACHAM & DEVIN LEWIS

editor
SANA AMANAT

senior editor
NICK LOWE

S.H.I.E.L.D. #2
writer **MARK WAID**
penciler **HUMBERTO RAMOS**
inker **VICTOR OLAZABA**
colorist **EDGAR DELGADO**
letterer **VC'S JOE CARAMAGNA**
cover art **JULIAN TOTINO TEDESCO**
assistant editor **JON MOISAN**
editors **TOM BREVOORT** with **ELLIE PYLE**

collection editor
JENNIFER GRÜNWALD
assistant editor
SARAH BRUNSTAD
associate managing editor
ALEX STARBUCK
editor, special projects
MARK D. BEAZLEY
senior editor, special projects
JEFF YOUNGQUIST
svp print, sales & marketing
DAVID GABRIEL

editor in chief
AXEL ALONSO
chief creative officer
JOE QUESADA
publisher
DAN BUCKLEY
executive producer
ALAN FINE

PREVIOUSLY

AFTER A STRANGE TERRIGEN MIST DESCENDED UPON JERSEY CITY,
KAMALA KHAN GOT POLYMORPH POWERS AND BECAME THE ALL-NEW...

MS.MARVEL

WITH STRICT PARENTS ON HER CASE, HER BEST FRIEND BRUNO BY HER
SIDE AND A WHOLE LOT OF WEIRD ENSNARING JERSEY CITY EVERY DAY,
KAMALA SOON REALIZED THAT BEING A SUPER HERO IS...COMPLICATED.

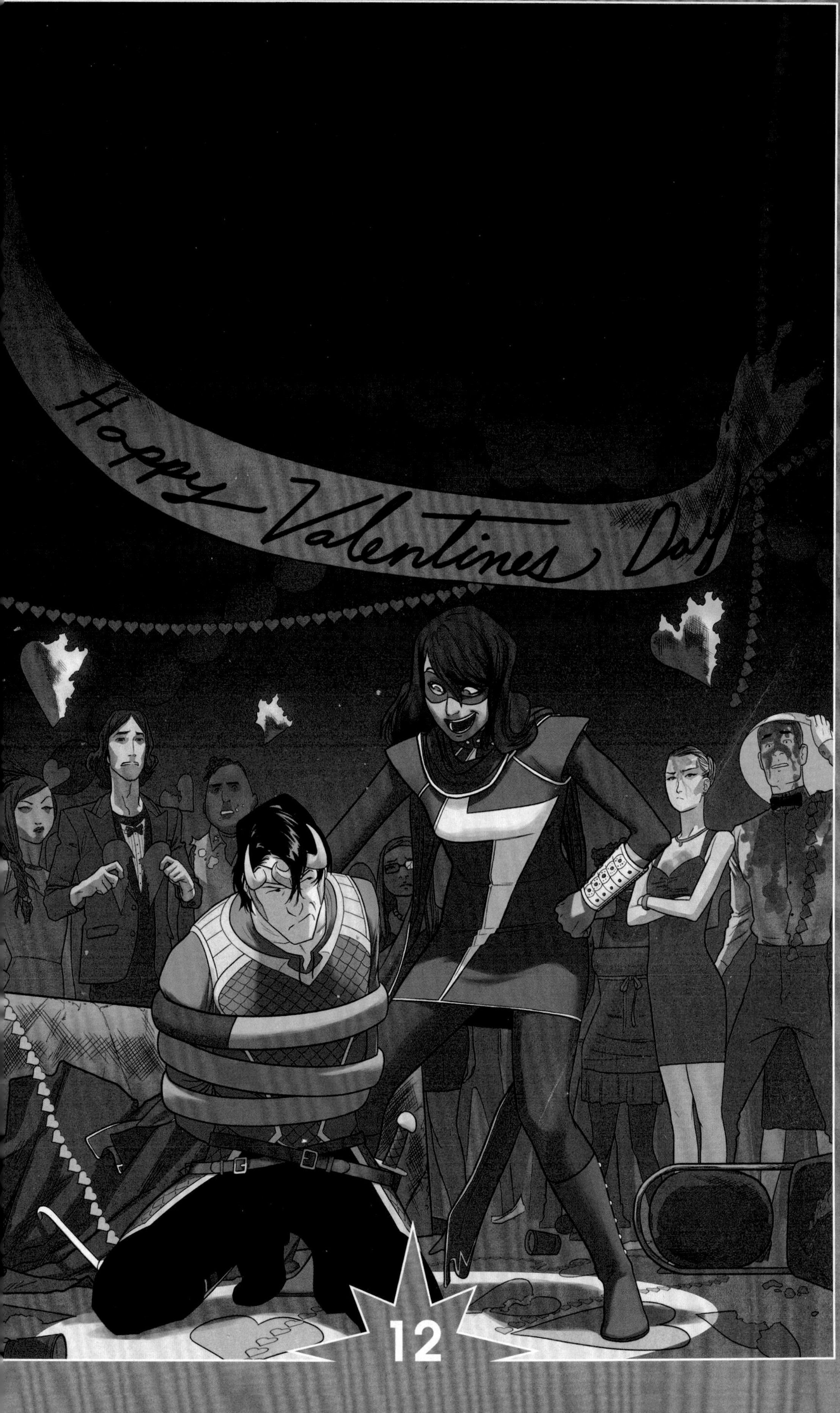
Happy Valentines Day
12

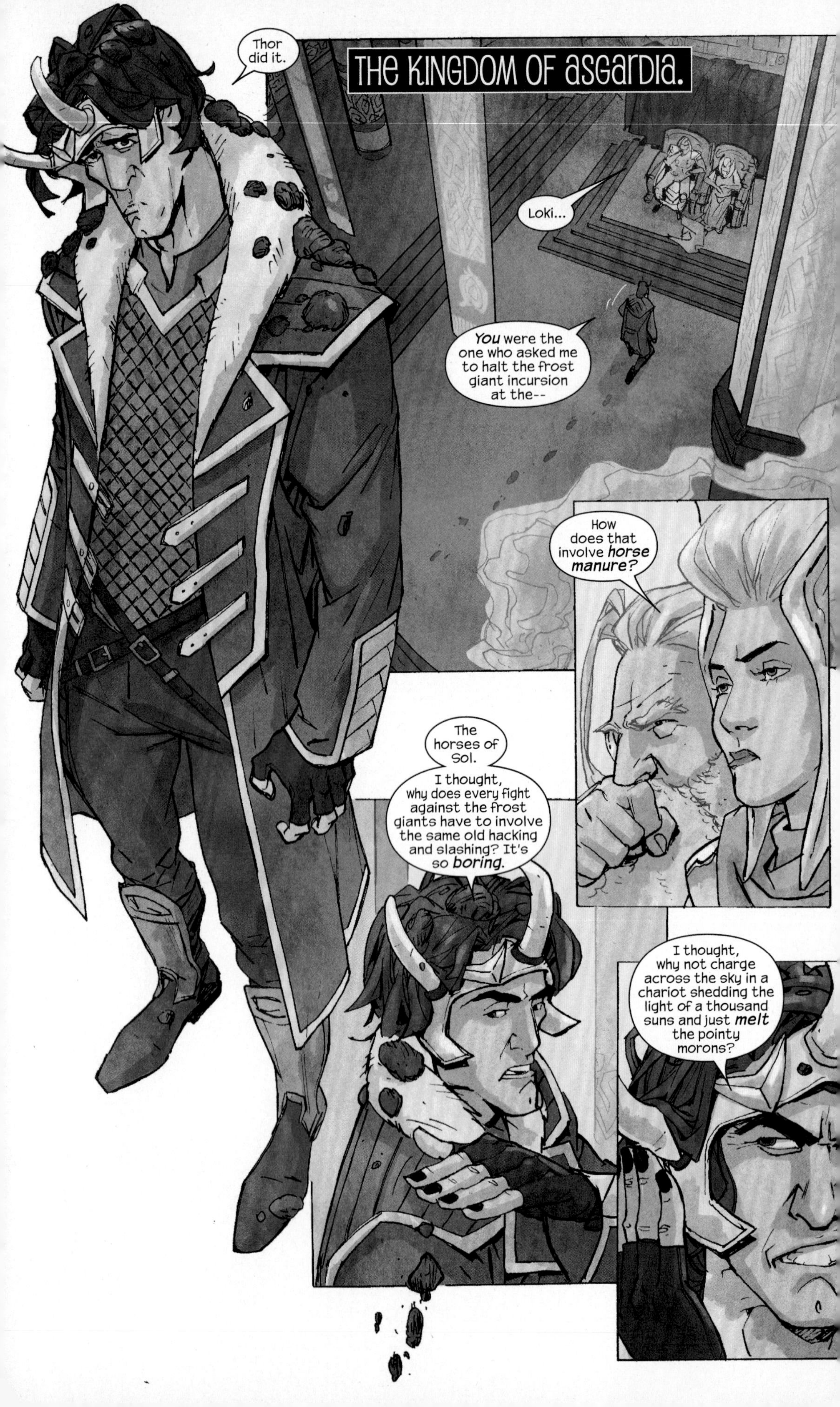
Thor did it.
THE KINGDOM OF ASGARDIA.
Loki...
You were the one who asked me to halt the frost giant incursion at the--
How does that involve ***horse manure?***
The horses of Sol.
I thought, why does every fight against the frost giants have to involve the same old hacking and slashing? It's so ***boring***.
I thought, why not charge across the sky in a chariot shedding the light of a thousand suns and just ***melt*** the pointy morons?

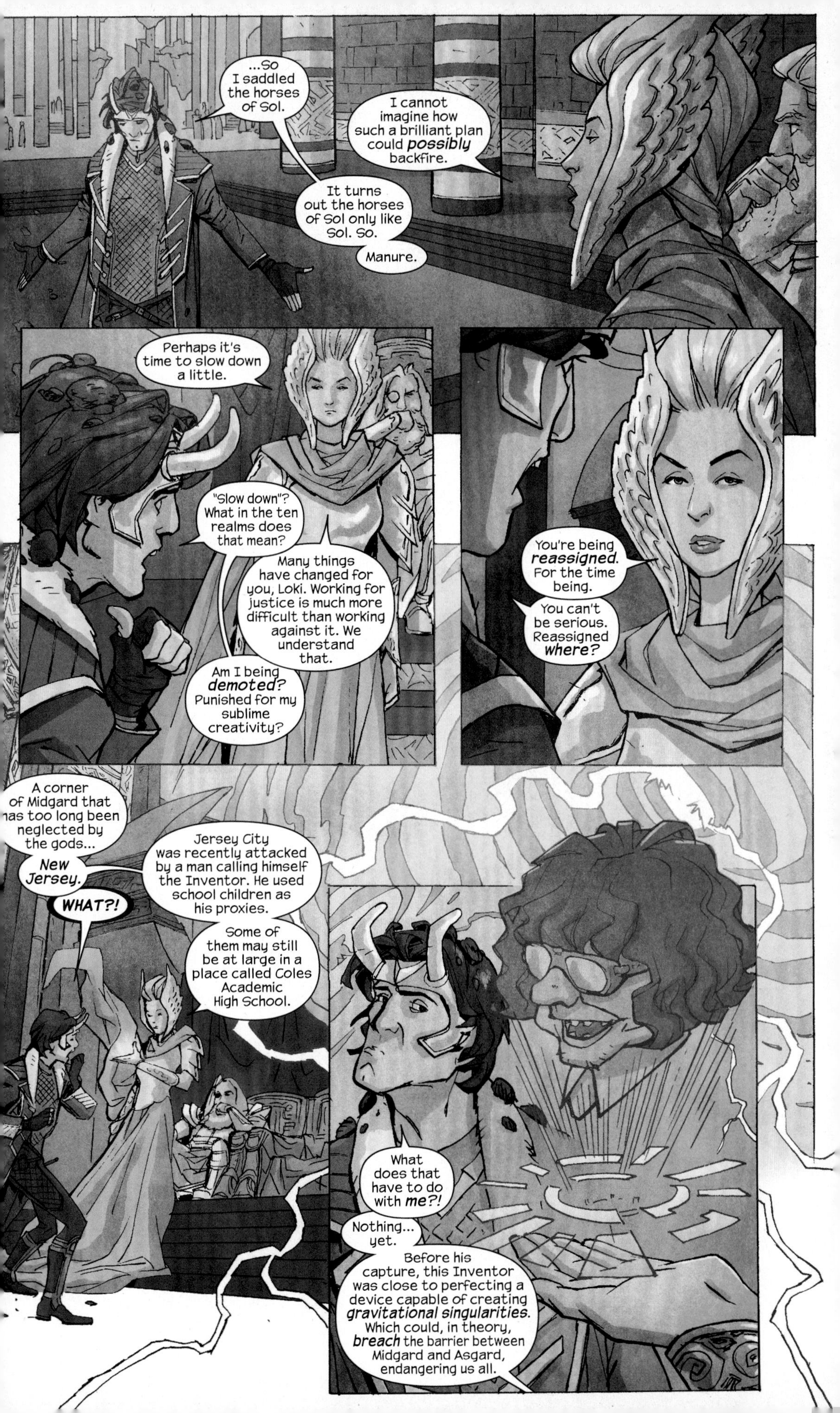
...So I saddled the horses of Sol.
I cannot imagine how such a brilliant plan could possibly backfire.
It turns out the horses of Sol only like Sol. So.
Manure.
Perhaps it's time to slow down a little.
"Slow down"? What in the ten realms does that mean?
Many things have changed for you, Loki. Working for justice is much more difficult than working against it. We understand that.
Am I being demoted? Punished for my sublime creativity?
You're being reassigned. For the time being.
You can't be serious. Reassigned where?
A corner of Midgard that has too long been neglected by the gods...
New Jersey.
WHAT?!
Jersey City was recently attacked by a man calling himself the Inventor. He used school children as his proxies.
Some of them may still be at large in a place called Coles Academic High School.
What does that have to do with me?!
Nothing... yet.
Before his capture, this Inventor was close to perfecting a device capable of creating gravitational singularities. Which could, in theory, breach the barrier between Midgard and Asgard, endangering us all.

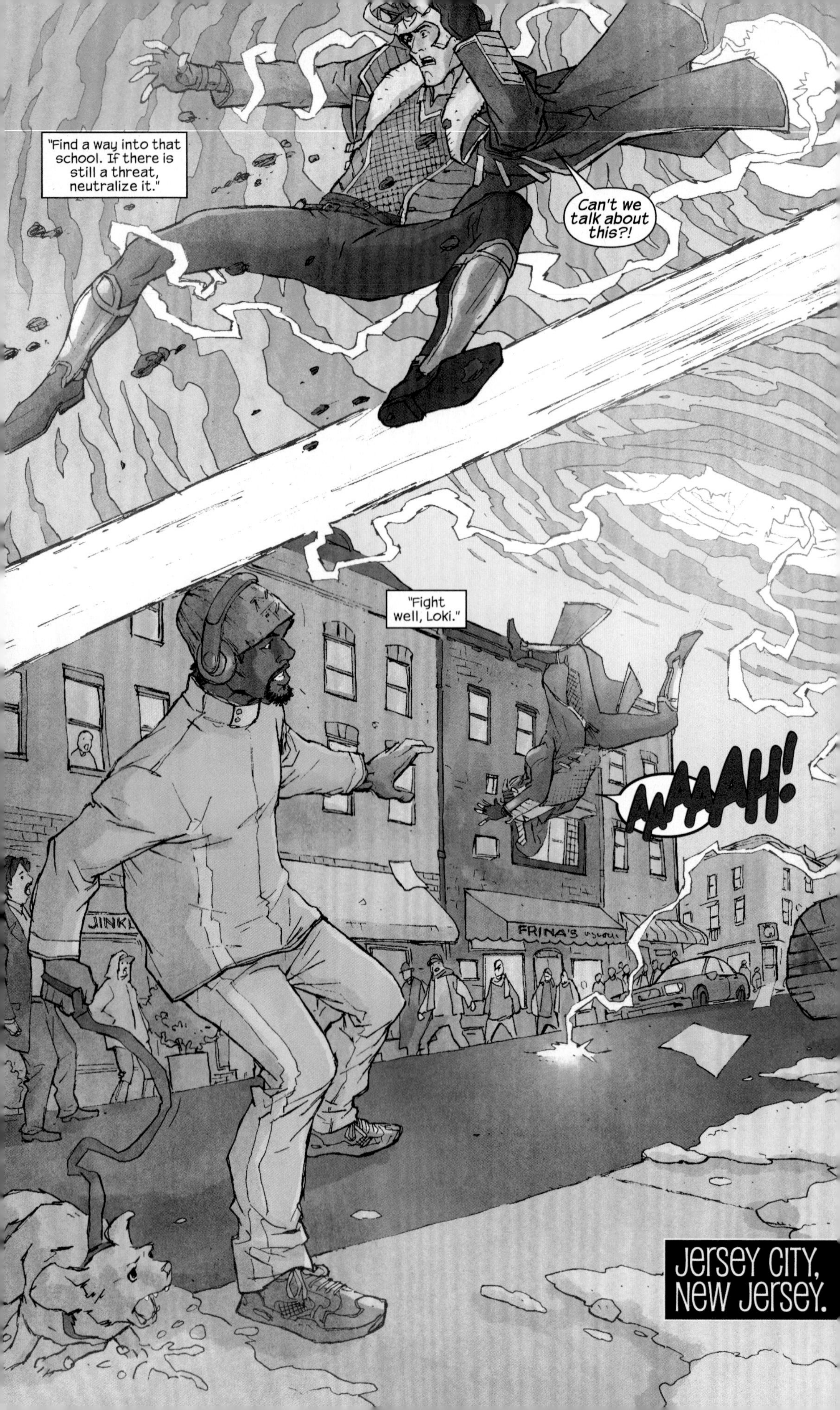
"Find a way into that school. If there is still a threat, neutralize it."
Can't we talk about this?!
"Fight well, Loki."
AAAAH!
Jersey City, New Jersey.

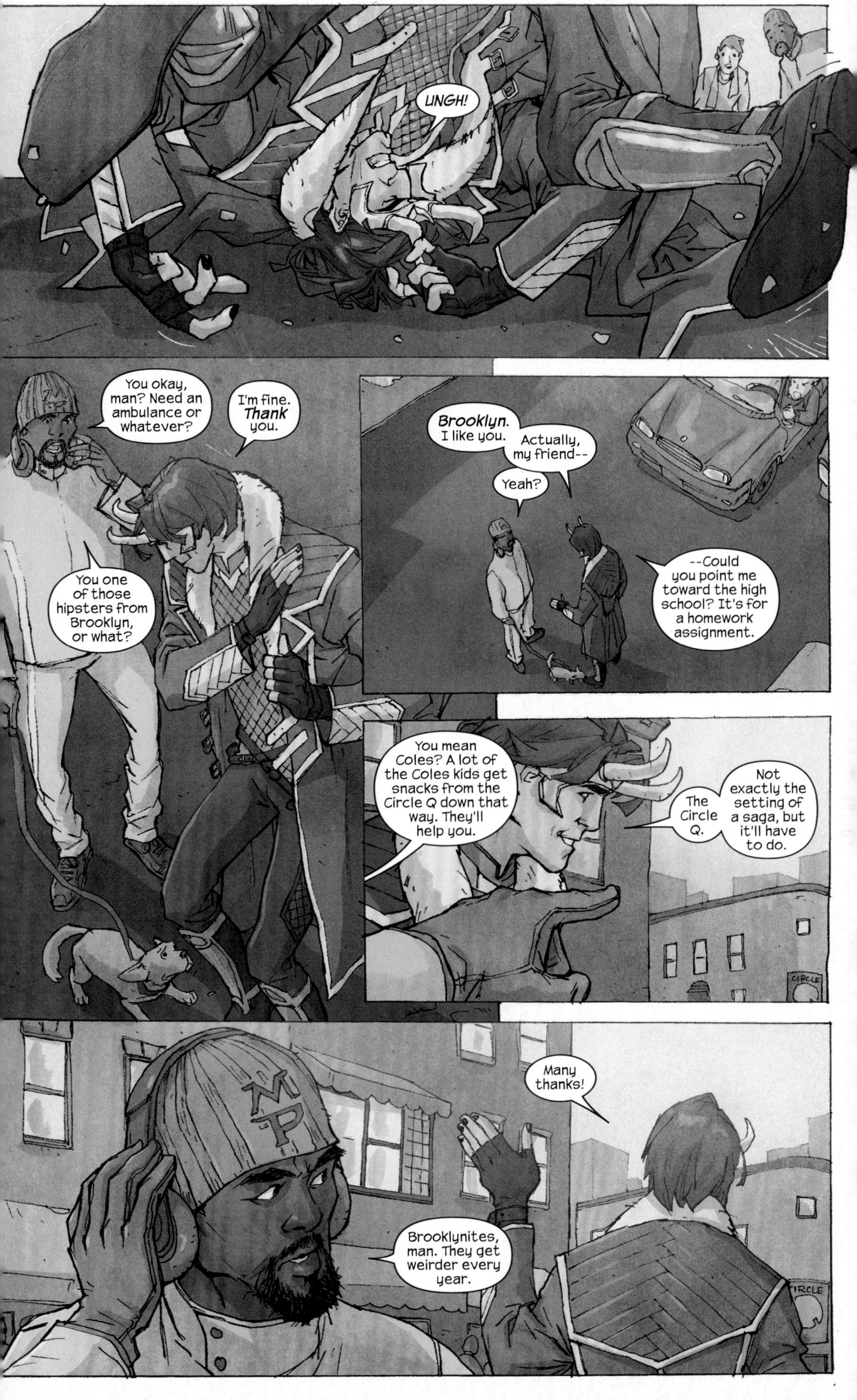

UNGH!
You okay, man? Need an ambulance or whatever?
I'm fine. *Thank* you.
You one of those hipsters from Brooklyn, or what?
Brooklyn. I like you.
Actually, my friend--
Yeah?
--Could you point me toward the high school? It's for a homework assignment.
You mean Coles? A lot of the Coles kids get snacks from the Circle Q down that way. They'll help you.
The Circle Q.
Not exactly the setting of a saga, but it'll have to do.
CIRCLE
Many thanks!
Brooklynites, man. They get weirder every year.
CIRCLE

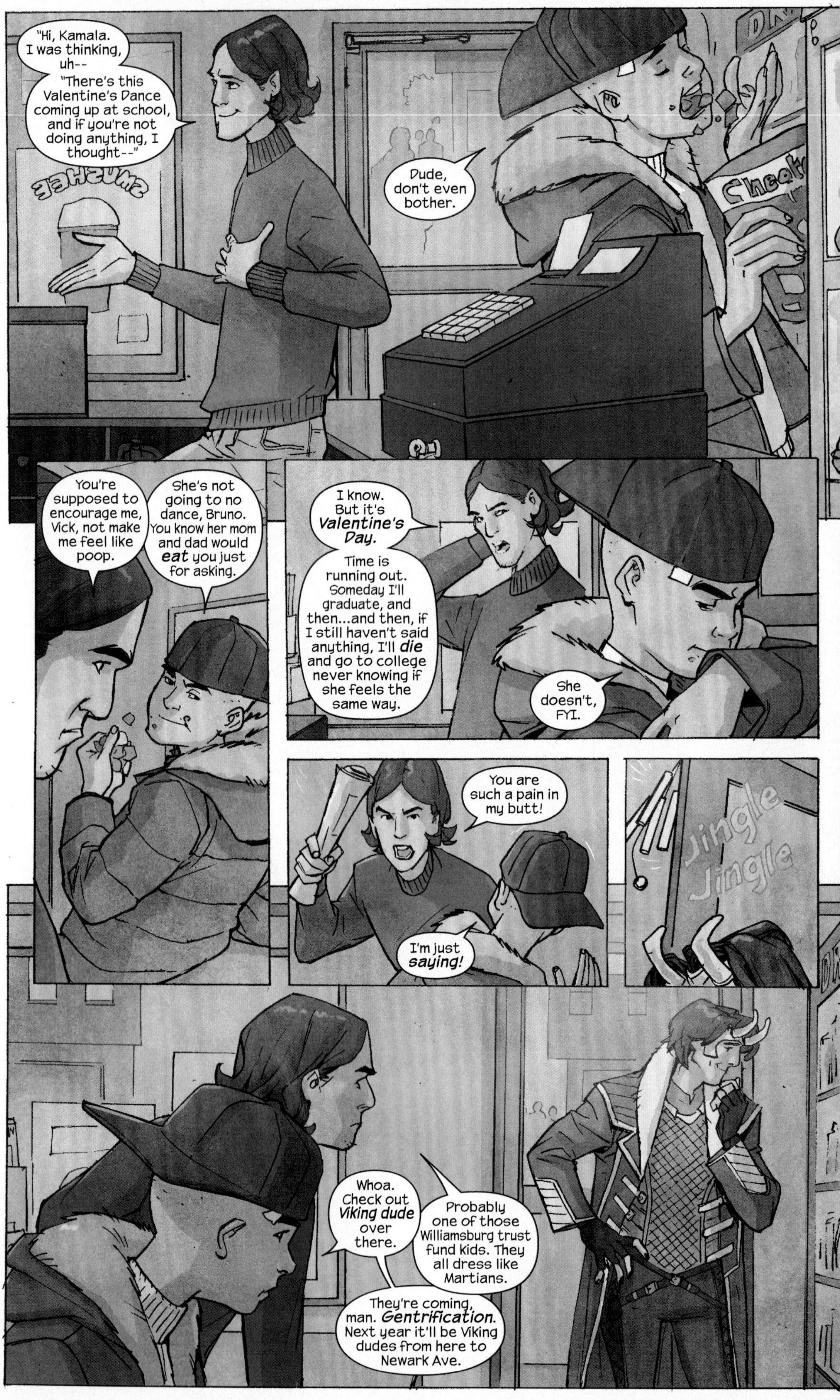
"Hi, Kamala. I was thinking, uh-- "There's this Valentine's Dance coming up at school, and if you're not doing anything, I thought--"
Dude, don't even bother.
You're supposed to encourage me, Vick, not make me feel like poop.
She's not going to no dance, Bruno. You know her mom and dad would *eat* you just for asking.
I know. But it's *Valentine's Day.*
Time is running out. Someday I'll graduate, and then...and then, if I still haven't said anything, I'll *die* and go to college never knowing if she feels the same way.
She doesn't, FYI.
You are such a pain in my butt!
I'm just *saying!*
Jingle Jingle
Whoa. Check out *Viking dude* over there.
Probably one of those Williamsburg trust fund kids. They all dress like Martians.
They're coming, man. *Gentrification.* Next year it'll be Viking dudes from here to Newark Ave.

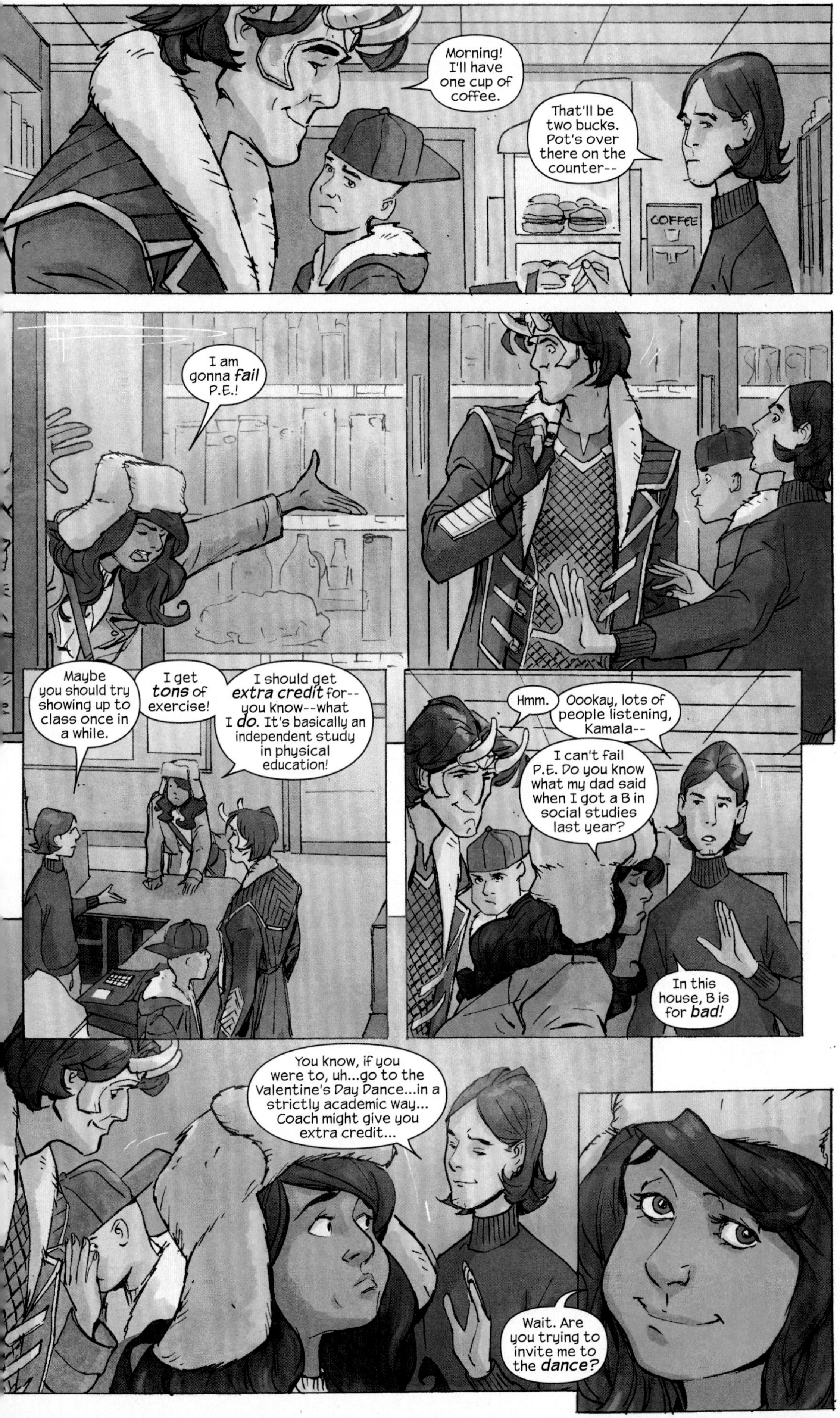
Morning! I'll have one cup of coffee.
That'll be two bucks. Pot's over there on the counter--
COFFEE
I am gonna *fail* P.E.!
Maybe you should try showing up to class once in a while.
I get *tons* of exercise!
I should get *extra credit* for-- you know--what I *do*. It's basically an independent study in physical education!
Hmm.
Oookay, lots of people listening, Kamala--
I can't fail P.E. Do you know what my dad said when I got a B in social studies last year?
In this house, B is for *bad!*
You know, if you were to, uh...go to the Valentine's Day Dance...in a strictly academic way... Coach might give you extra credit...
Wait. Are you trying to invite me to the *dance?*

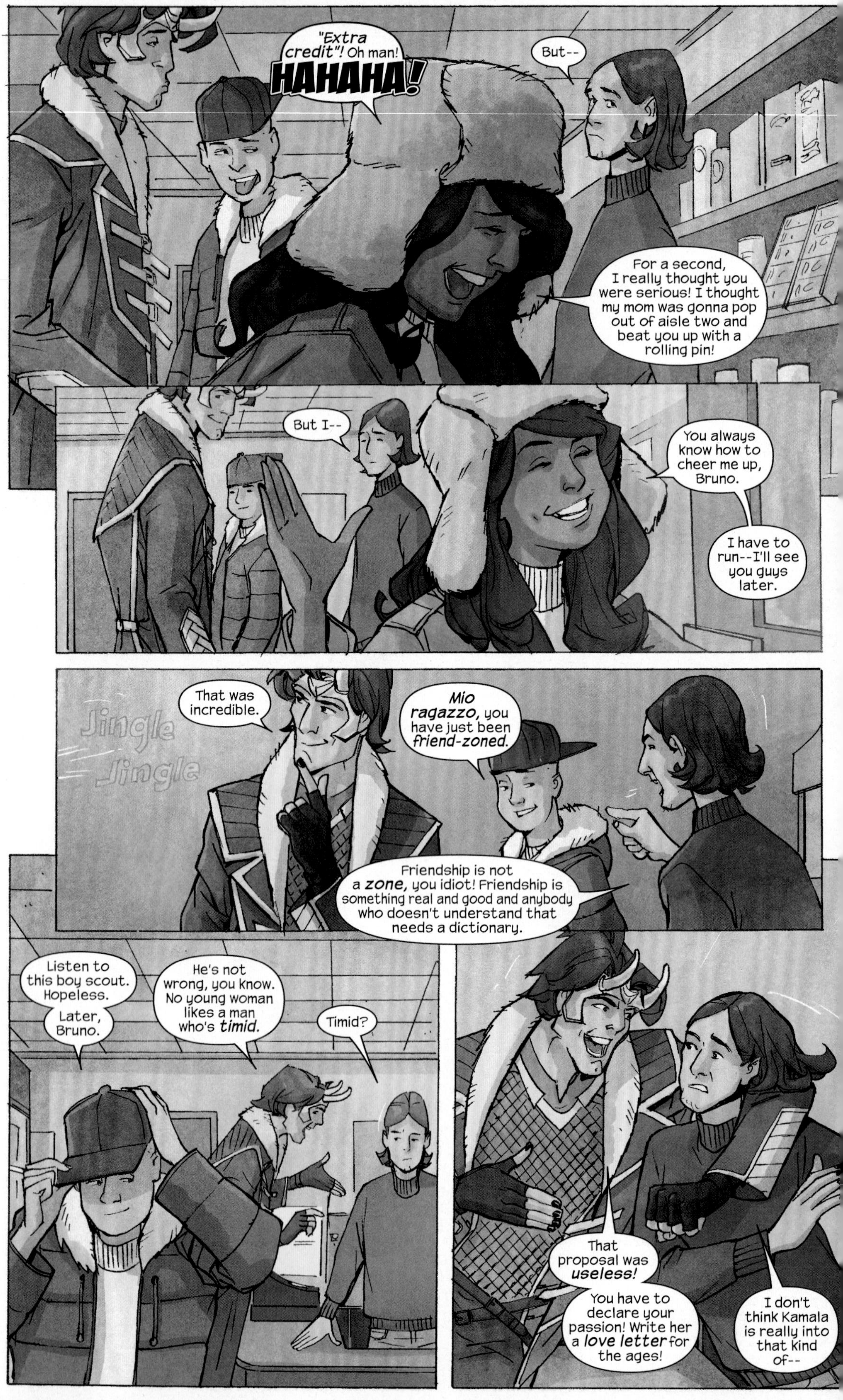

"Extra credit"! Oh man!
HAHAHA!
But--
For a second, I really thought you were serious! I thought my mom was gonna pop out of aisle two and beat you up with a rolling pin!
But I--
You always know how to cheer me up, Bruno.
I have to run--I'll see you guys later.
Jingle Jingle
That was incredible.
Mio ragazzo, you have just been *friend-zoned*.
Friendship is not a *zone*, you idiot! Friendship is something real and good and anybody who doesn't understand that needs a dictionary.
Listen to this boy scout. Hopeless.
Later, Bruno.
He's not wrong, you know. No young woman likes a man who's *timid*.
Timid?
That proposal was *useless!*
You have to declare your passion! Write her a *love letter* for the ages!
I don't think Kamala is really into that kind of--

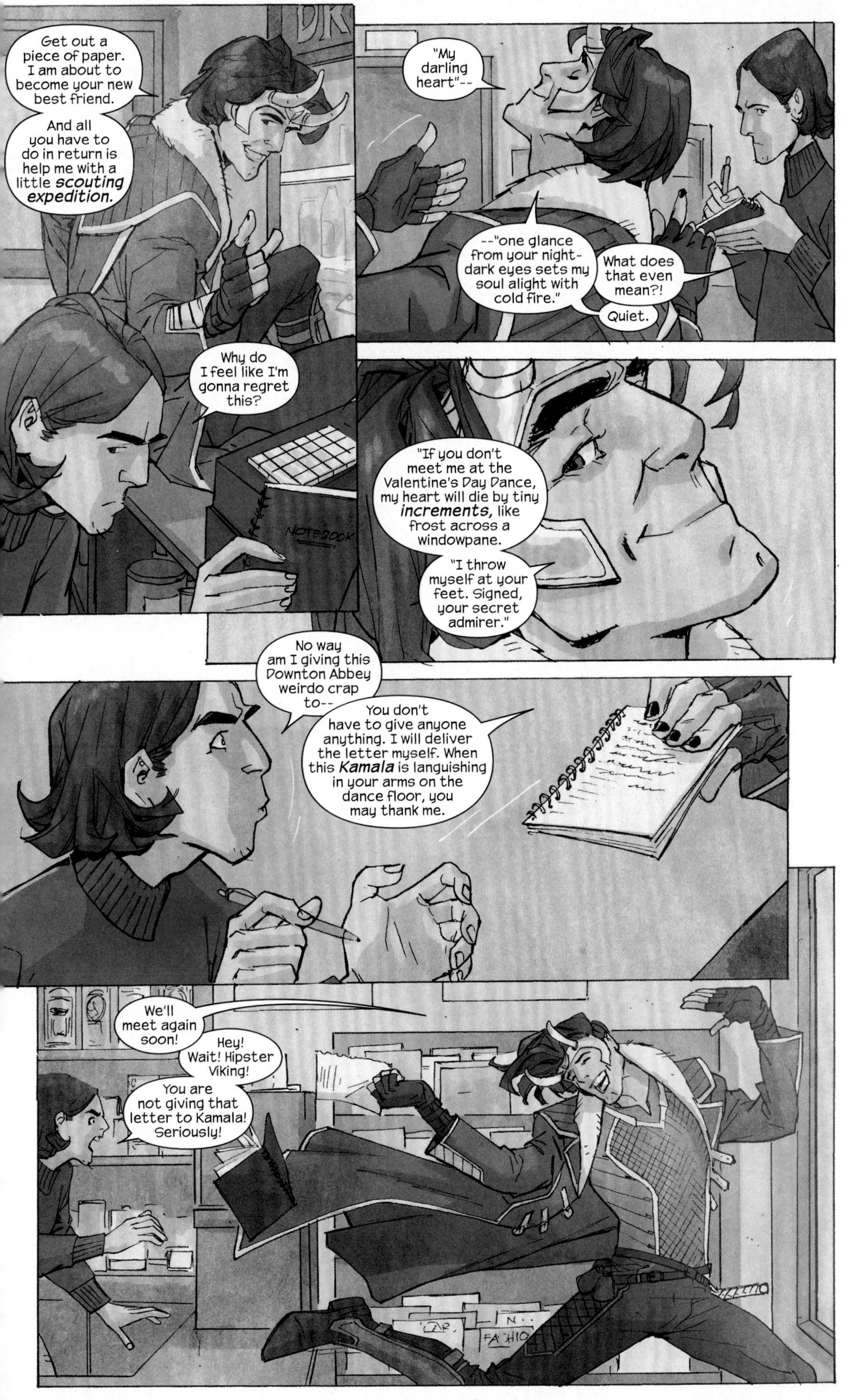
Get out a piece of paper. I am about to become your new best friend.
And all you have to do in return is help me with a little *scouting expedition.*
Why do I feel like I'm gonna regret this?
NOTEBOOK
"My darling heart"--
--"one glance from your night-dark eyes sets my soul alight with cold fire."
What does that even mean?!
Quiet.
"If you don't meet me at the Valentine's Day Dance, my heart will die by tiny *increments,* like frost across a windowpane.
"I throw myself at your feet. Signed, your secret admirer."
No way am I giving this Downton Abbey weirdo crap to--
You don't have to give anyone anything. I will deliver the letter myself. When this *Kamala* is languishing in your arms on the dance floor, you may thank me.
We'll meet again soon!
Hey! Wait! Hipster Viking!
You are not giving that letter to Kamala! Seriously!

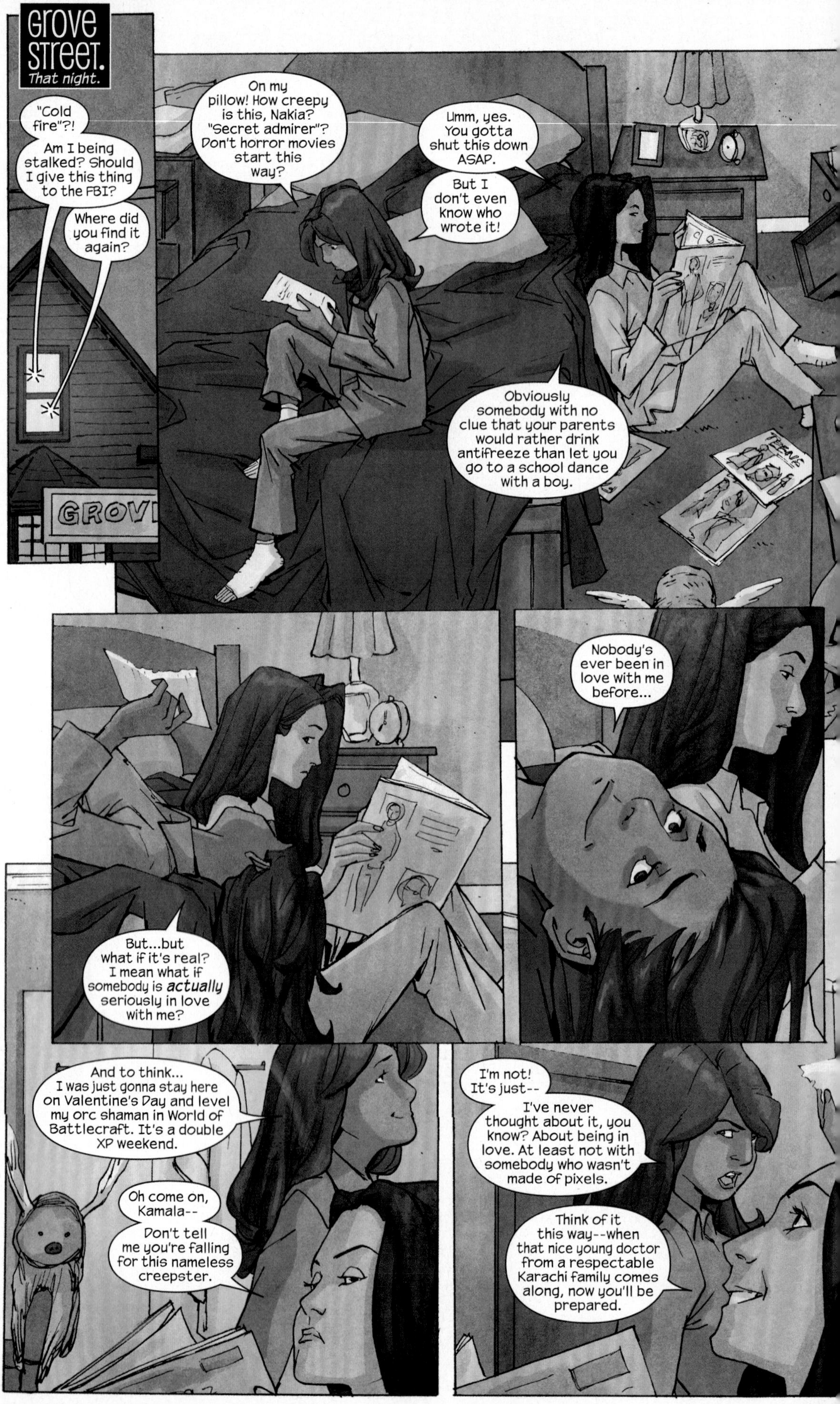

Grove Street. That night.
"Cold fire"?!
Am I being stalked? Should I give this thing to the FBI?
Where did you find it again?
GROV
On my pillow! How creepy is this, Nakia? "Secret admirer"? Don't horror movies start this way?
Umm, yes. You gotta shut this down ASAP.
But I don't even know who wrote it!
Obviously somebody with no clue that your parents would rather drink antifreeze than let you go to a school dance with a boy.
But...but what if it's real? I mean what if somebody is *actually* seriously in love with me?
Nobody's ever been in love with me before...
And to think... I was just gonna stay here on Valentine's Day and level my orc shaman in World of Battlecraft. It's a double XP weekend.
Oh come on, Kamala--
Don't tell me you're falling for this nameless creepster.
I'm not! It's just--
I've never thought about it, you know? About being in love. At least not with somebody who wasn't made of pixels.
Think of it this way--when that nice young doctor from a respectable Karachi family comes along, now you'll be prepared.

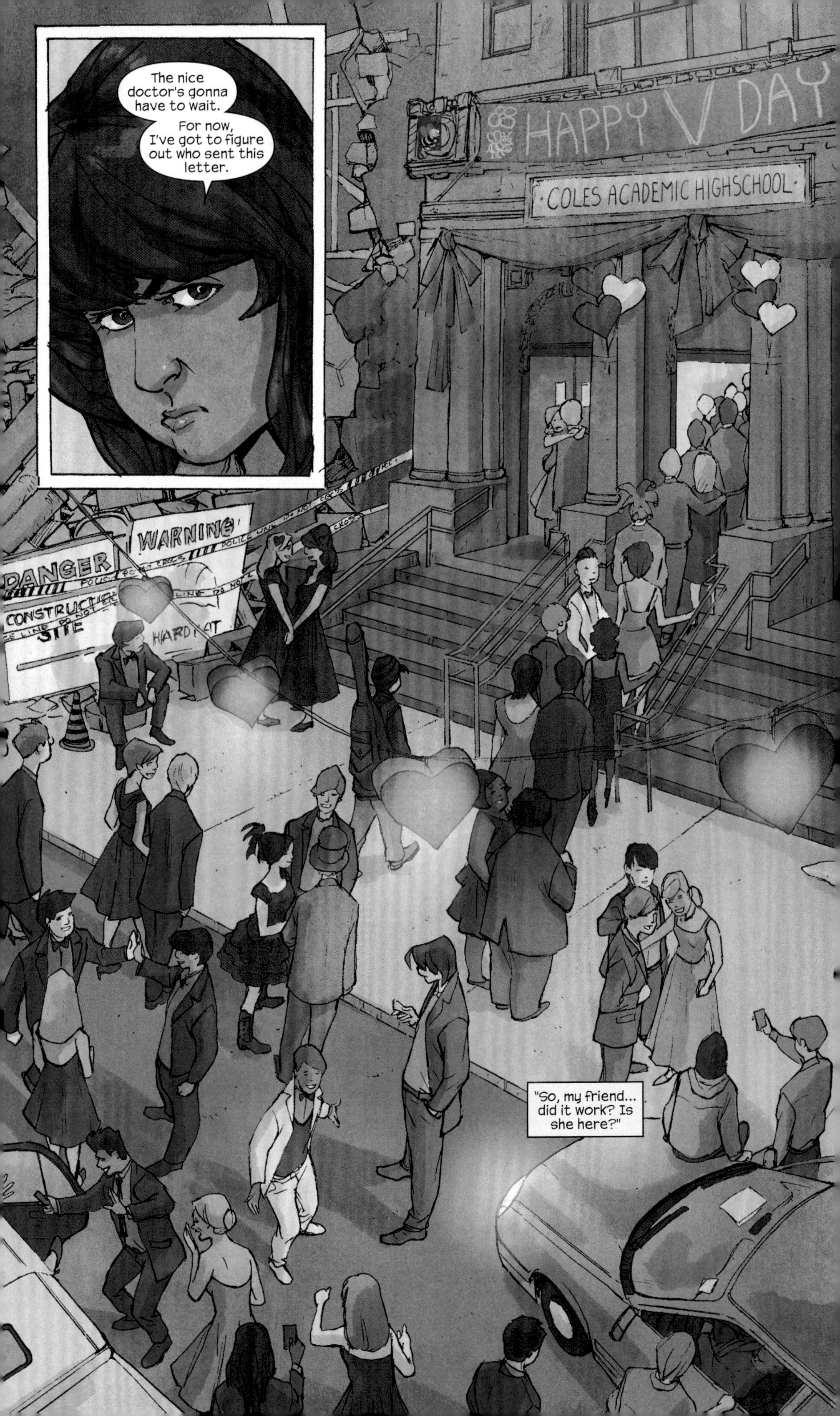
The nice doctor's gonna have to wait.
For now, I've got to figure out who sent this letter.
HAPPY V DAY
COLES ACADEMIC HIGHSCHOOL
WARNING
DANGER
CONSTRUCTION SITE
"So, my friend... did it work? Is she here?"

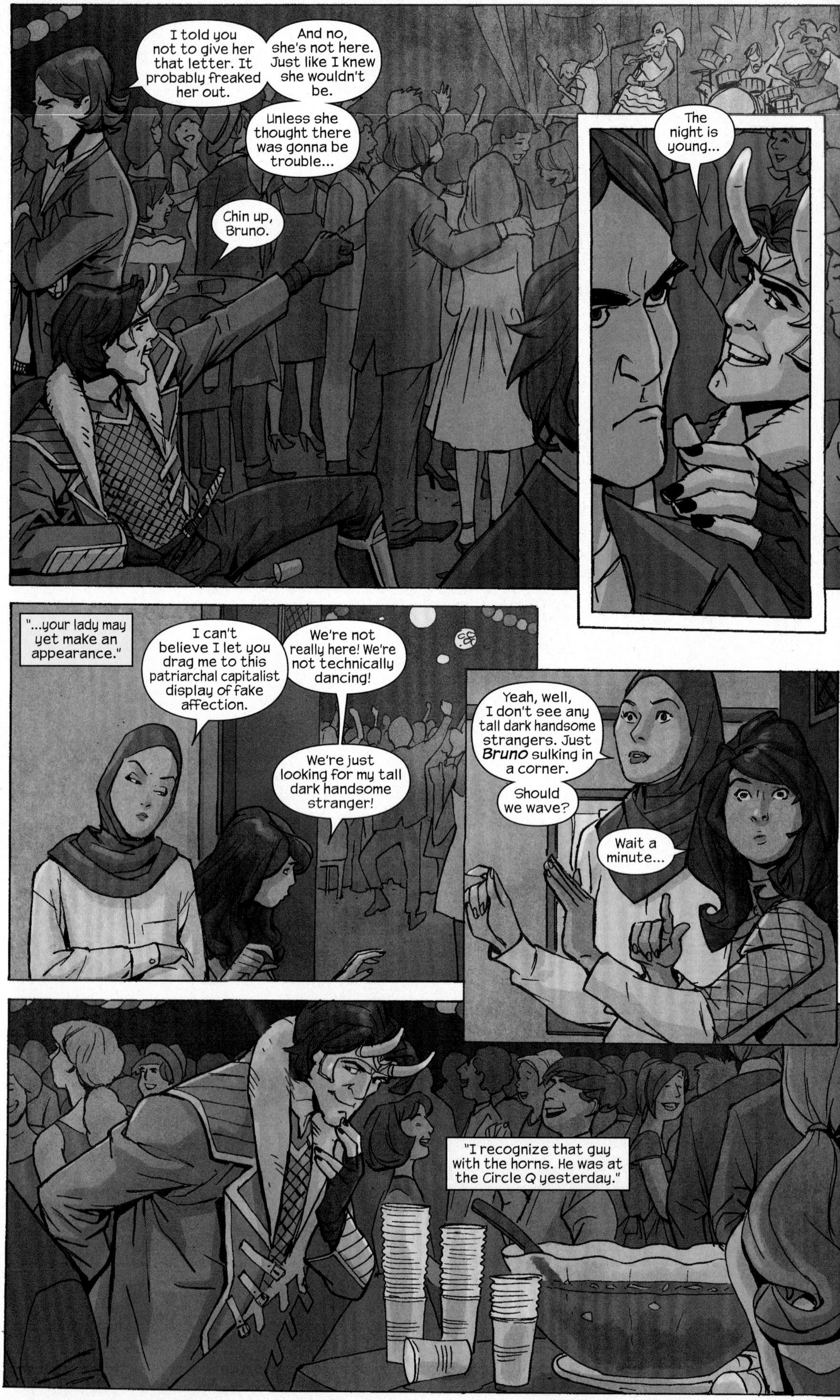

I told you not to give her that letter. It probably freaked her out.
And no, she's not here. Just like I knew she wouldn't be.
Unless she thought there was gonna be trouble...
Chin up, Bruno.
The night is young...
"...your lady may yet make an appearance."
I can't believe I let you drag me to this patriarchal capitalist display of fake affection.
We're not really here! We're not technically dancing!
We're just looking for my tall dark handsome stranger!
Yeah, well, I don't see any tall dark handsome strangers. Just *Bruno* sulking in a corner.
Should we wave?
Wait a minute...
"I recognize that guy with the horns. He was at the Circle Q yesterday."

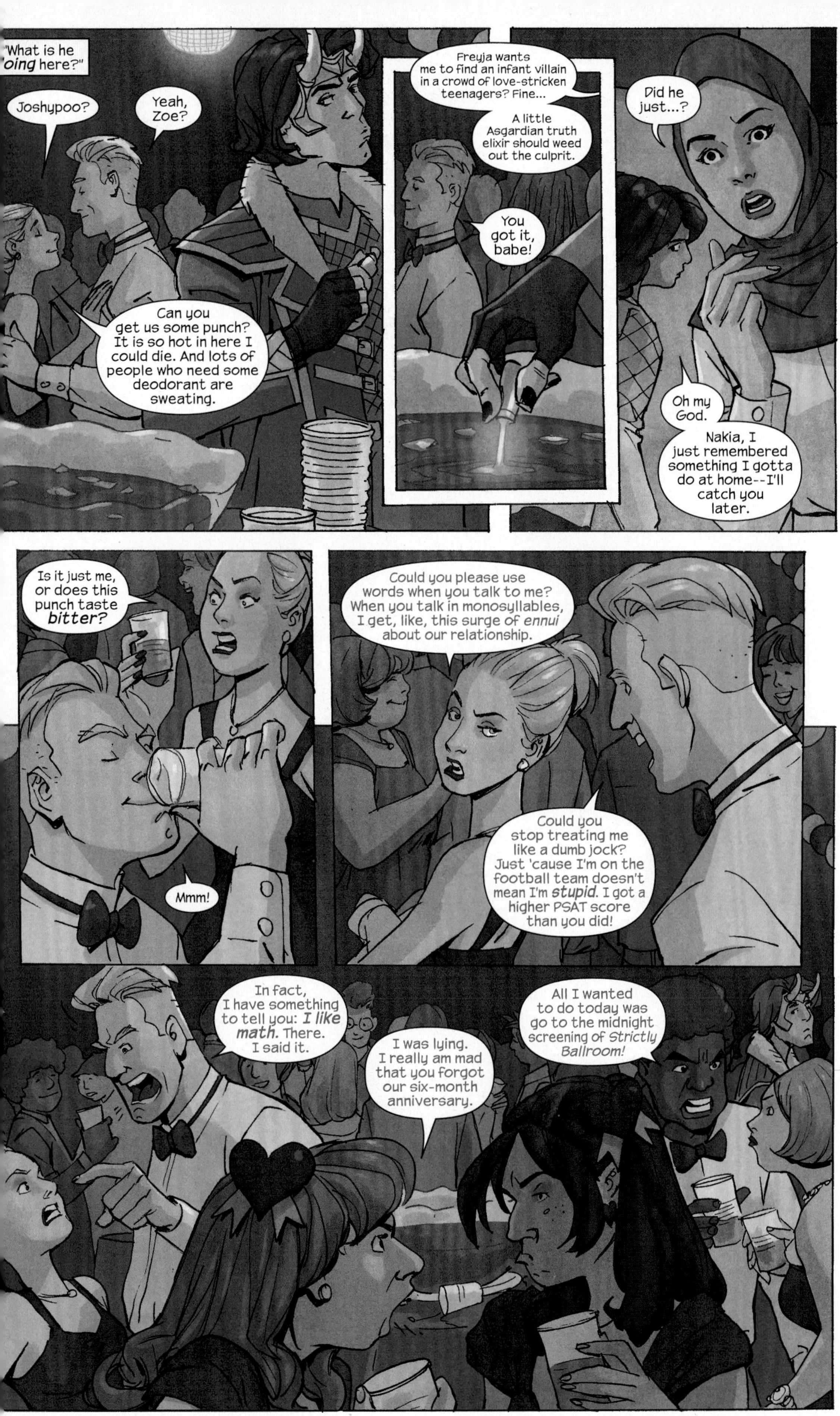
"What is he
oing here?"
Joshypoo?
Yeah, Zoe?
Can you get us some punch? It is so hot in here I could die. And lots of people who need some deodorant are sweating.
Freyja wants me to find an infant villain in a crowd of love-stricken teenagers? Fine...
A little Asgardian truth elixir should weed out the culprit.
You got it, babe!
Did he just...?
Oh my God.
Nakia, I just remembered something I gotta do at home--I'll catch you later.
Is it just me, or does this punch taste *bitter*?
Mmm!
Could you please use words when you talk to me? When you talk in monosyllables, I get, like, this surge of *ennui* about our relationship.
Could you stop treating me like a dumb jock? Just 'cause I'm on the football team doesn't mean I'm *stupid*. I got a higher PSAT score than you did!
In fact, I have something to tell you: *I like math*. There. I said it.
I was lying. I really am mad that you forgot our six-month anniversary.
All I wanted to do today was go to the midnight screening of *Strictly Ballroom!*

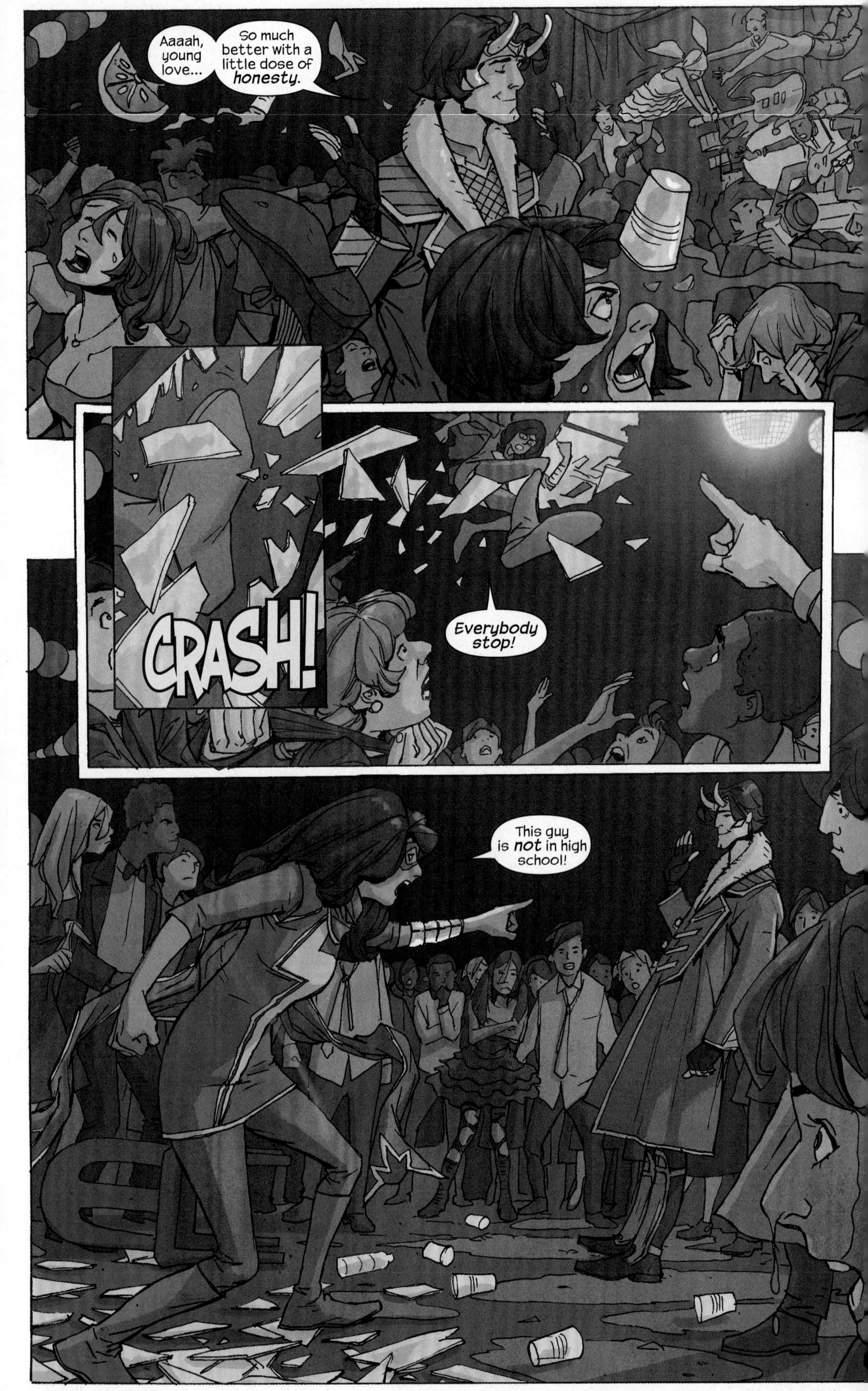
Aaaah, young love...
So much better with a little dose of *honesty*.
CRASH!
Everybody stop!
This guy is **not** in high school!

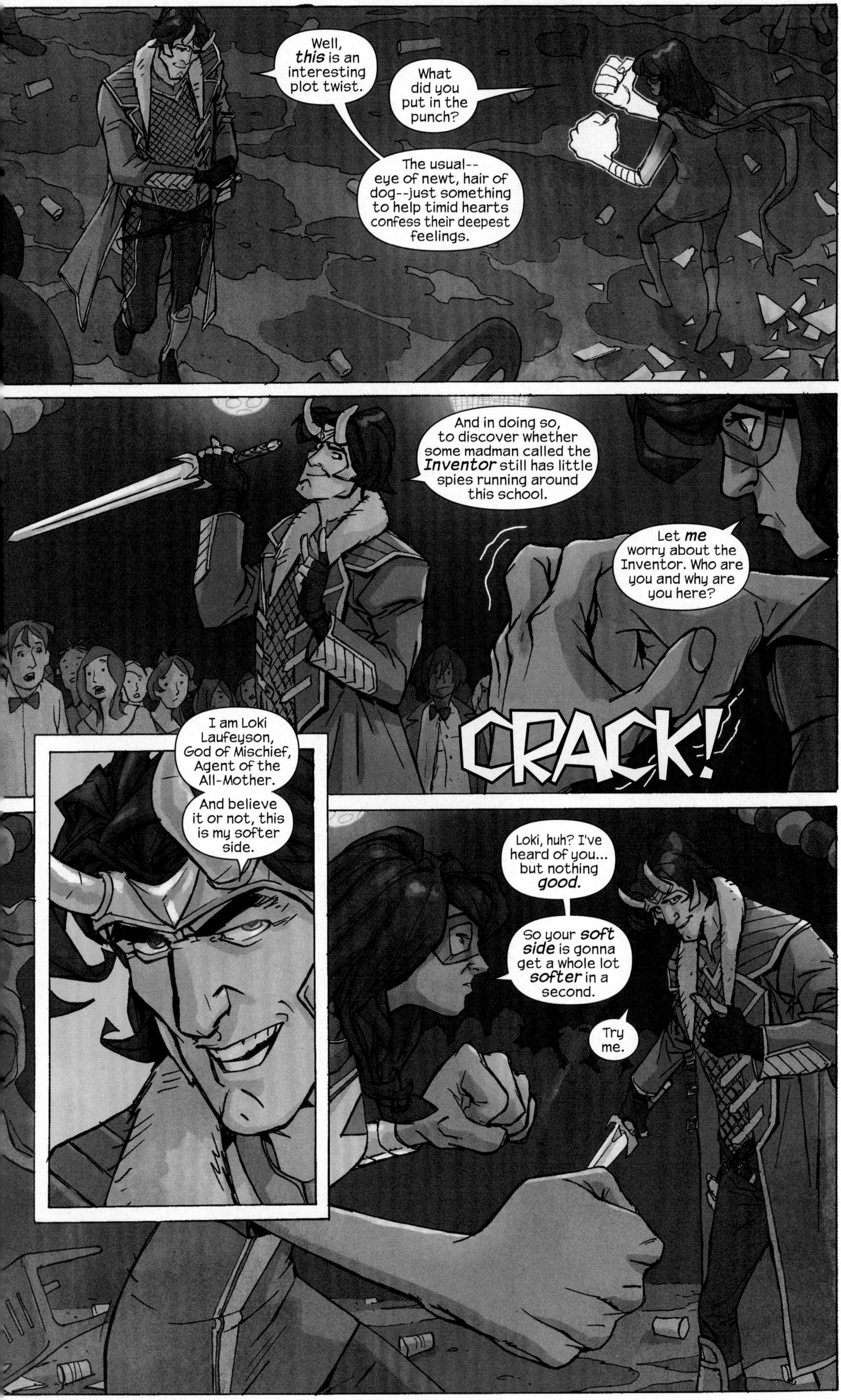
Well, this is an interesting plot twist.
What did you put in the punch?
The usual--eye of newt, hair of dog--just something to help timid hearts confess their deepest feelings.
And in doing so, to discover whether some madman called the Inventor still has little spies running around this school.
Let me worry about the Inventor. Who are you and why are you here?
CRACK!
I am Loki Laufeyson, God of Mischief, Agent of the All-Mother.
And believe it or not, this is my softer side.
Loki, huh? I've heard of you... but nothing good.
So your soft side is gonna get a whole lot softer in a second.
Try me.

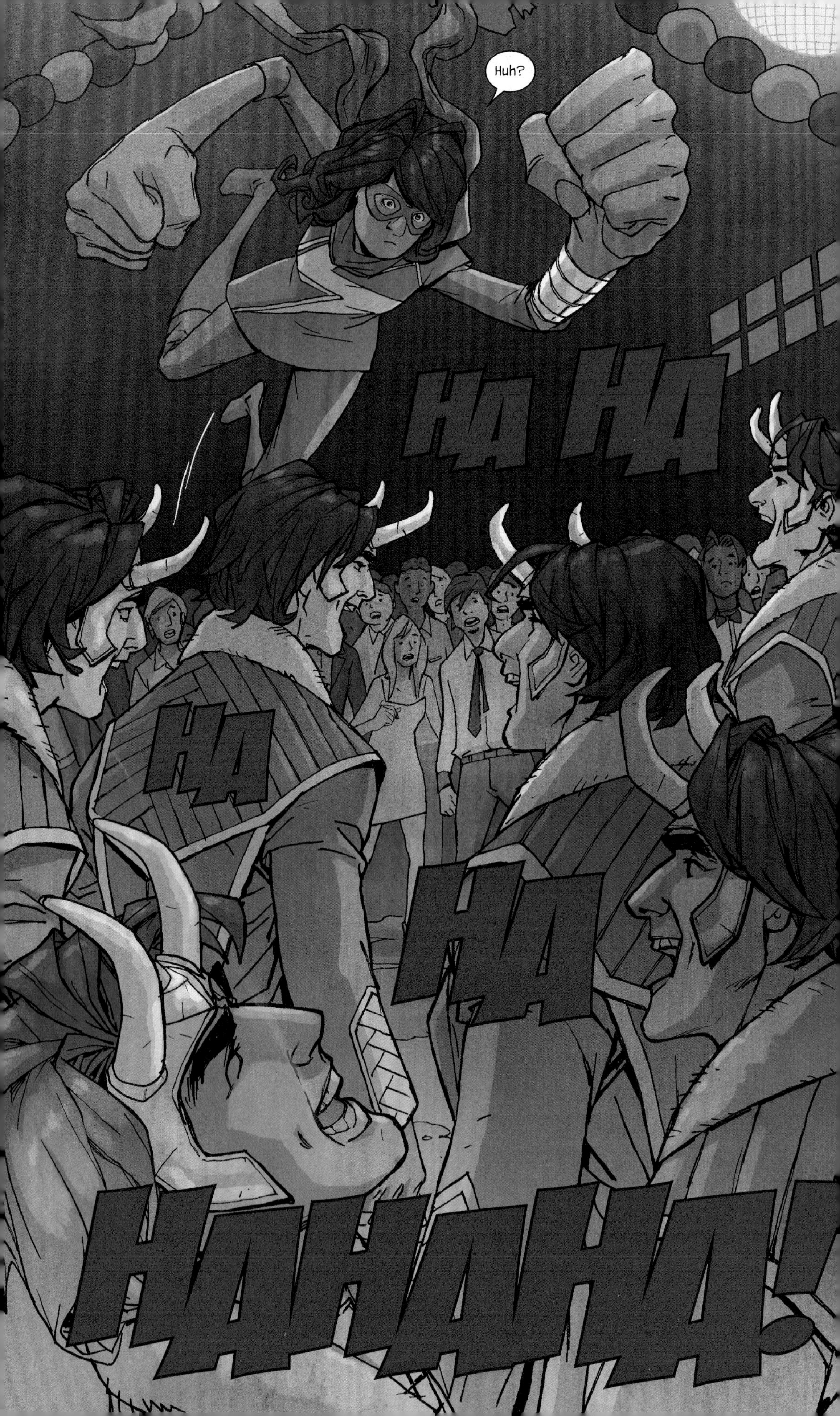
Huh?
HA HA
HA
HA
HAHAHA!

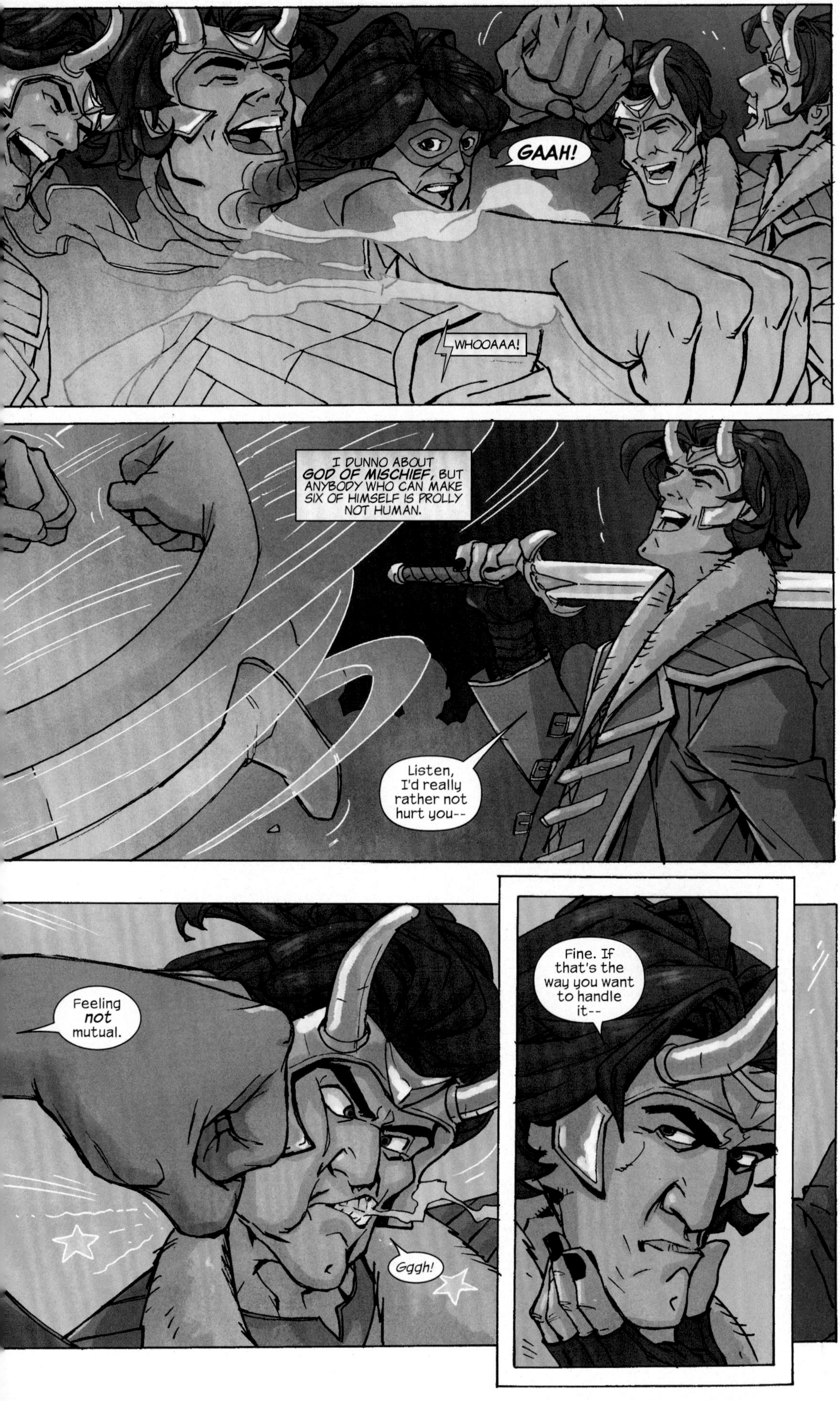
GAAH!
WHOOAAA!
I DUNNO ABOUT GOD OF MISCHIEF, BUT ANYBODY WHO CAN MAKE SIX OF HIMSELF IS PROLLY NOT HUMAN.
Listen, I'd really rather not hurt you--
Feeling not mutual.
Gggh!
Fine. If that's the way you want to handle it--

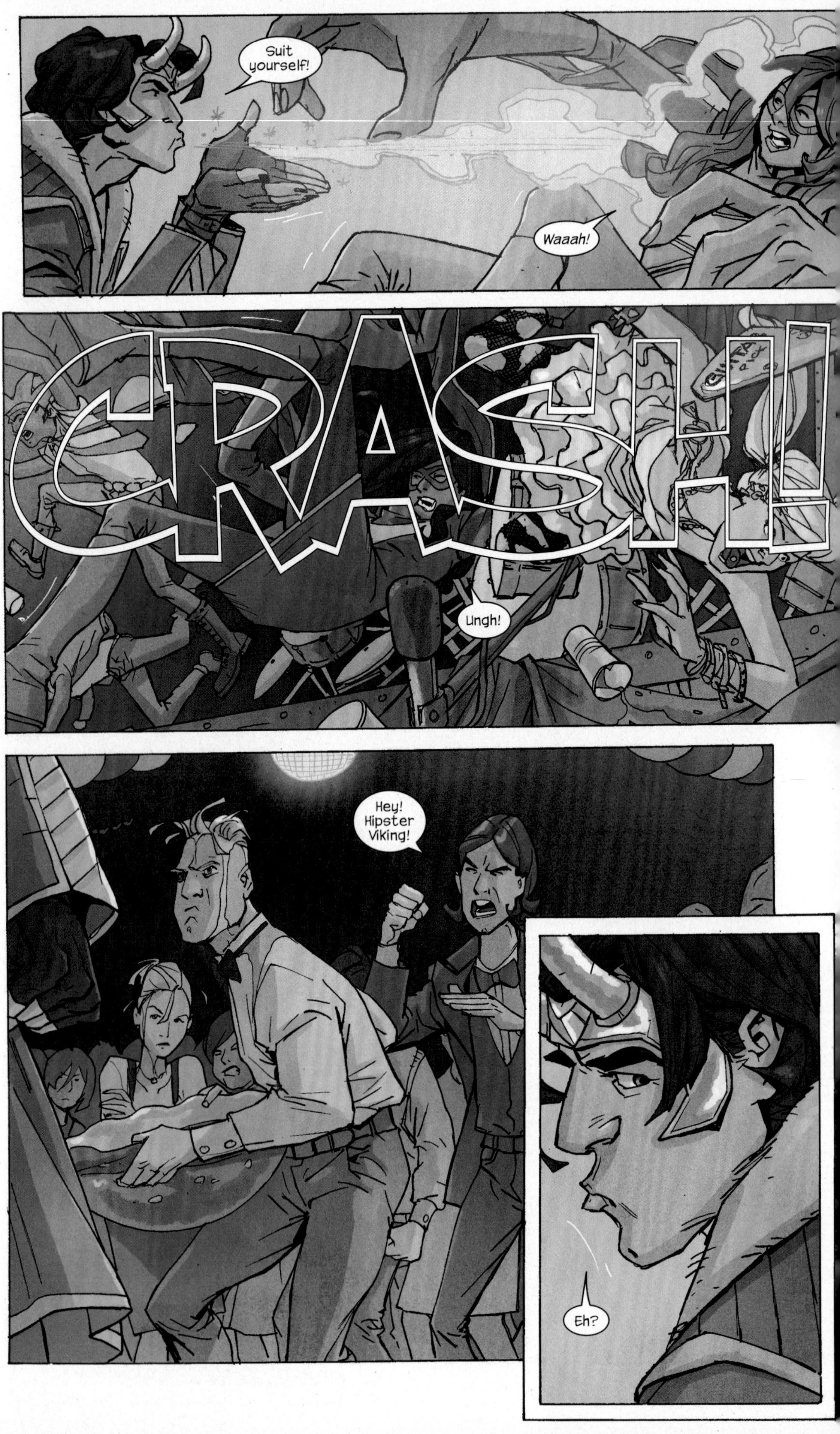
Suit yourself!
Waaah!
CRASH!
Ungh!
Hey! Hipster Viking!
Eh?

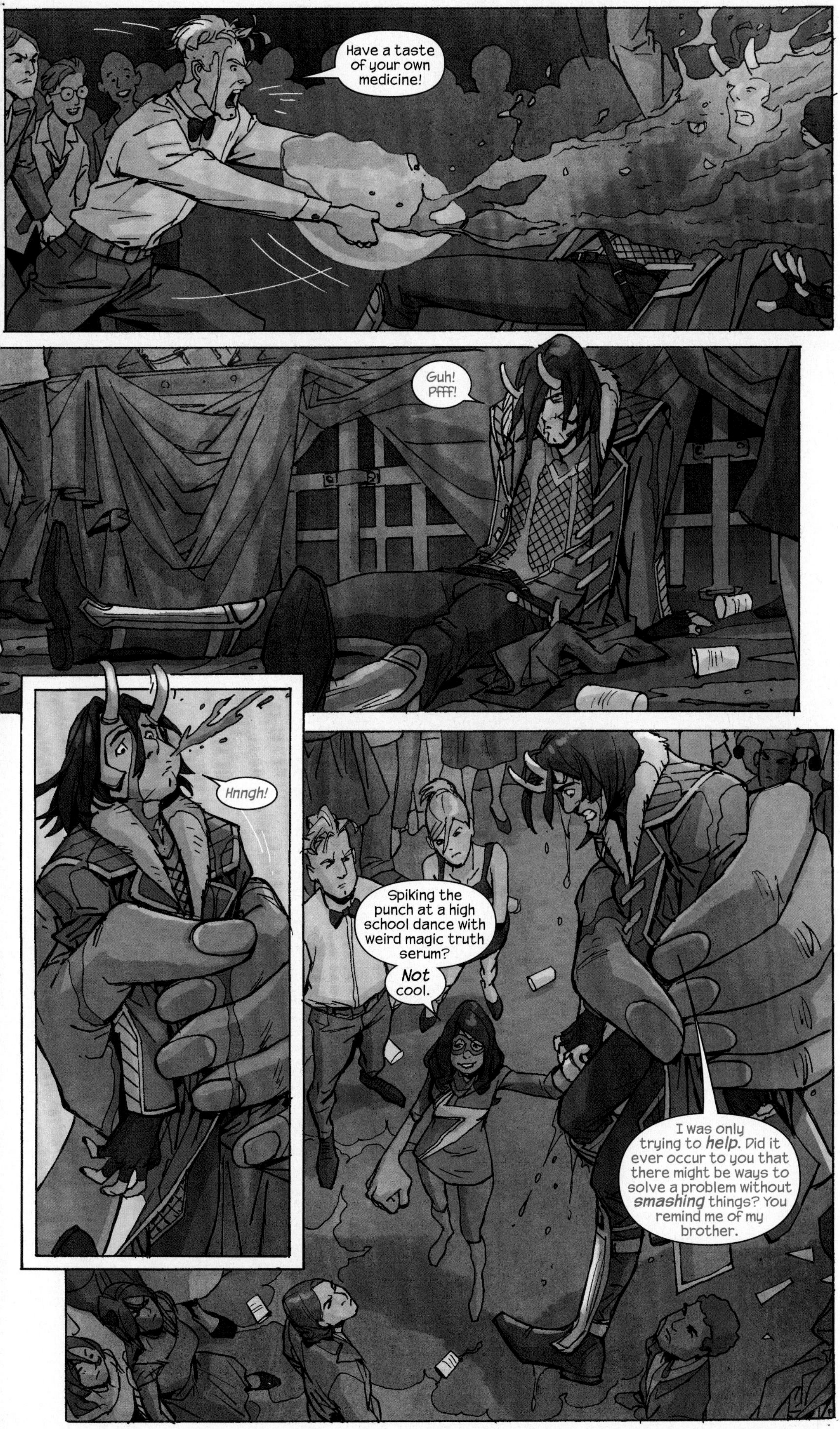
Have a taste of your own medicine!
Guh! Pfff!
Hnngh!
Spiking the punch at a high school dance with weird magic truth serum?
Not cool.
I was only trying to help. Did it ever occur to you that there might be ways to solve a problem without smashing things? You remind me of my brother.

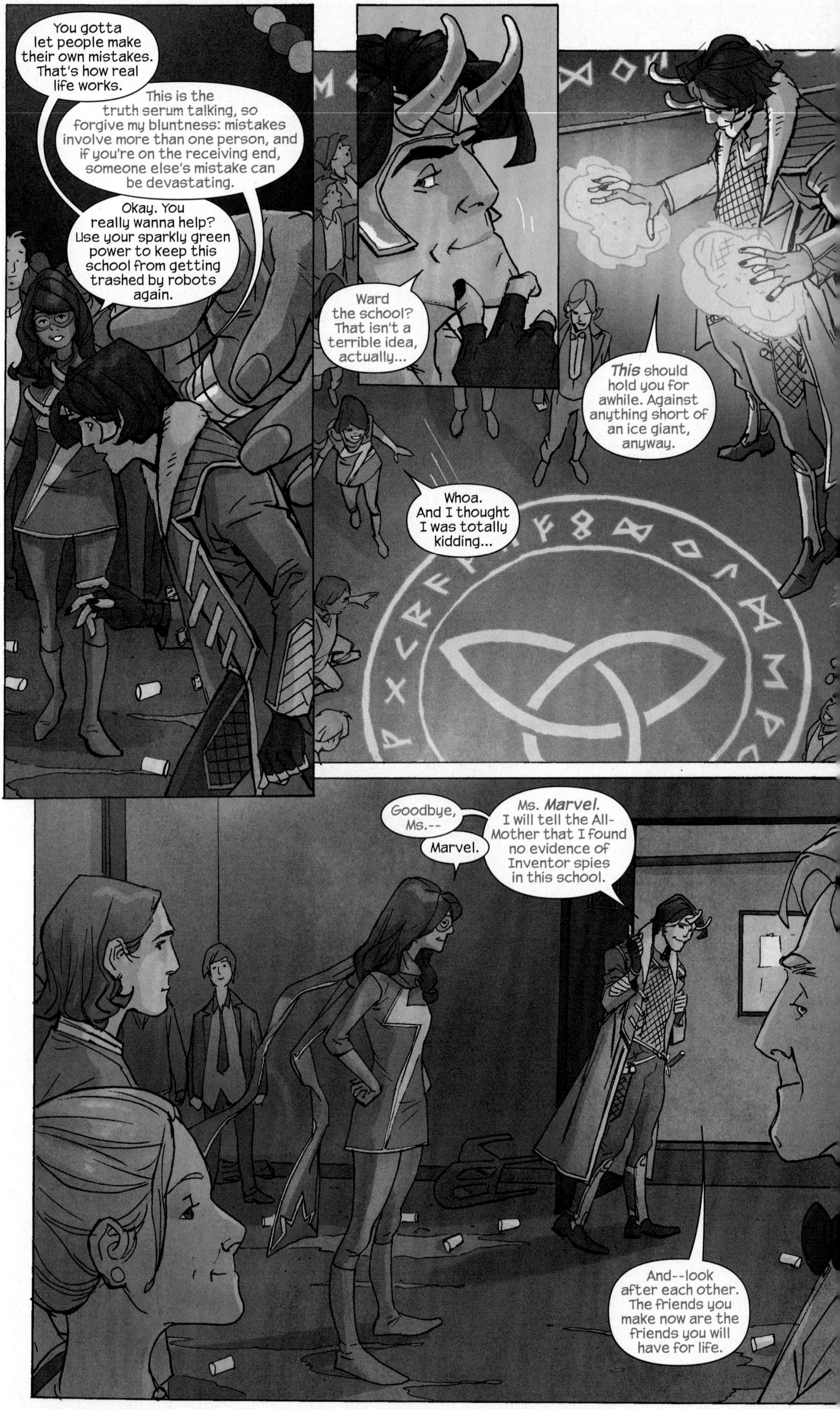

You gotta let people make their own mistakes. That's how real life works.
This is the truth serum talking, so forgive my bluntness: mistakes involve more than one person, and if you're on the receiving end, someone else's mistake can be devastating.
Okay. You really wanna help? Use your sparkly green power to keep this school from getting trashed by robots again.
Ward the school? That isn't a terrible idea, actually...
This should hold you for awhile. Against anything short of an ice giant, anyway.
Whoa. And I thought I was totally kidding...
Goodbye, Ms.--
Marvel.
Ms. Marvel. I will tell the All-Mother that I found no evidence of Inventor spies in this school.
And--look after each other. The friends you make now are the friends you will have for life.

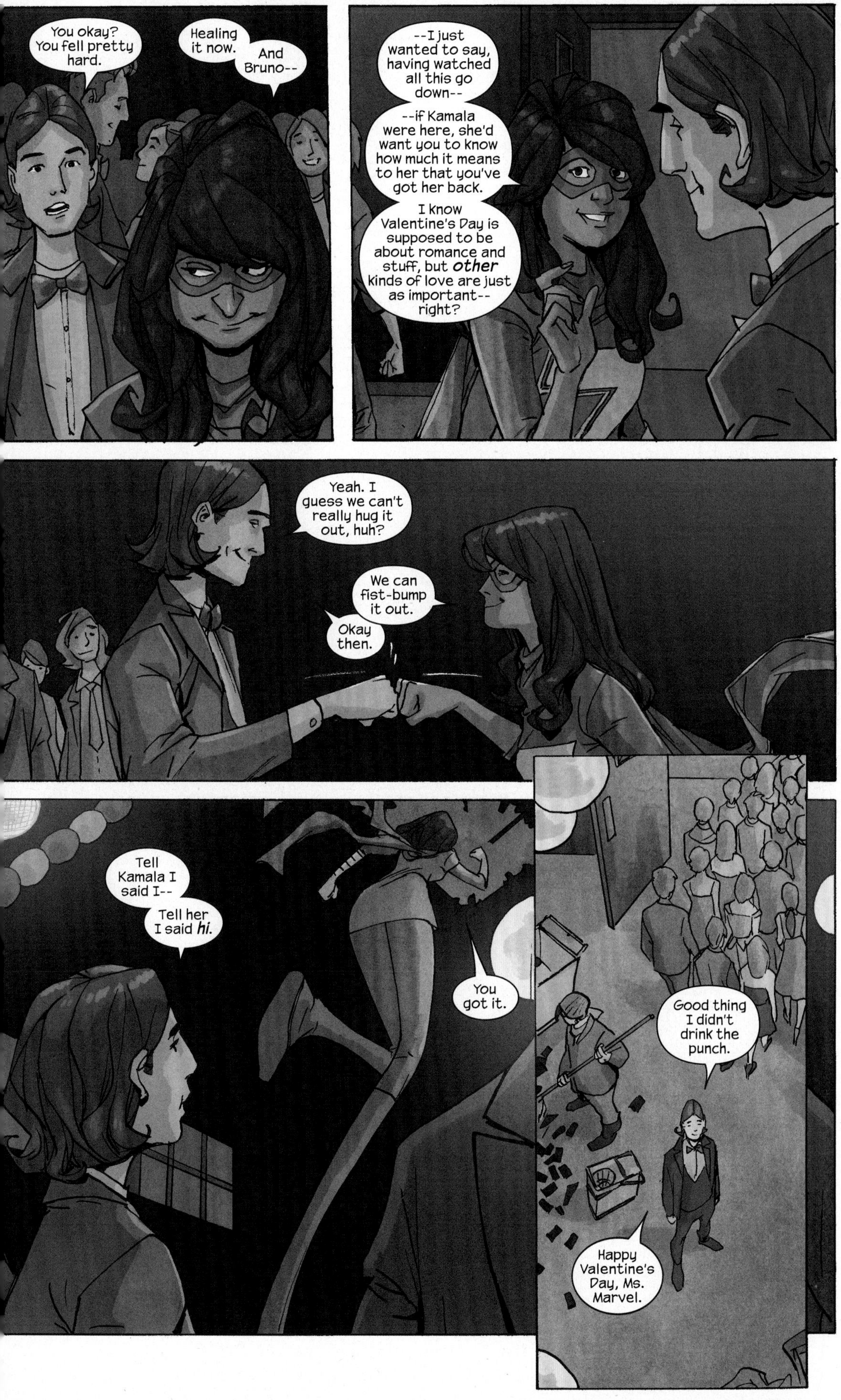

You okay? You fell pretty hard.
Healing it now.
And Bruno--
--I just wanted to say, having watched all this go down--
--if Kamala were here, she'd want you to know how much it means to her that you've got her back.
I know Valentine's Day is supposed to be about romance and stuff, but *other* kinds of love are just as important--right?
Yeah. I guess we can't really hug it out, huh?
We can fist-bump it out.
Okay then.
Tell Kamala I said I--
Tell her I said *hi*.
You got it.
Good thing I didn't drink the punch.
Happy Valentine's Day, Ms. Marvel.

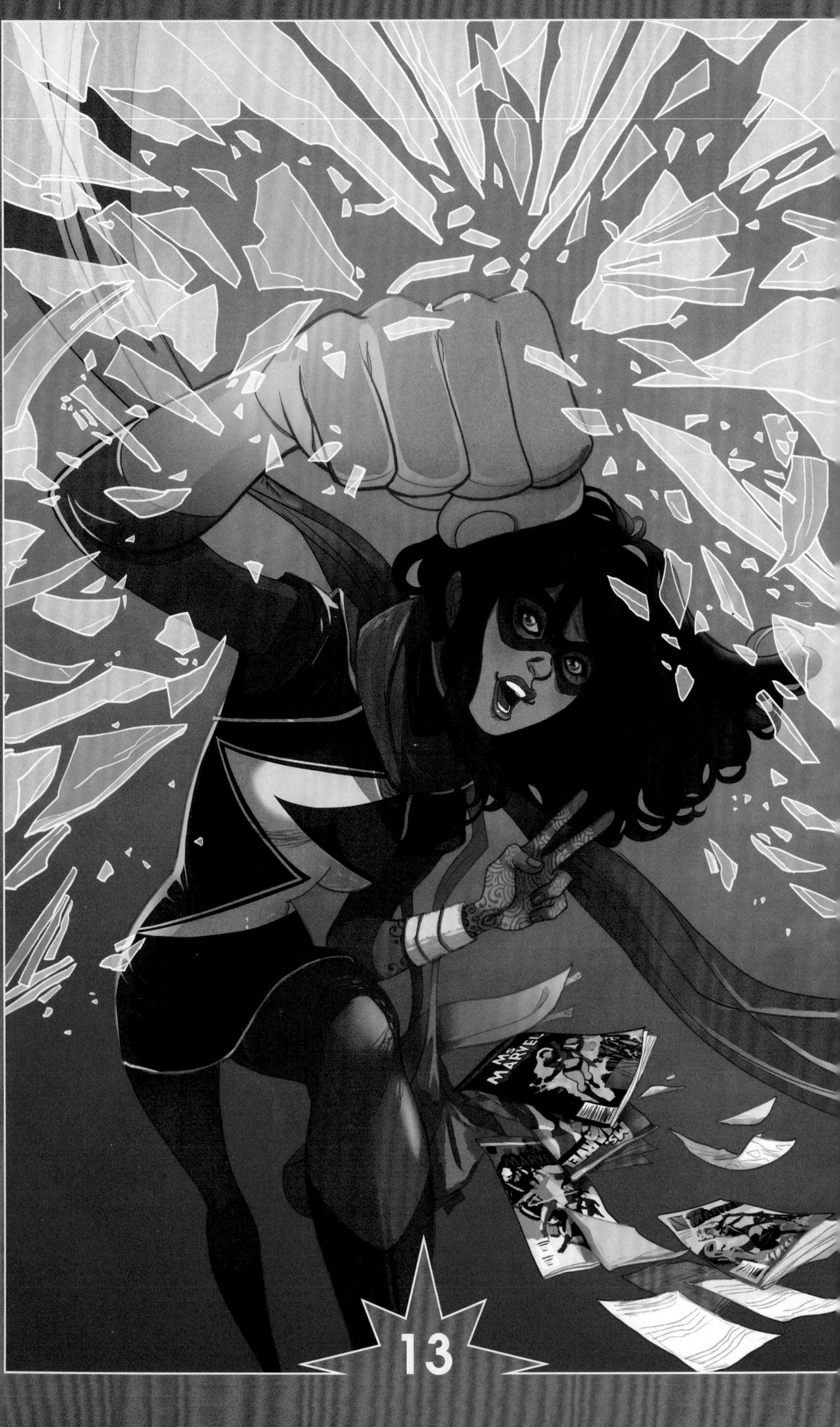
Ms MARVEL
13

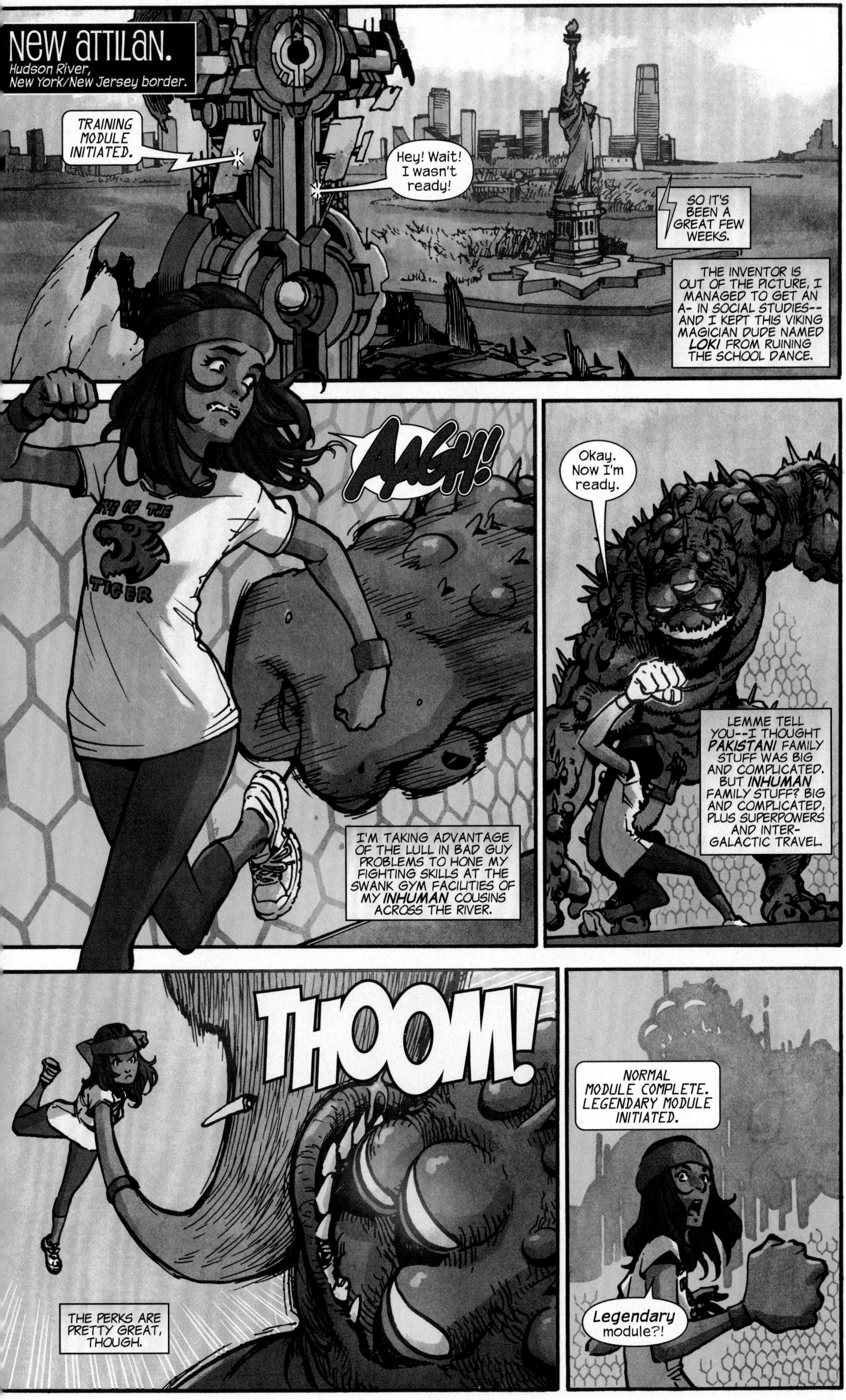
New Attilan.
Hudson River, New York/New Jersey border.
TRAINING MODULE INITIATED.
Hey! Wait! I wasn't ready!
SO IT'S BEEN A GREAT FEW WEEKS.
THE INVENTOR IS OUT OF THE PICTURE, I MANAGED TO GET AN A- IN SOCIAL STUDIES-- AND I KEPT THIS VIKING MAGICIAN DUDE NAMED LOKI FROM RUINING THE SCHOOL DANCE.
AAGH!
I'M TAKING ADVANTAGE OF THE LULL IN BAD GUY PROBLEMS TO HONE MY FIGHTING SKILLS AT THE SWANK GYM FACILITIES OF MY INHUMAN COUSINS ACROSS THE RIVER.
Okay. Now I'm ready.
LEMME TELL YOU--I THOUGHT PAKISTANI FAMILY STUFF WAS BIG AND COMPLICATED. BUT INHUMAN FAMILY STUFF? BIG AND COMPLICATED, PLUS SUPERPOWERS AND INTER-GALACTIC TRAVEL.
THOOM!
THE PERKS ARE PRETTY GREAT, THOUGH.
NORMAL MODULE COMPLETE. LEGENDARY MODULE INITIATED.
Legendary module?!

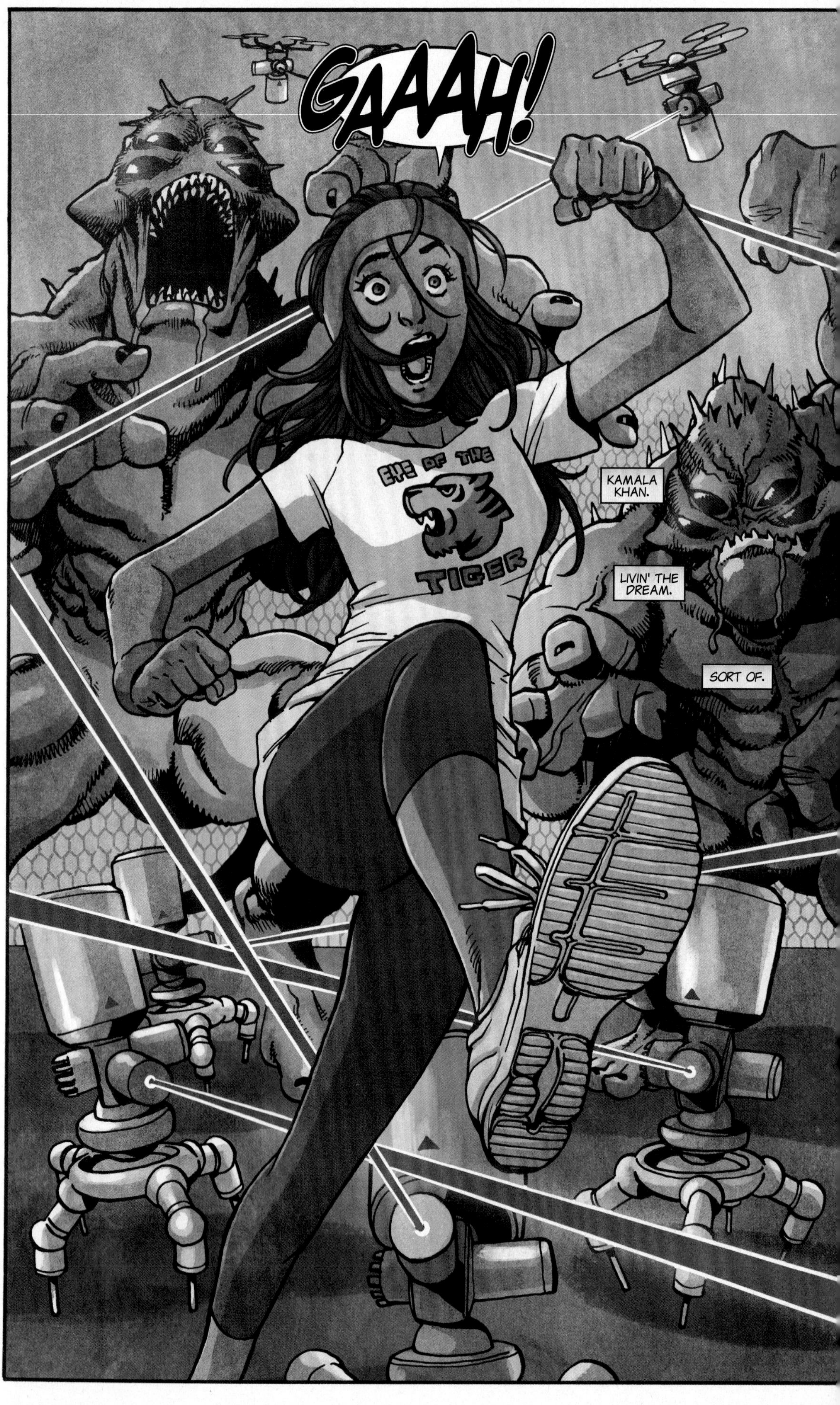
GAAAH!
EYE OF THE
TIGER
KAMALA KHAN.
LIVIN' THE DREAM.
SORT OF.

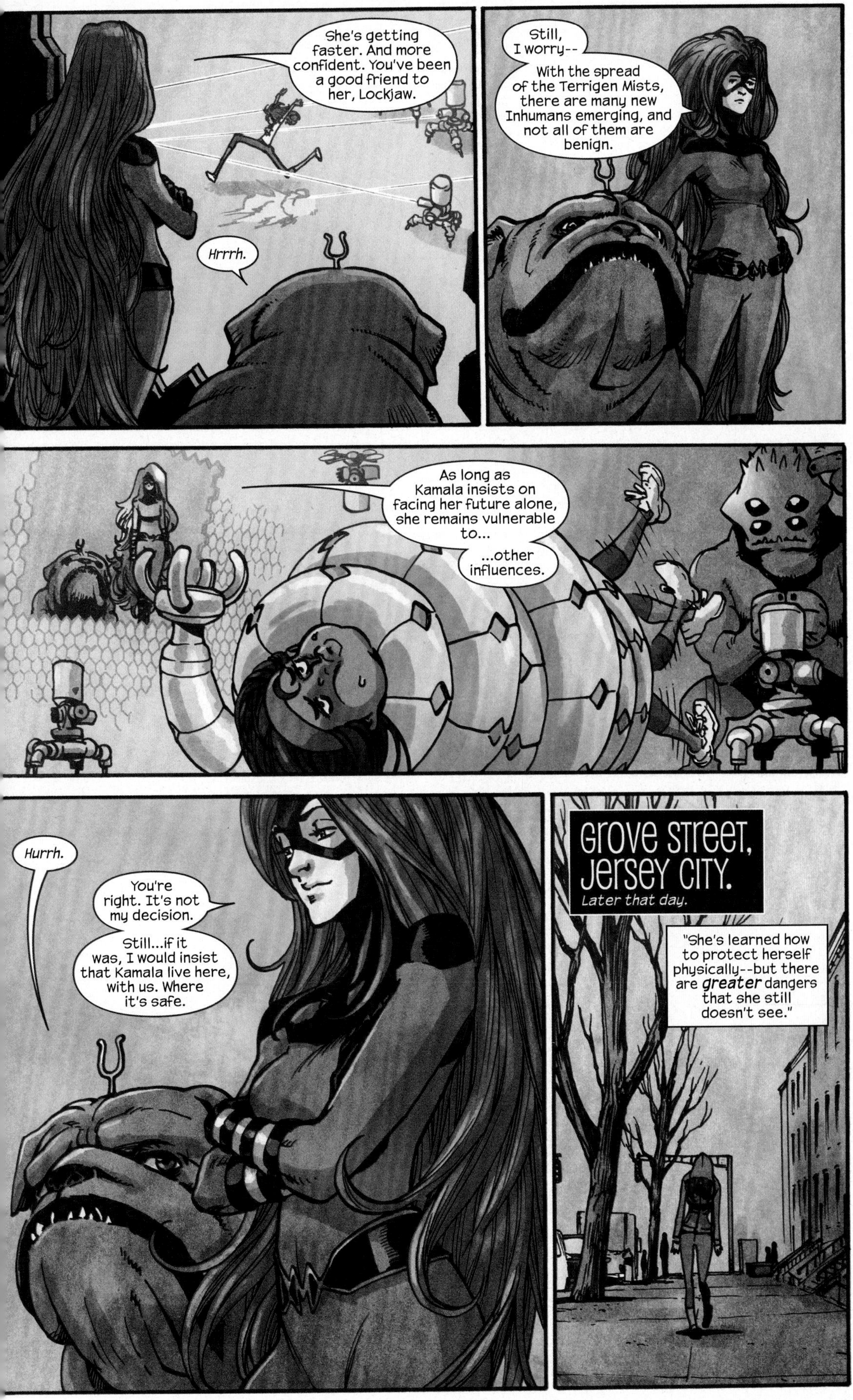

She's getting faster. And more confident. You've been a good friend to her, Lockjaw.
Hrrrh.
Still, I worry--
With the spread of the Terrigen Mists, there are many new Inhumans emerging, and not all of them are benign.
As long as Kamala insists on facing her future alone, she remains vulnerable to...
...other influences.
Hurrh.
You're right. It's not my decision.
Still...if it was, I would insist that Kamala live here, with us. Where it's safe.
GROVE STREET, JERSEY CITY.
Later that day.
"She's learned how to protect herself physically--but there are greater dangers that she still doesn't see."

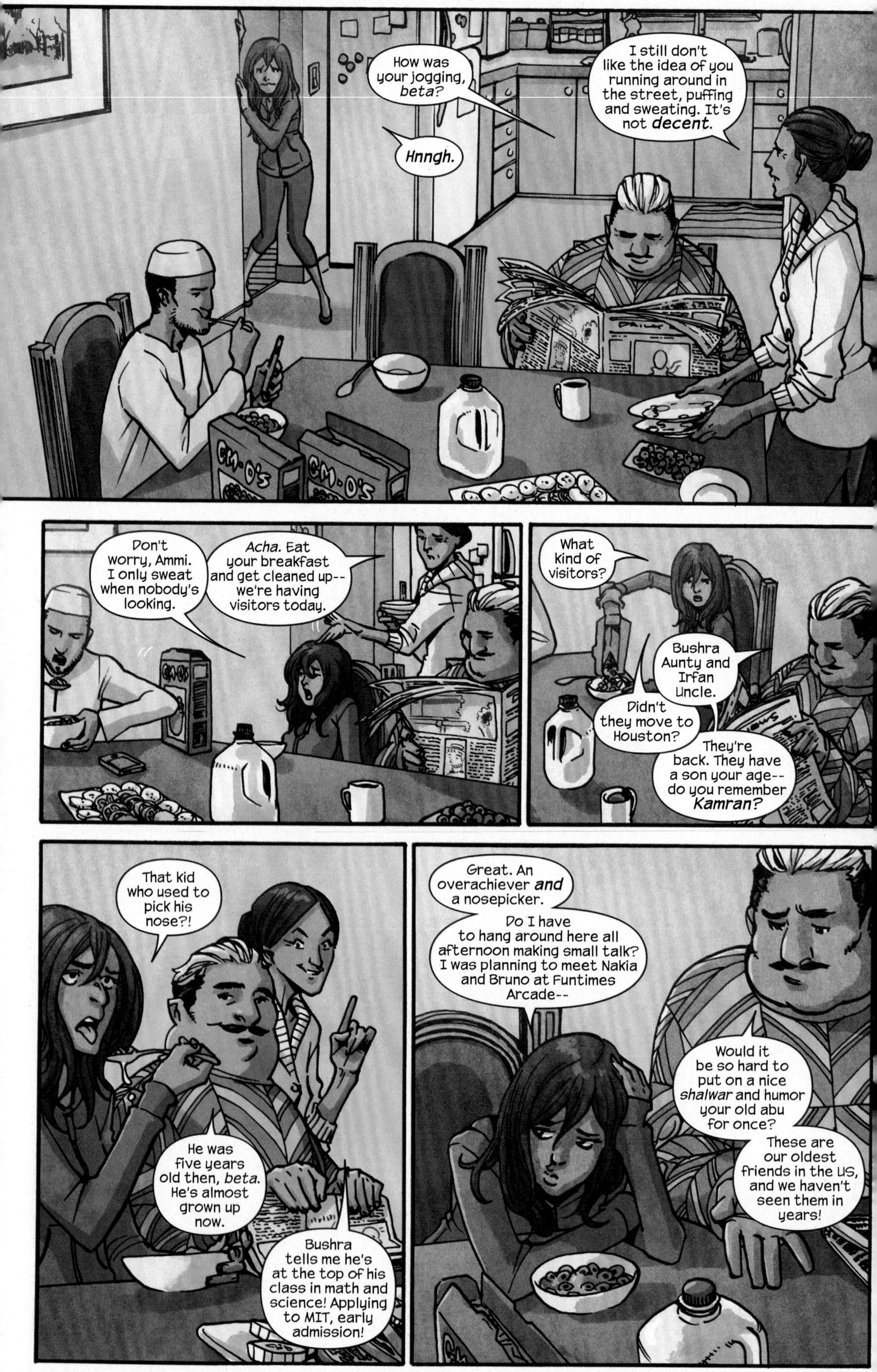
How was your jogging, *beta?*
Hnngh.
I still don't like the idea of you running around in the street, puffing and sweating. It's not ***decent***.
Don't worry, Ammi. I only sweat when nobody's looking.
Acha. Eat your breakfast and get cleaned up--we're having visitors today.
What kind of visitors?
Bushra Aunty and Irfan Uncle.
Didn't they move to Houston?
They're back. They have a son your age--do you remember ***Kamran?***
That kid who used to pick his nose?!
He was five years old then, *beta.* He's almost grown up now.
Bushra tells me he's at the top of his class in math and science! Applying to MIT, early admission!
Great. An overachiever ***and*** a nosepicker.
Do I have to hang around here all afternoon making small talk? I was planning to meet Nakia and Bruno at Funtimes Arcade--
Would it be so hard to put on a nice *shalwar* and humor your old abu for once?
These are our oldest friends in the US, and we haven't seen them in years!

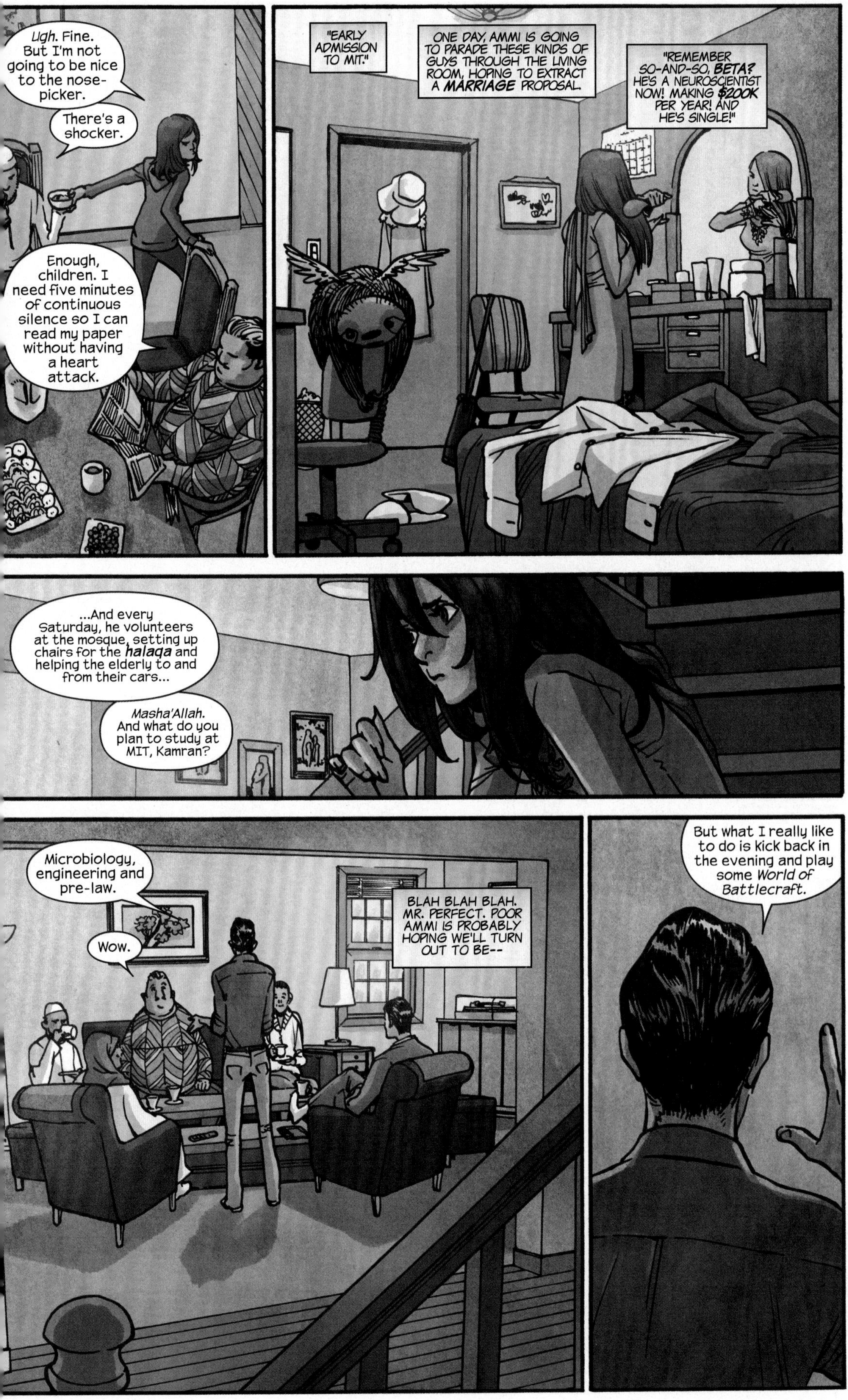
Ugh. Fine. But I'm not going to be nice to the nose-picker.
There's a shocker.
Enough, children. I need five minutes of continuous silence so I can read my paper without having a heart attack.
"EARLY ADMISSION TO MIT."
ONE DAY, AMMI IS GOING TO PARADE THESE KINDS OF GUYS THROUGH THE LIVING ROOM, HOPING TO EXTRACT A MARRIAGE PROPOSAL.
"REMEMBER SO-AND-SO, BETA? HE'S A NEUROSCIENTIST NOW! MAKING $200K PER YEAR! AND HE'S SINGLE!"
...And every Saturday, he volunteers at the mosque, setting up chairs for the halaqa and helping the elderly to and from their cars...
Masha'Allah. And what do you plan to study at MIT, Kamran?
Microbiology, engineering and pre-law.
Wow.
BLAH BLAH BLAH. MR. PERFECT. POOR AMMI IS PROBABLY HOPING WE'LL TURN OUT TO BE--
But what I really like to do is kick back in the evening and play some World of Battlecraft.

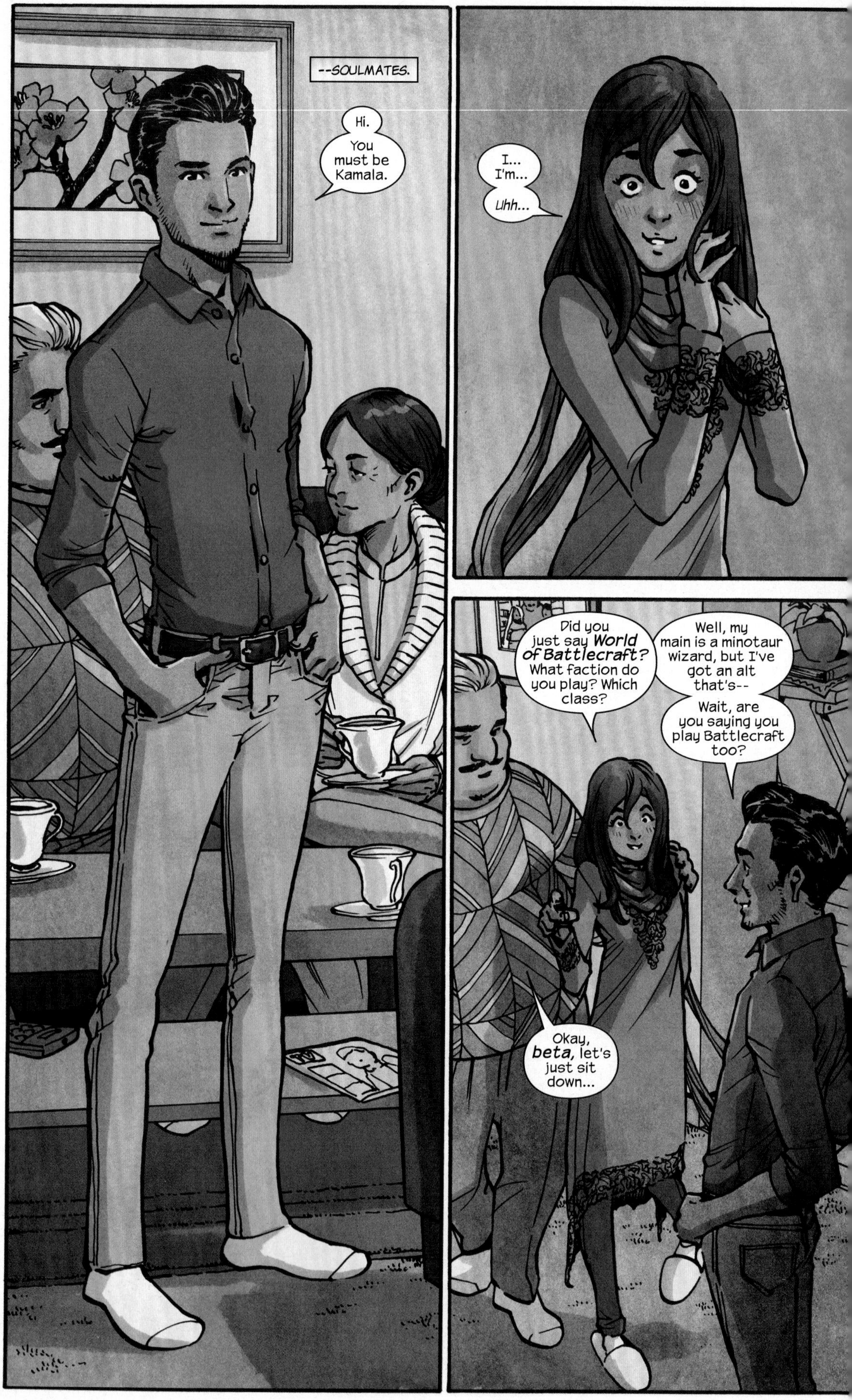
--SOULMATES.
Hi.
You must be Kamala.
I... I'm...
Uhh...
Did you just say World of Battlecraft? What faction do you play? Which class?
Well, my main is a minotaur wizard, but I've got an alt that's--
Wait, are you saying you play Battlecraft too?
Okay, beta, let's just sit down...

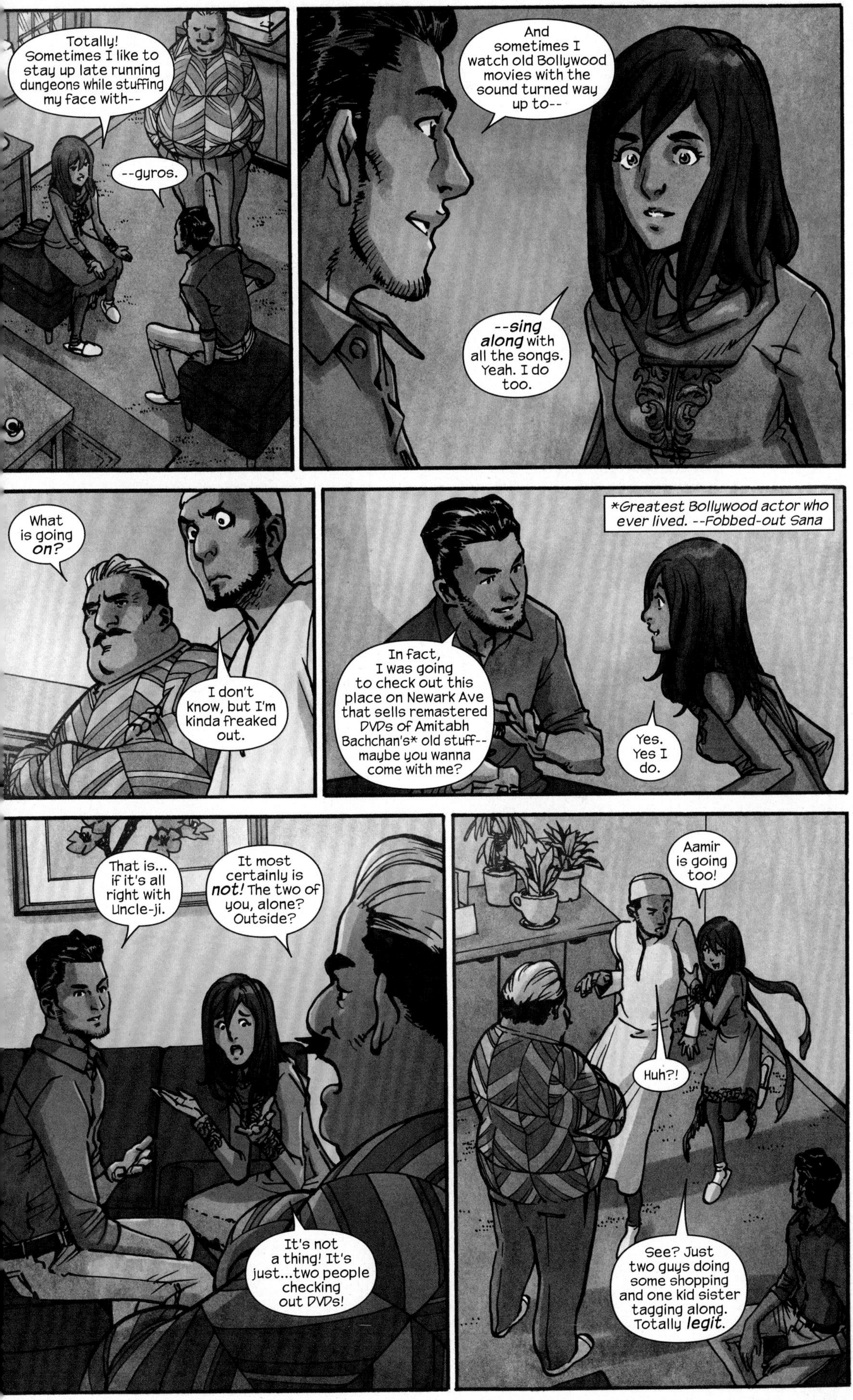

Totally! Sometimes I like to stay up late running dungeons while stuffing my face with--
--gyros.
And sometimes I watch old Bollywood movies with the sound turned way up to--
--sing along with all the songs. Yeah. I do too.
What is going on?
I don't know, but I'm kinda freaked out.
*Greatest Bollywood actor who ever lived. --Fobbed-out Sana
In fact, I was going to check out this place on Newark Ave that sells remastered DVDs of Amitabh Bachchan's* old stuff-- maybe you wanna come with me?
Yes. Yes I do.
That is... if it's all right with Uncle-ji.
It most certainly is not! The two of you, alone? Outside?
It's not a thing! It's just...two people checking out DVDs!
Aamir is going too!
Huh?!
See? Just two guys doing some shopping and one kid sister tagging along. Totally legit.

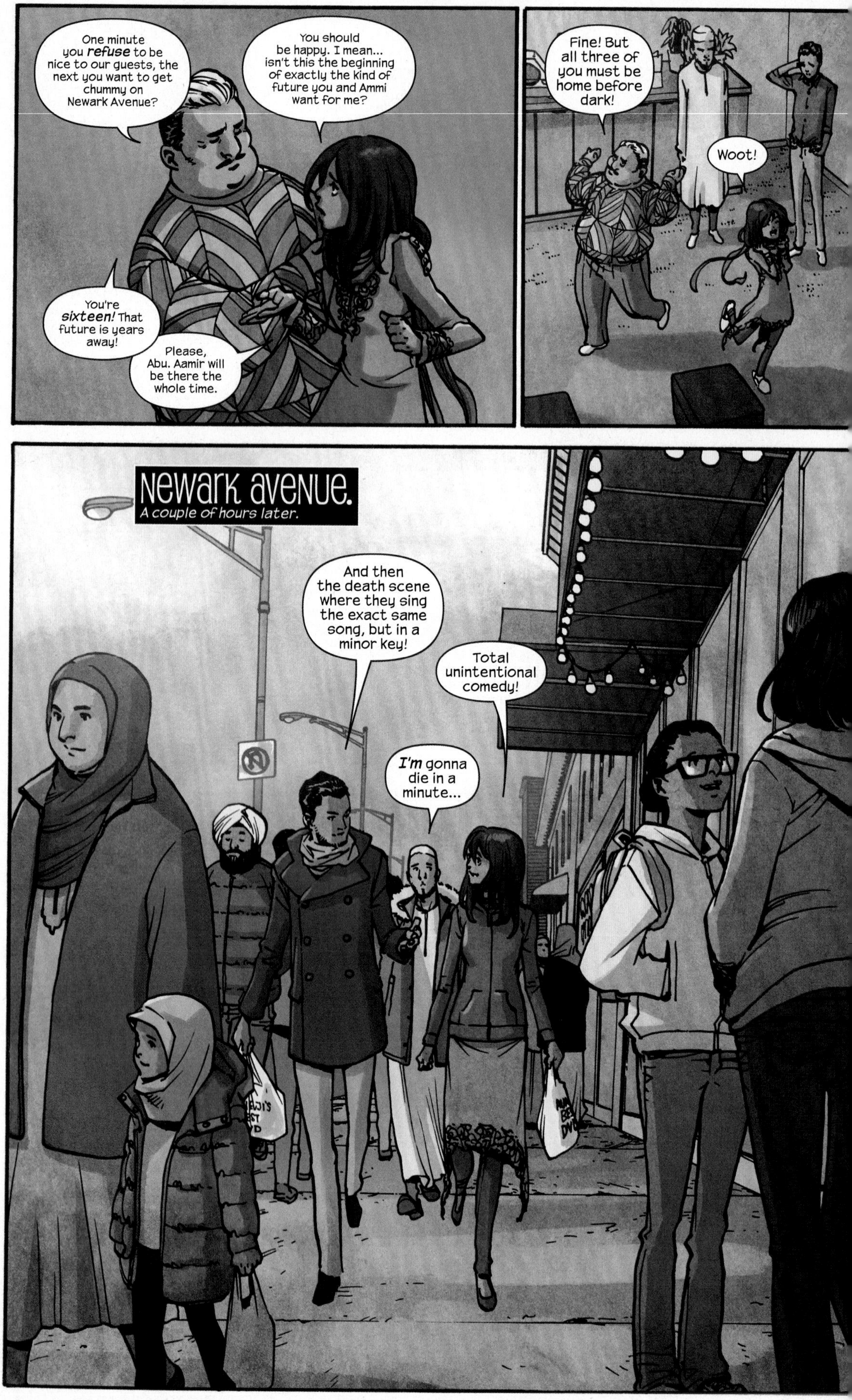
One minute you *refuse* to be nice to our guests, the next you want to get chummy on Newark Avenue?
You should be happy. I mean... isn't this the beginning of exactly the kind of future you and Ammi want for me?
You're *sixteen!* That future is years away!
Please, Abu. Aamir will be there the whole time.
Fine! But all three of you must be home before dark!
Woot!
Newark avenue.
A couple of hours later.
And then the death scene where they sing the exact same song, but in a minor key!
Total unintentional comedy!
I'm gonna die in a minute...

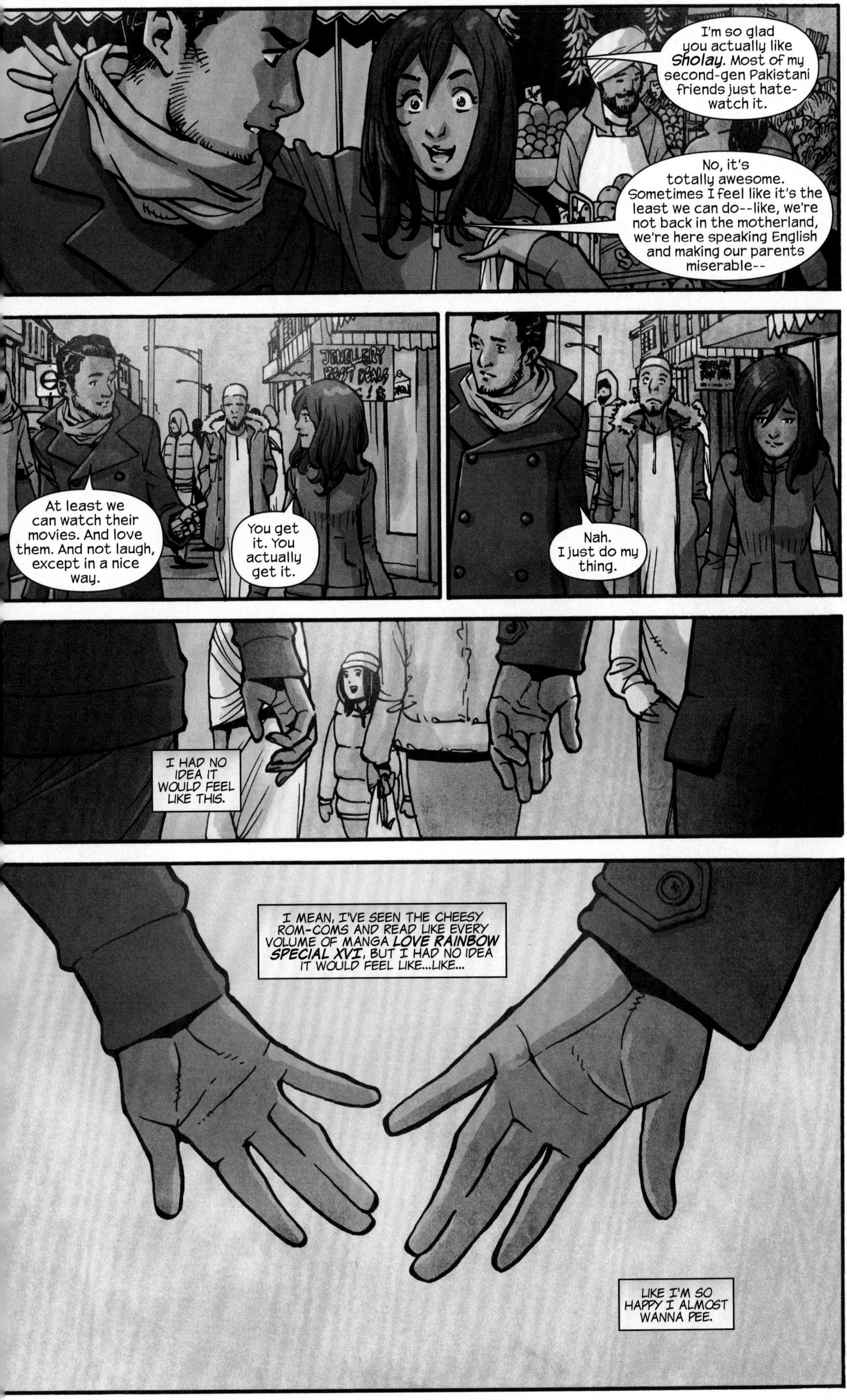
I'm so glad you actually like *Sholay*. Most of my second-gen Pakistani friends just hate-watch it.
No, it's totally awesome. Sometimes I feel like it's the least we can do--like, we're not back in the motherland, we're here speaking English and making our parents miserable--
At least we can watch their movies. And love them. And not laugh, except in a nice way.
You get it. You actually get it.
Nah. I just do my thing.
I HAD NO IDEA IT WOULD FEEL LIKE THIS.
I MEAN, I'VE SEEN THE CHEESY ROM-COMS AND READ LIKE EVERY VOLUME OF MANGA *LOVE RAINBOW SPECIAL XVI*, BUT I HAD NO IDEA IT WOULD FEEL LIKE...LIKE...
LIKE I'M SO HAPPY I ALMOST WANNA PEE.

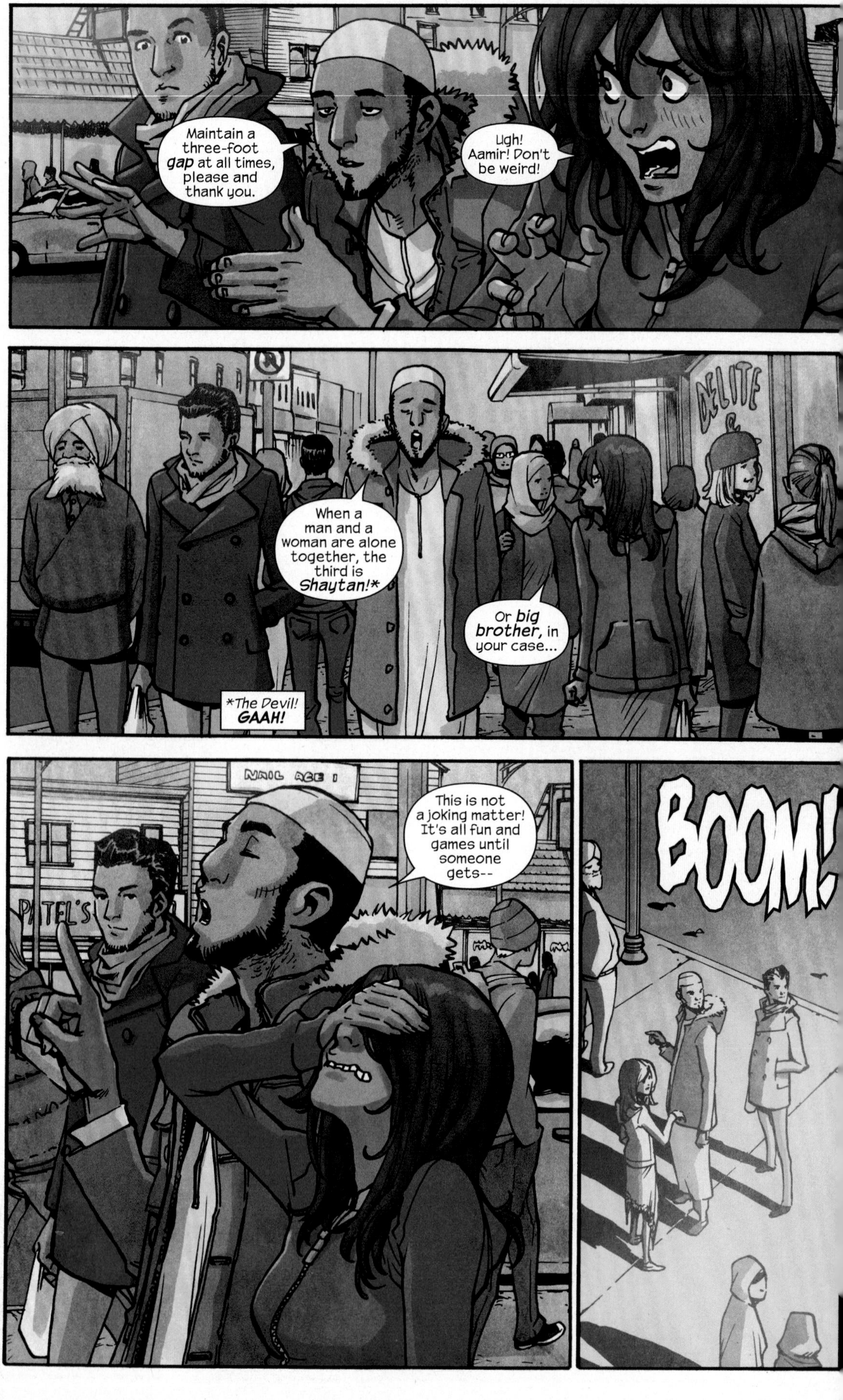

Maintain a three-foot *gap* at all times, please and thank you.
Ugh! Aamir! Don't be weird!
When a man and a woman are alone together, the third is *Shaytan!**
Or *big brother,* in your case...
*The Devil! **GAAH!**
DELITE
This is not a joking matter! It's all fun and games until someone gets--
PATEL'S
BOOM!

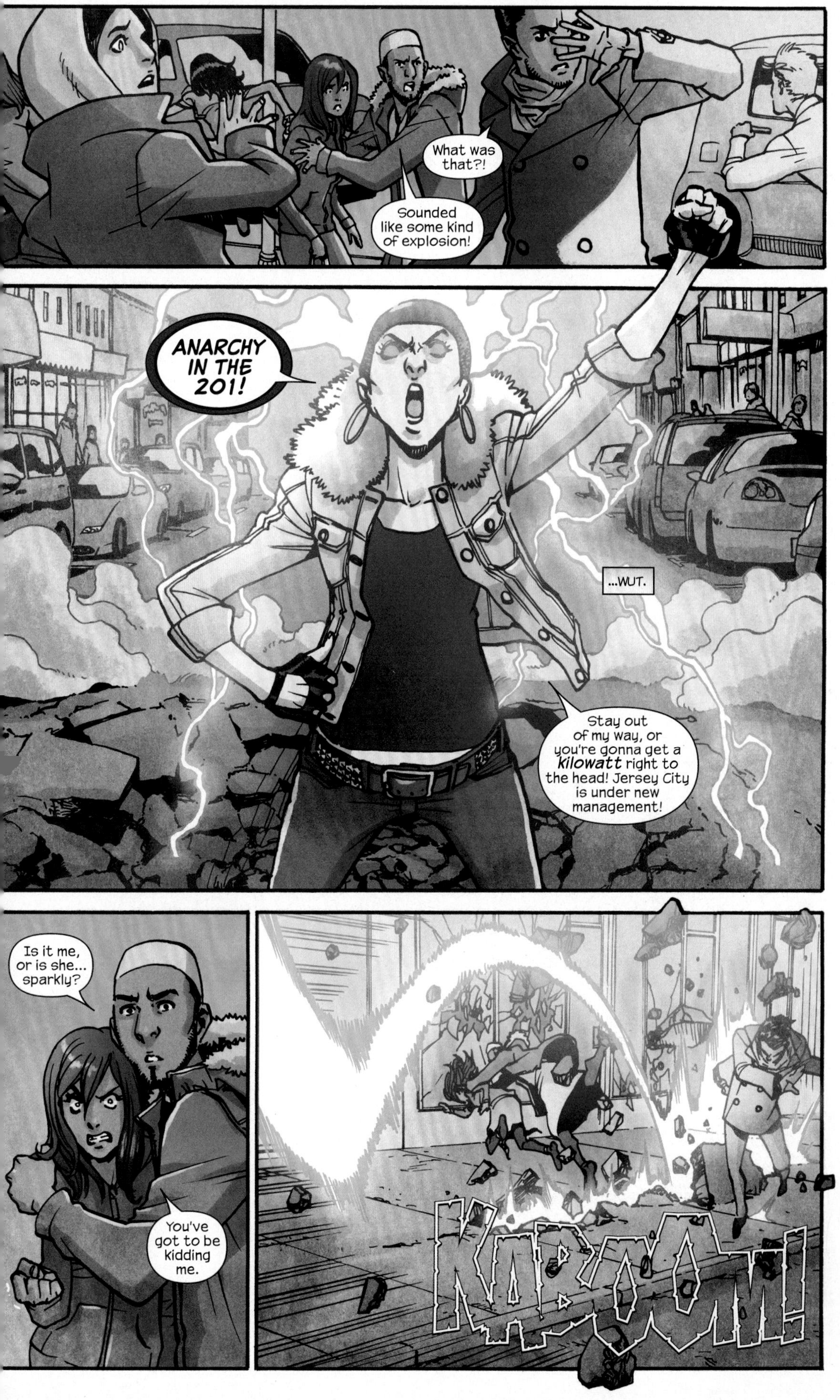
What was that?!
Sounded like some kind of explosion!
ANARCHY IN THE 201!
...WUT.
Stay out of my way, or you're gonna get a *kilowatt* right to the head! Jersey City is under new management!
Is it me, or is she... sparkly?
You've got to be kidding me.
KA-BOOM!

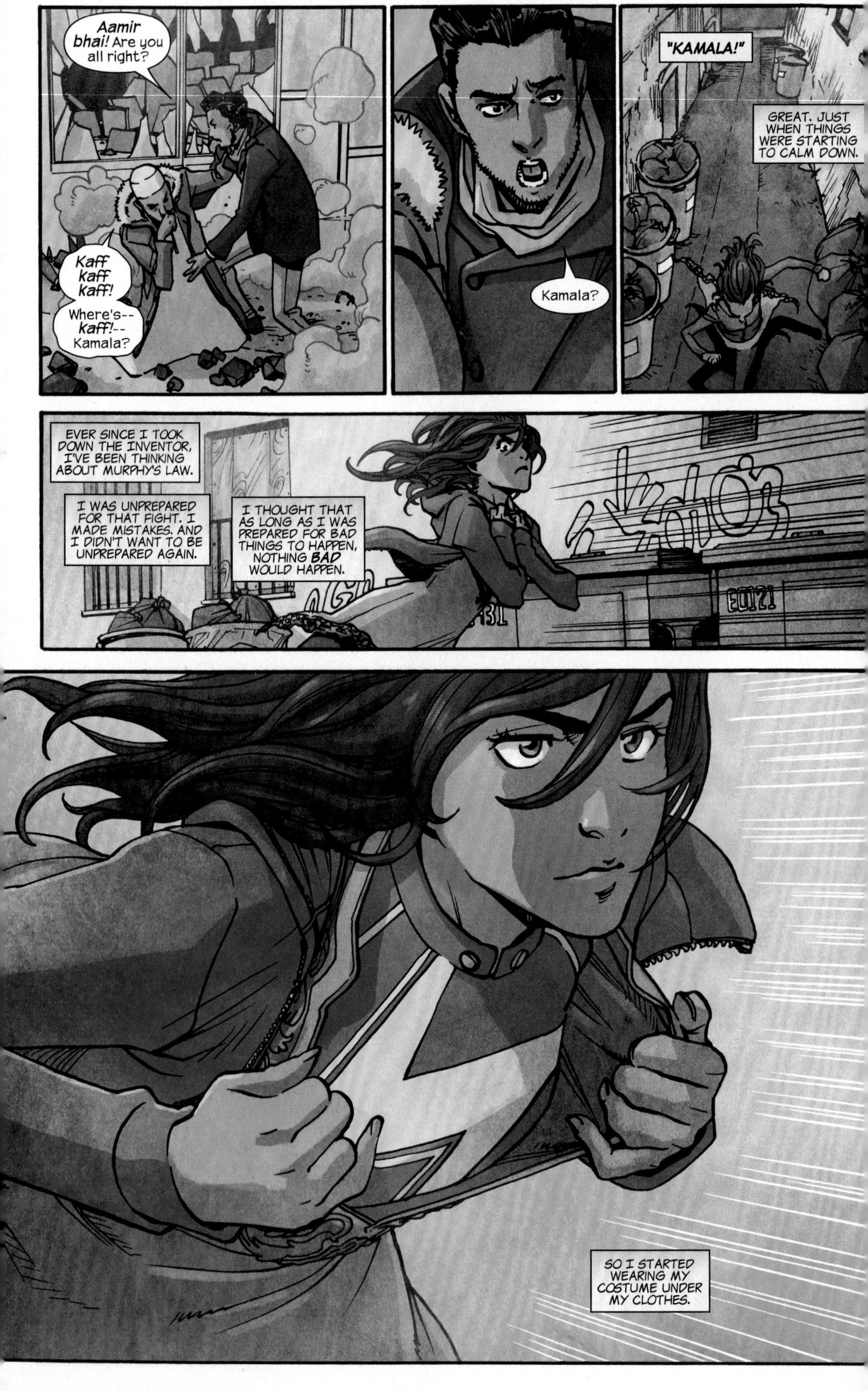
Aamir bhai! Are you all right?
Kaff kaff kaff!
Where's-- kaff!-- Kamala?
Kamala?
"KAMALA!"
GREAT. JUST WHEN THINGS WERE STARTING TO CALM DOWN.
EVER SINCE I TOOK DOWN THE INVENTOR, I'VE BEEN THINKING ABOUT MURPHY'S LAW.
I WAS UNPREPARED FOR THAT FIGHT. I MADE MISTAKES. AND I DIDN'T WANT TO BE UNPREPARED AGAIN.
I THOUGHT THAT AS LONG AS I WAS PREPARED FOR BAD THINGS TO HAPPEN, NOTHING BAD WOULD HAPPEN.
SO I STARTED WEARING MY COSTUME UNDER MY CLOTHES.

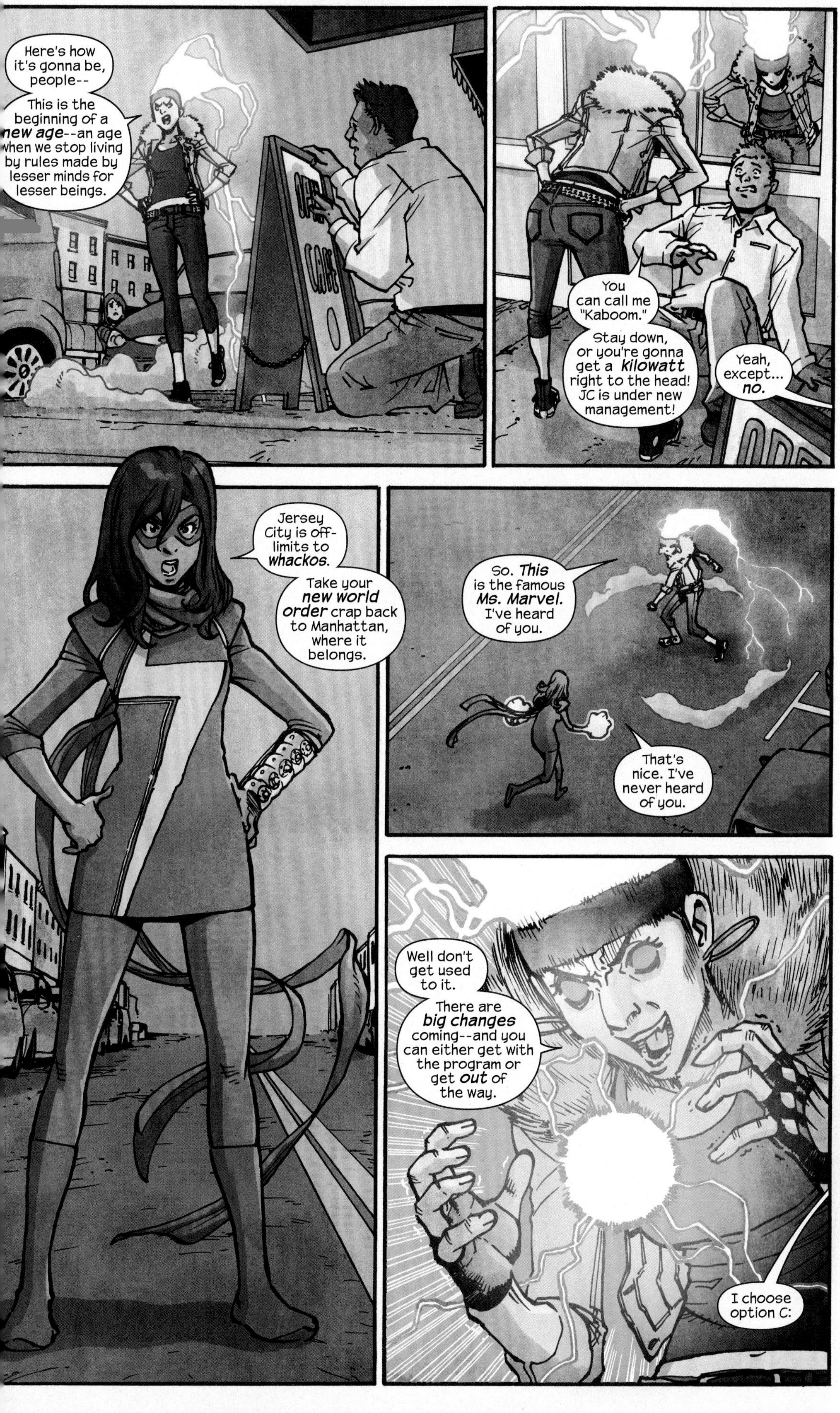
Here's how it's gonna be, people--
This is the beginning of a *new age*--an age when we stop living by rules made by lesser minds for lesser beings.
You can call me "Kaboom."
Stay down, or you're gonna get a *kilowatt* right to the head! JC is under new management!
Yeah, except... *no.*
Jersey City is off-limits to *whackos.*
Take your *new world order* crap back to Manhattan, where it belongs.
So. *This* is the famous *Ms. Marvel.* I've heard of you.
That's nice. I've never heard of you.
Well don't get used to it.
There are *big changes* coming--and you can either get with the program or get *out* of the way.
I choose option C:

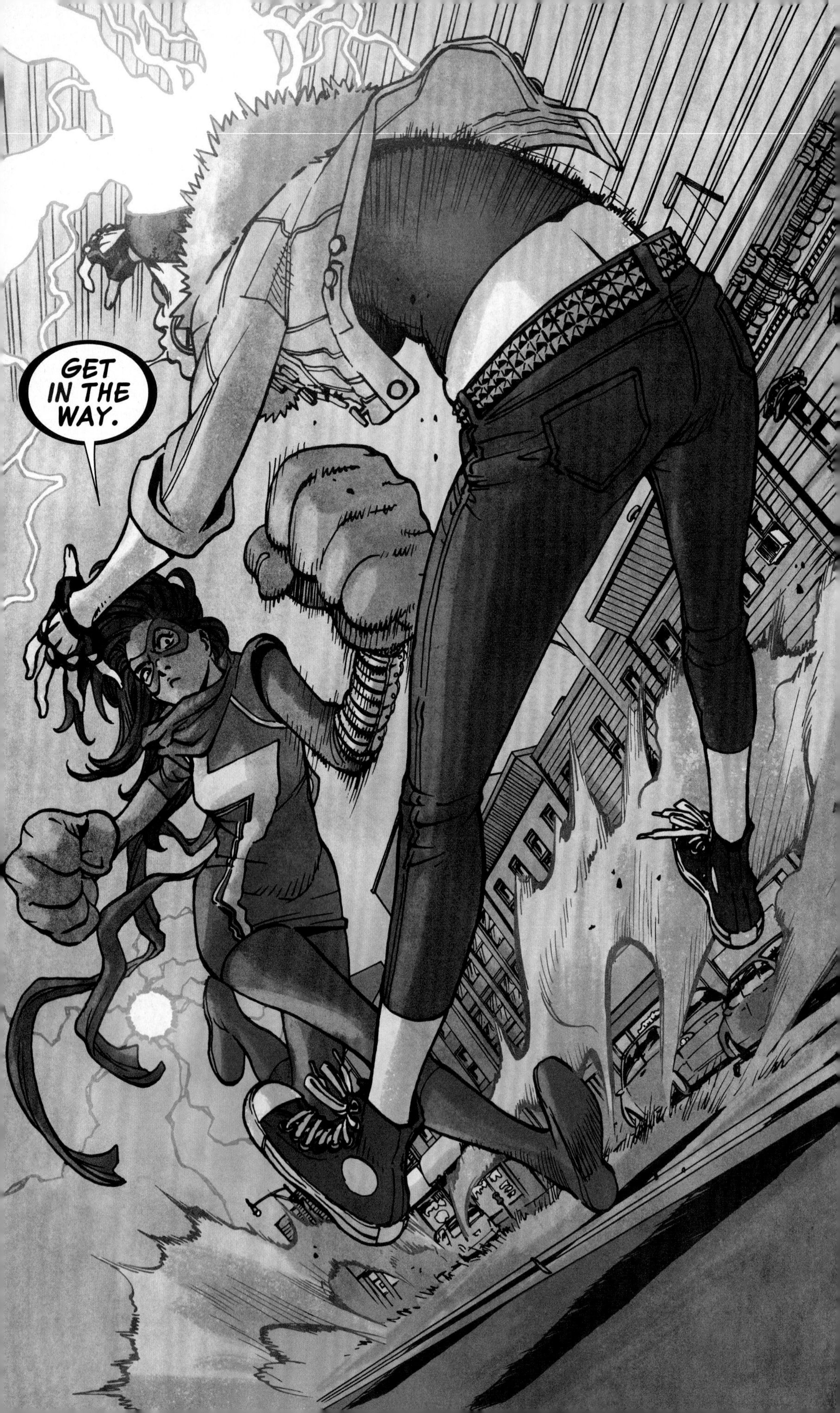
GET IN THE WAY.

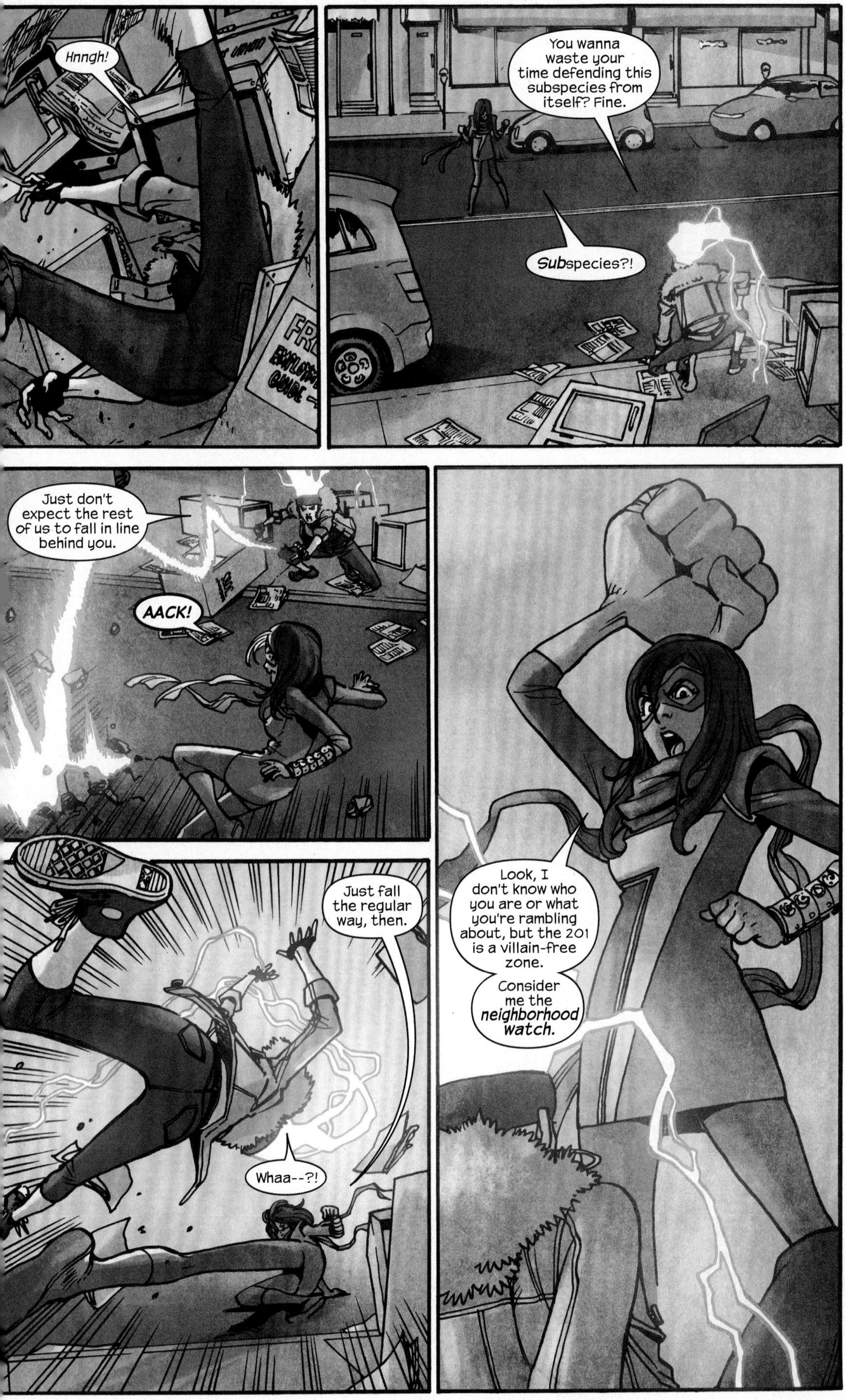
Hnngh!
You wanna waste your time defending this subspecies from itself? Fine.
Subspecies?!
Just don't expect the rest of us to fall in line behind you.
AACK!
Just fall the regular way, then.
Whaa--?!
Look, I don't know who you are or what you're rambling about, but the 201 is a villain-free zone.
Consider me the neighborhood watch.

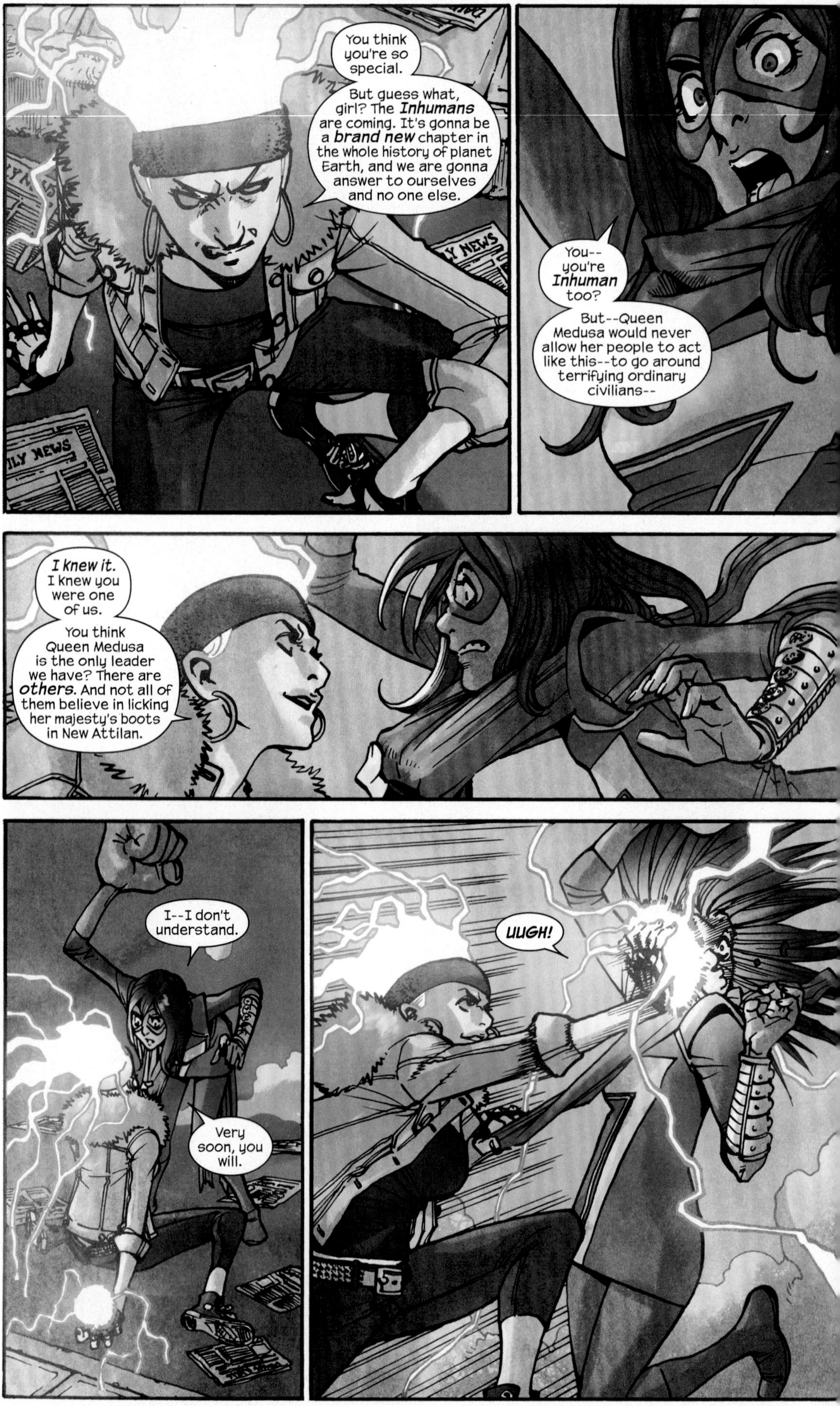
You think you're so special.
But guess what, girl? The *Inhumans* are coming. It's gonna be a ***brand new*** chapter in the whole history of planet Earth, and we are gonna answer to ourselves and no one else.
You-- you're *Inhuman* too?
But--Queen Medusa would never allow her people to act like this--to go around terrifying ordinary civilians--
I knew it. I knew you were one of us.
You think Queen Medusa is the only leader we have? There are ***others***. And not all of them believe in licking her majesty's boots in New Attilan.
I--I don't understand.
Very soon, you will.
UUGH!

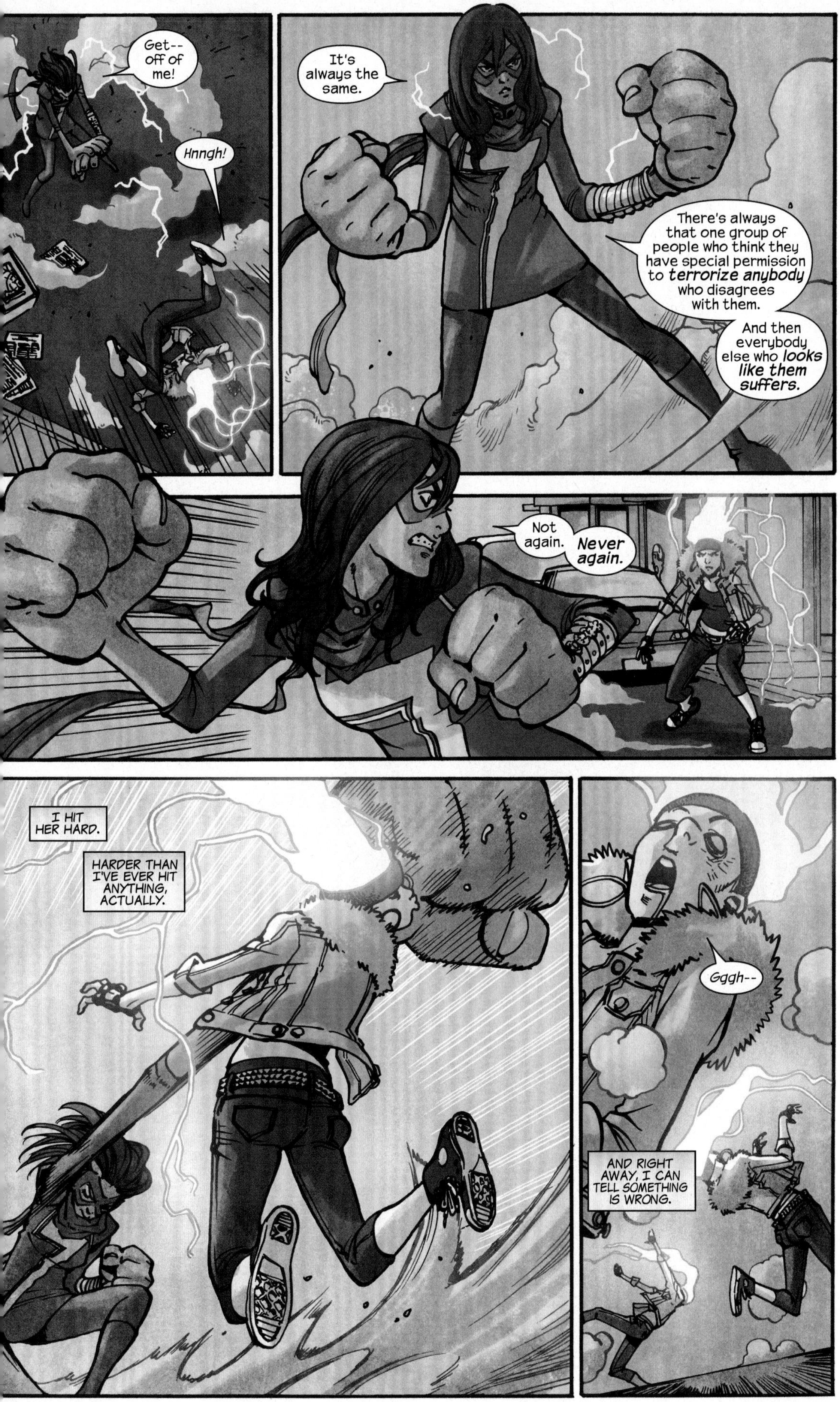
Get-- off of me!
Hnngh!
It's always the same.
There's always that one group of people who think they have special permission to terrorize anybody who disagrees with them.
And then everybody else who looks like them suffers.
Not again.
Never again.
I HIT HER HARD.
HARDER THAN I'VE EVER HIT ANYTHING, ACTUALLY.
Gggh--
AND RIGHT AWAY, I CAN TELL SOMETHING IS WRONG.

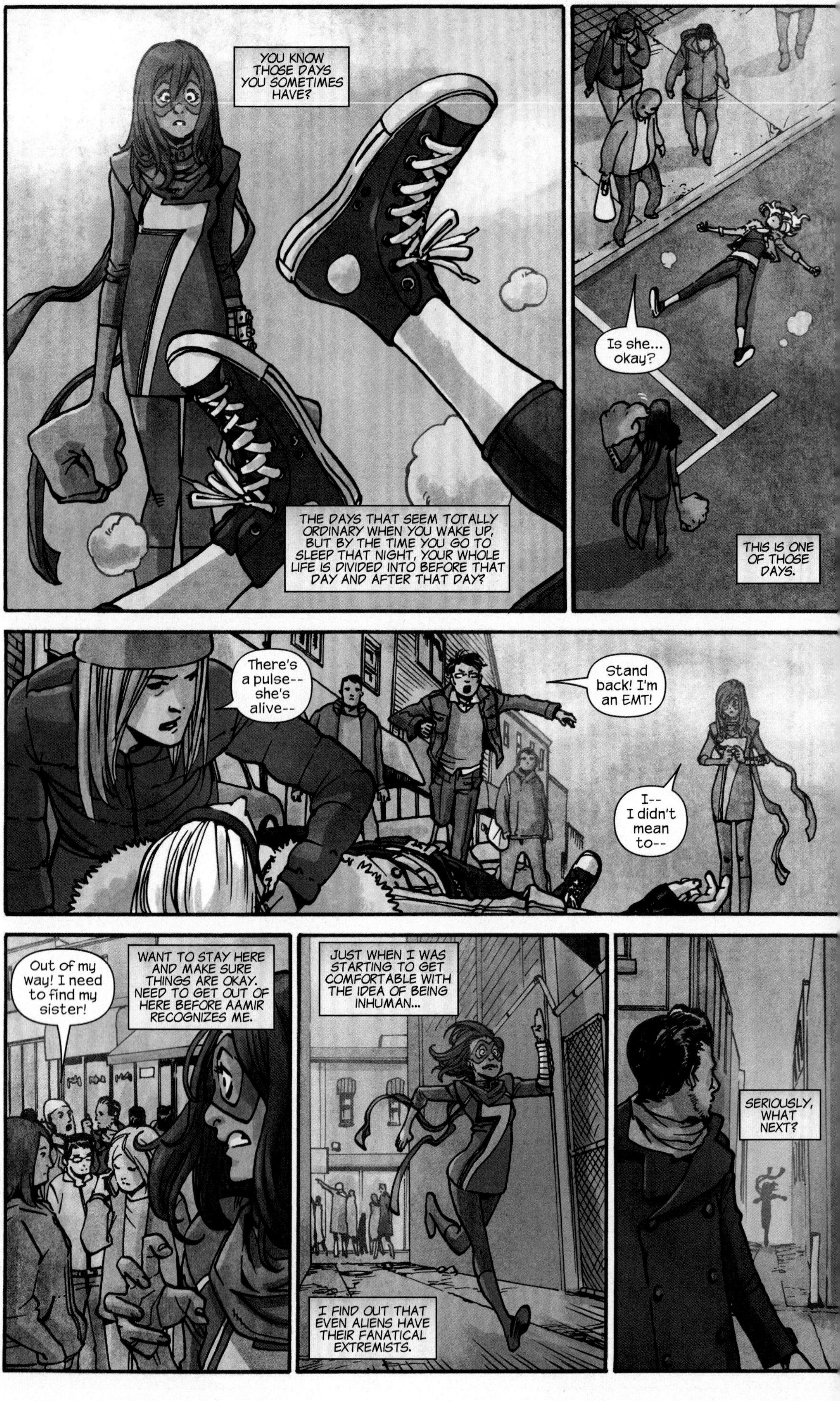

YOU KNOW THOSE DAYS YOU SOMETIMES HAVE?
THE DAYS THAT SEEM TOTALLY ORDINARY WHEN YOU WAKE UP, BUT BY THE TIME YOU GO TO SLEEP THAT NIGHT, YOUR WHOLE LIFE IS DIVIDED INTO BEFORE THAT DAY AND AFTER THAT DAY?
Is she... okay?
THIS IS ONE OF THOSE DAYS.
There's a pulse--she's alive--
Stand back! I'm an EMT!
I-- I didn't mean to--
Out of my way! I need to find my sister!
WANT TO STAY HERE AND MAKE SURE THINGS ARE OKAY. NEED TO GET OUT OF HERE BEFORE AAMIR RECOGNIZES ME.
JUST WHEN I WAS STARTING TO GET COMFORTABLE WITH THE IDEA OF BEING INHUMAN...
I FIND OUT THAT EVEN ALIENS HAVE THEIR FANATICAL EXTREMISTS.
SERIOUSLY, WHAT NEXT?

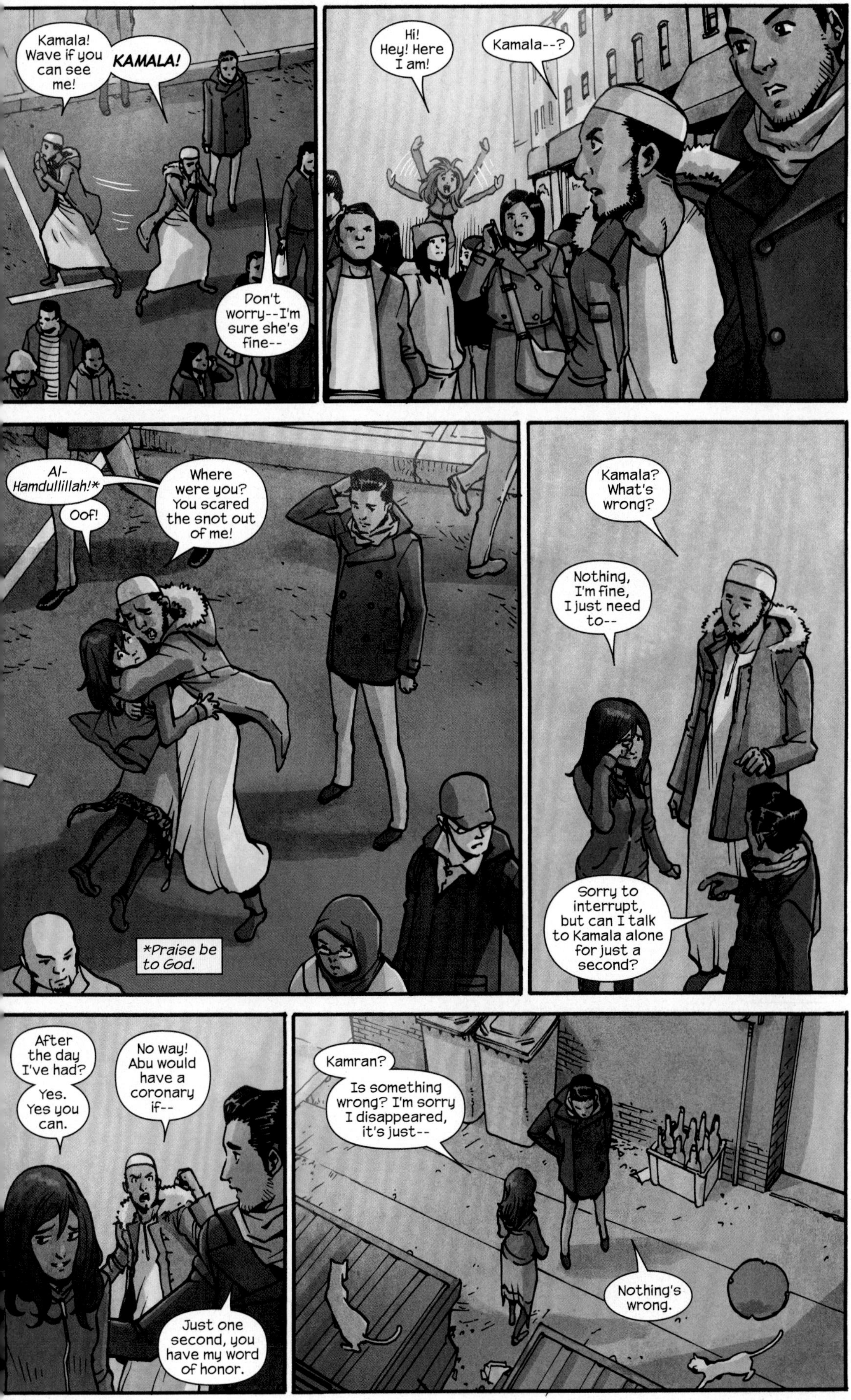
Kamala! Wave if you can see me!
KAMALA!
Don't worry--I'm sure she's fine--
Hi! Hey! Here I am!
Kamala--?
Al-Hamdullillah!*
Oof!
Where were you? You scared the snot out of me!
*Praise be to God.
Kamala? What's wrong?
Nothing, I'm fine, I just need to--
Sorry to interrupt, but can I talk to Kamala alone for just a second?
After the day I've had?
Yes. Yes you can.
No way! Abu would have a coronary if--
Just one second, you have my word of honor.
Kamran?
Is something wrong? I'm sorry I disappeared, it's just--
Nothing's wrong.

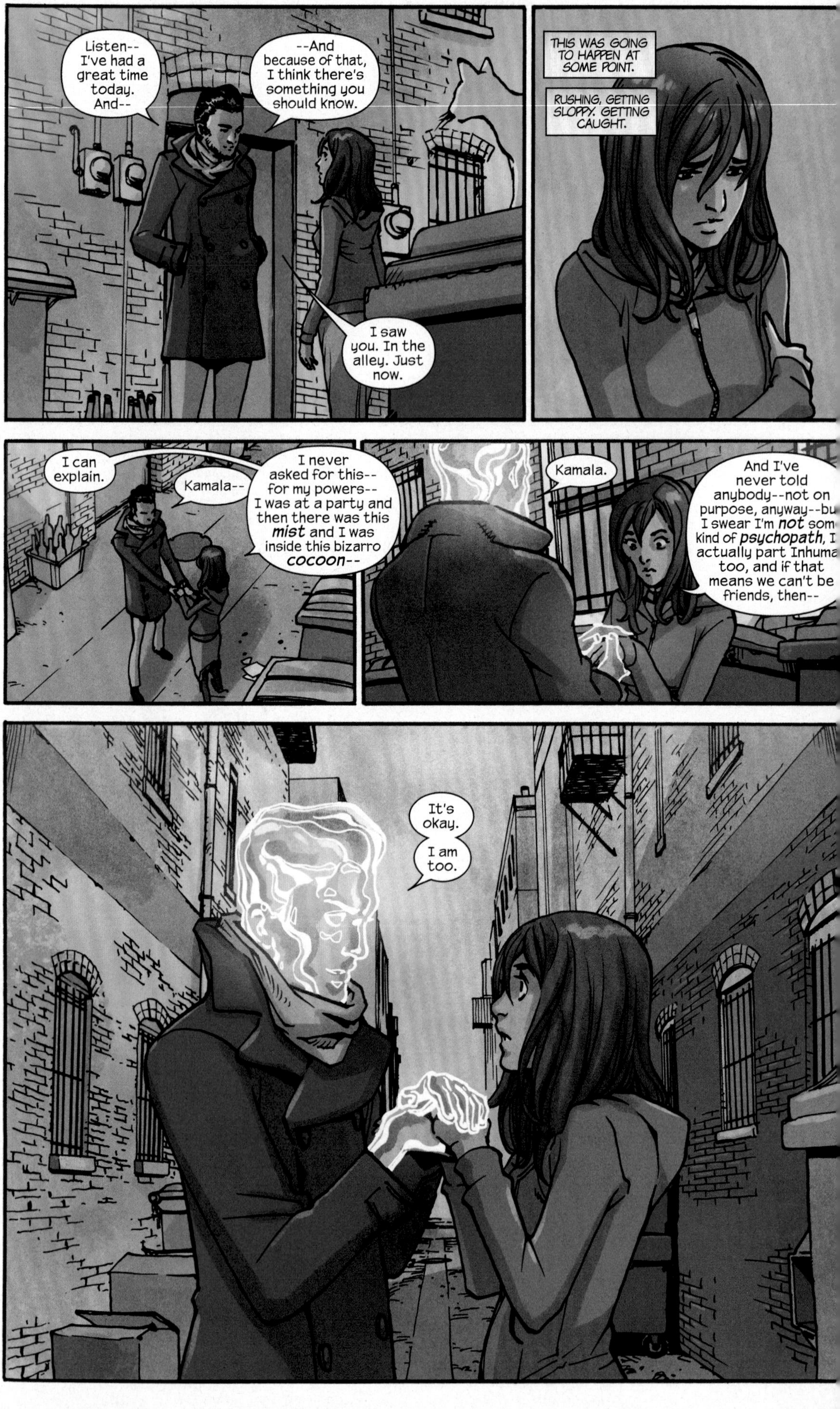
Listen-- I've had a great time today. And--
--And because of that, I think there's something you should know.
I saw you. In the alley. Just now.
THIS WAS GOING TO HAPPEN AT SOME POINT.
RUSHING, GETTING SLOPPY. GETTING CAUGHT.
I can explain.
Kamala--
I never asked for this-- for my powers-- I was at a party and then there was this *mist* and I was inside this bizarro *cocoon*--
Kamala.
And I've never told anybody--not on purpose, anyway--bu I swear I'm *not* som kind of *psychopath*, I actually part Inhuma too, and if that means we can't be friends, then--
It's okay.
I am too.

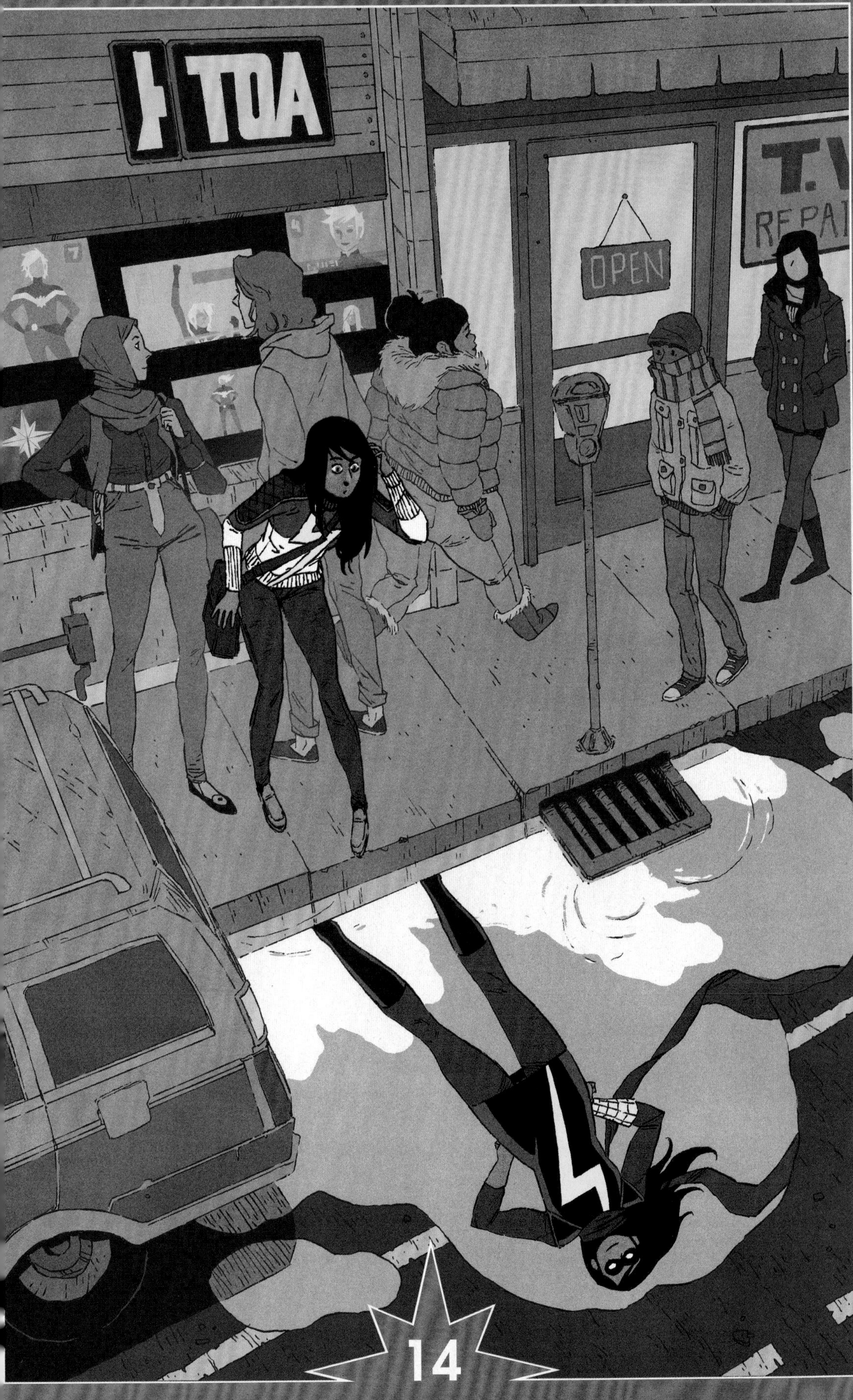
OPEN
14

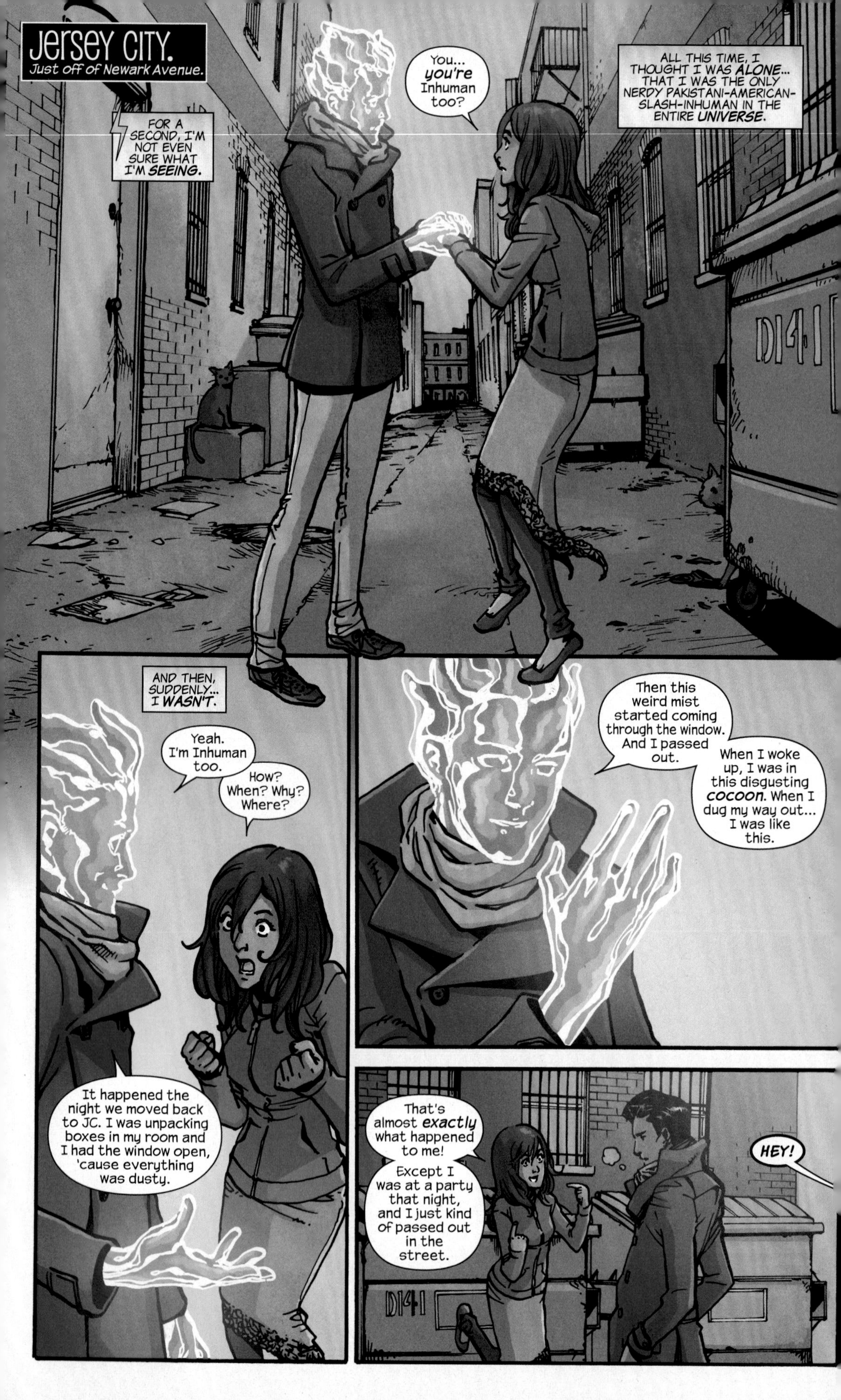
JERSEY CITY.
Just off of Newark Avenue.
FOR A SECOND, I'M NOT EVEN SURE WHAT I'M SEEING.
You... you're Inhuman too?
ALL THIS TIME, I THOUGHT I WAS ALONE... THAT I WAS THE ONLY NERDY PAKISTANI-AMERICAN-SLASH-INHUMAN IN THE ENTIRE UNIVERSE.
AND THEN, SUDDENLY... I WASN'T.
Yeah. I'm Inhuman too.
How? When? Why? Where?
It happened the night we moved back to JC. I was unpacking boxes in my room and I had the window open, 'cause everything was dusty.
Then this weird mist started coming through the window. And I passed out.
When I woke up, I was in this disgusting cocoon. When I dug my way out... I was like this.
That's almost exactly what happened to me!
Except I was at a party that night, and I just kind of passed out in the street.
HEY!

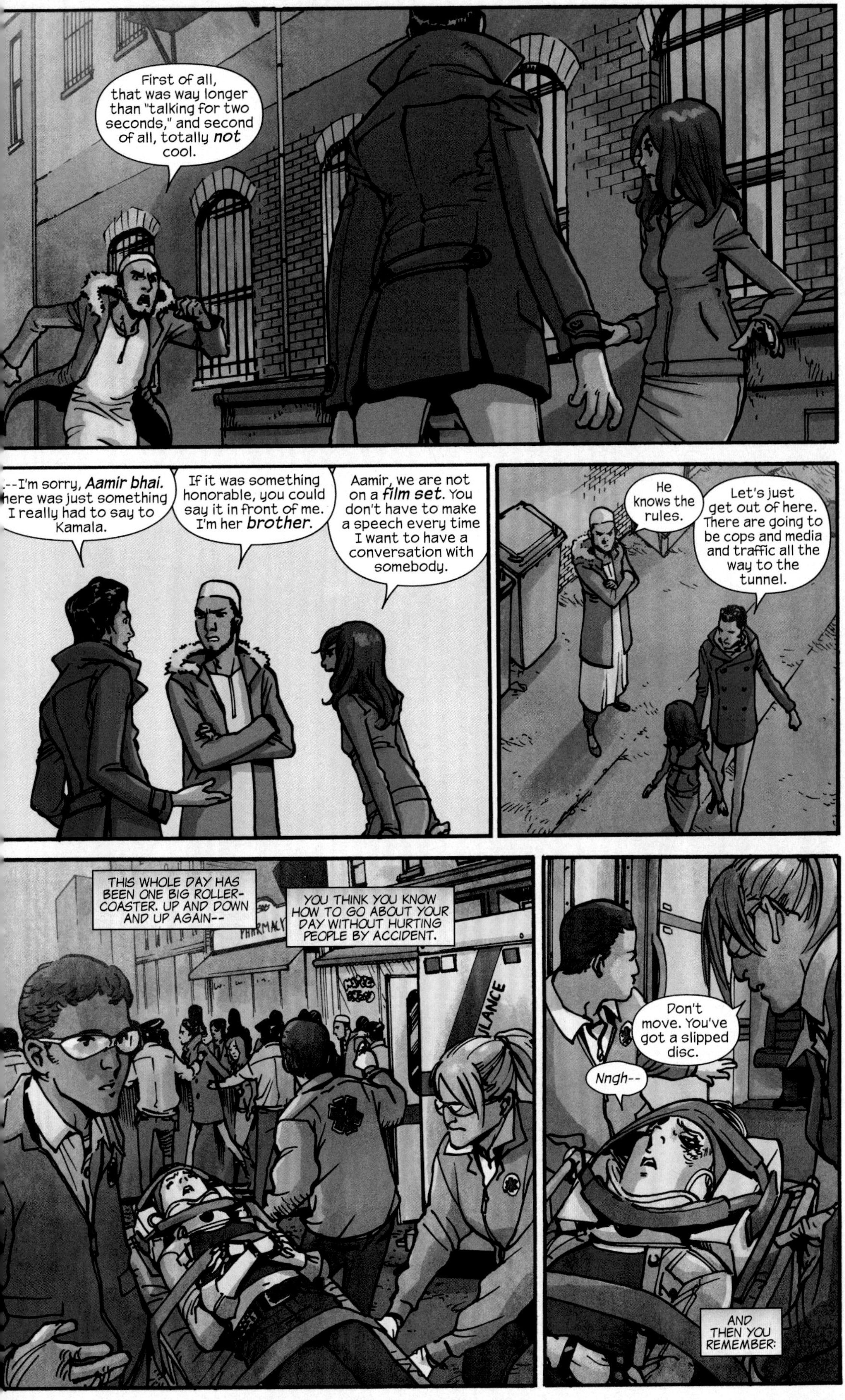
First of all, that was way longer than "talking for two seconds," and second of all, totally *not* cool.
--I'm sorry, *Aamir bhai.* here was just something I really had to say to Kamala.
If it was something honorable, you could say it in front of me. I'm her *brother*.
Aamir, we are not on a *film set*. You don't have to make a speech every time I want to have a conversation with somebody.
He knows the rules.
Let's just get out of here. There are going to be cops and media and traffic all the way to the tunnel.
THIS WHOLE DAY HAS BEEN ONE BIG ROLLER-COASTER. UP AND DOWN AND UP AGAIN--
YOU THINK YOU KNOW HOW TO GO ABOUT YOUR DAY WITHOUT HURTING PEOPLE BY ACCIDENT.
PHARMACY
Don't move. You've got a slipped disc.
Nngh--
AND THEN YOU REMEMBER:

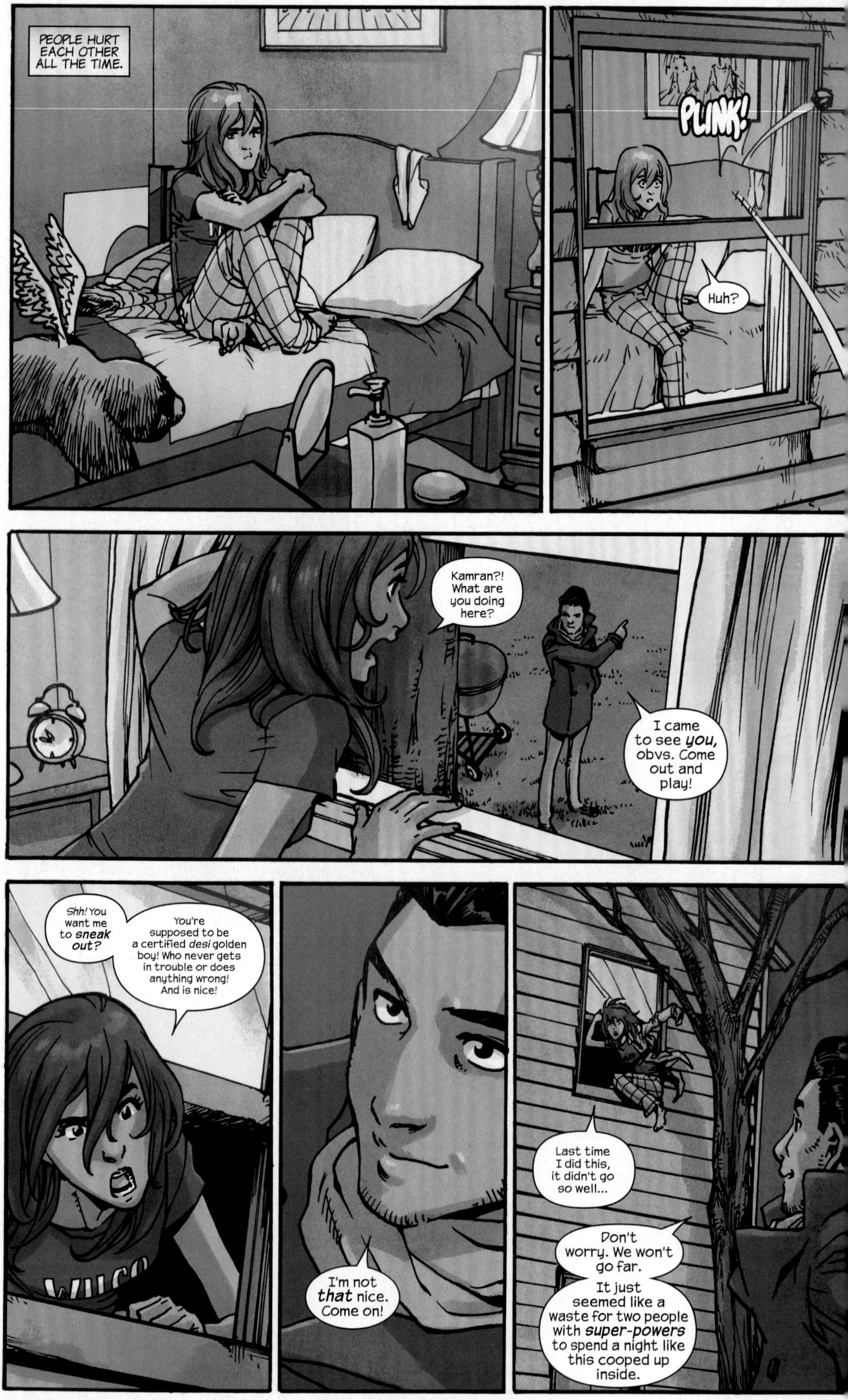
PEOPLE HURT EACH OTHER ALL THE TIME.
PLINK!
Huh?
Kamran?! What are you doing here?
I came to see *you,* obvs. Come out and play!
Shh! You want me to ***sneak out?***
You're supposed to be a certified *desi* golden boy! Who never gets in trouble or does anything wrong! And is nice!
I'm not ***that*** nice. Come on!
Last time I did this, it didn't go so well...
Don't worry. We won't go far.
It just seemed like a waste for two people with ***super-powers*** to spend a night like this cooped up inside.
WILCO

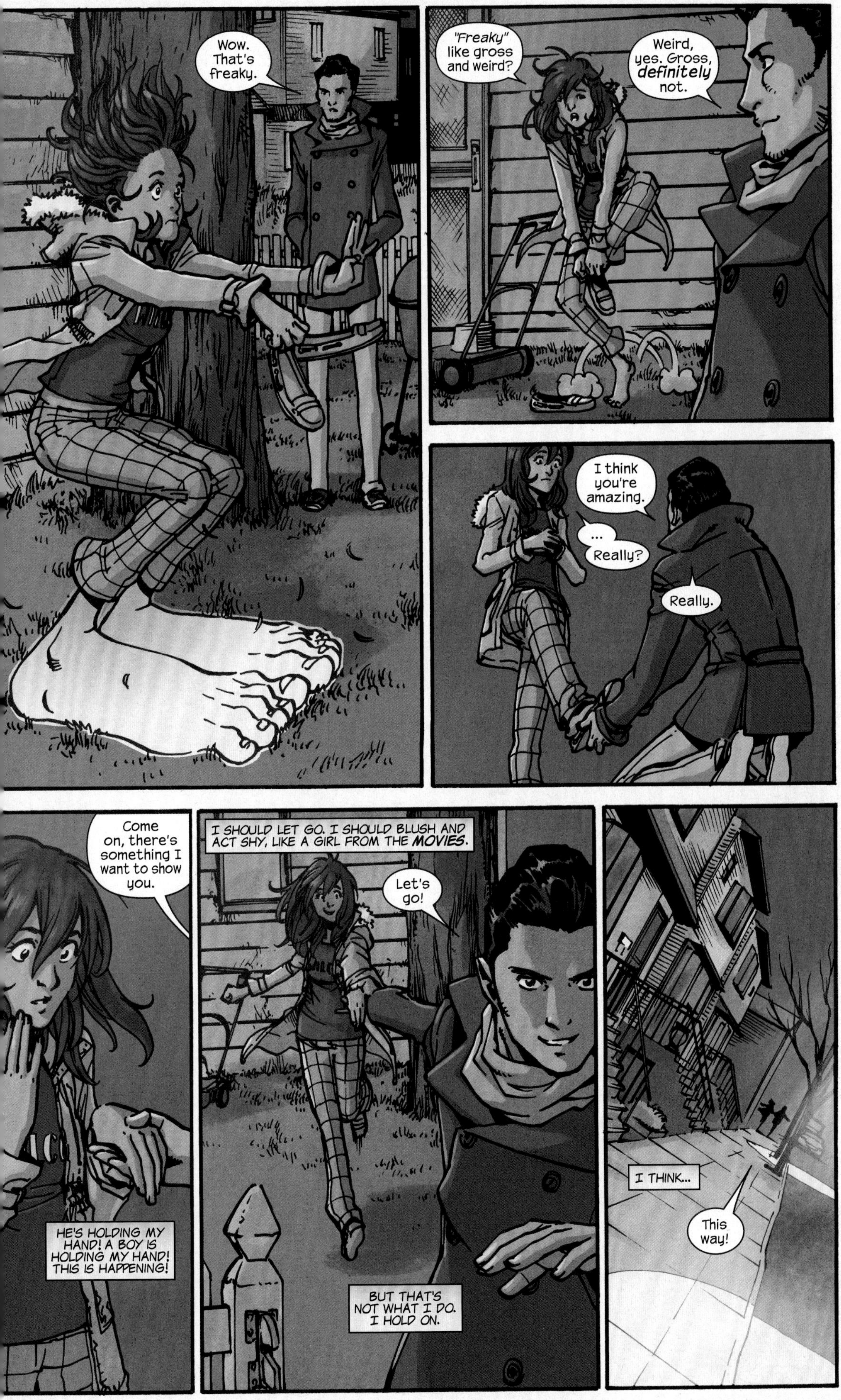
Wow. That's freaky.
"Freaky" like gross and weird?
Weird, yes. Gross, *definitely* not.
I think you're amazing.
... Really?
Really.
Come on, there's something I want to show you.
HE'S HOLDING MY HAND! A BOY IS HOLDING MY HAND! THIS IS HAPPENING!
I SHOULD LET GO. I SHOULD BLUSH AND ACT SHY, LIKE A GIRL FROM THE *MOVIES*.
Let's go!
BUT THAT'S NOT WHAT I DO. I HOLD ON.
I THINK...
This way!

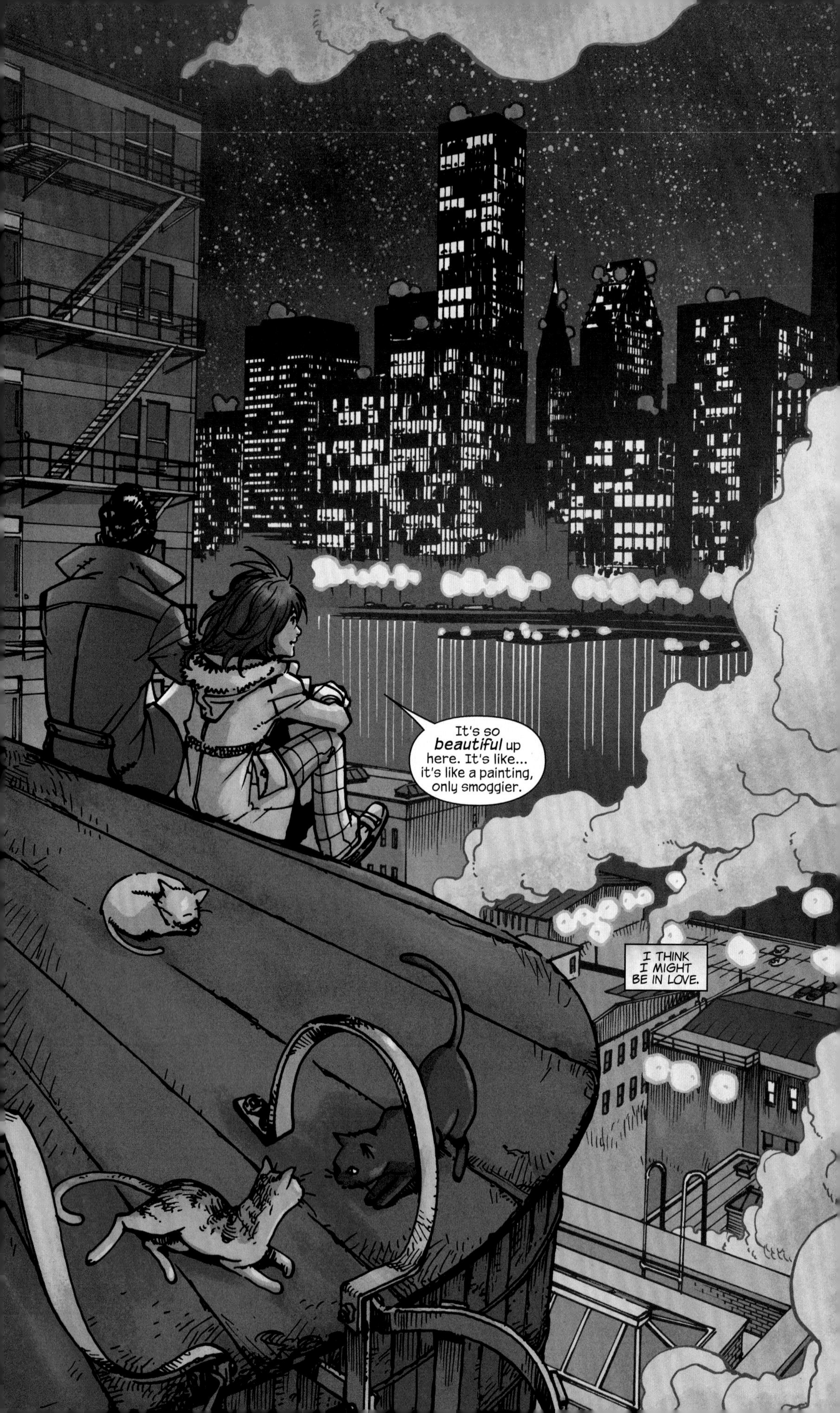
It's so *beautiful* up here. It's like... it's like a painting, only smoggier.
I THINK I MIGHT BE IN LOVE.

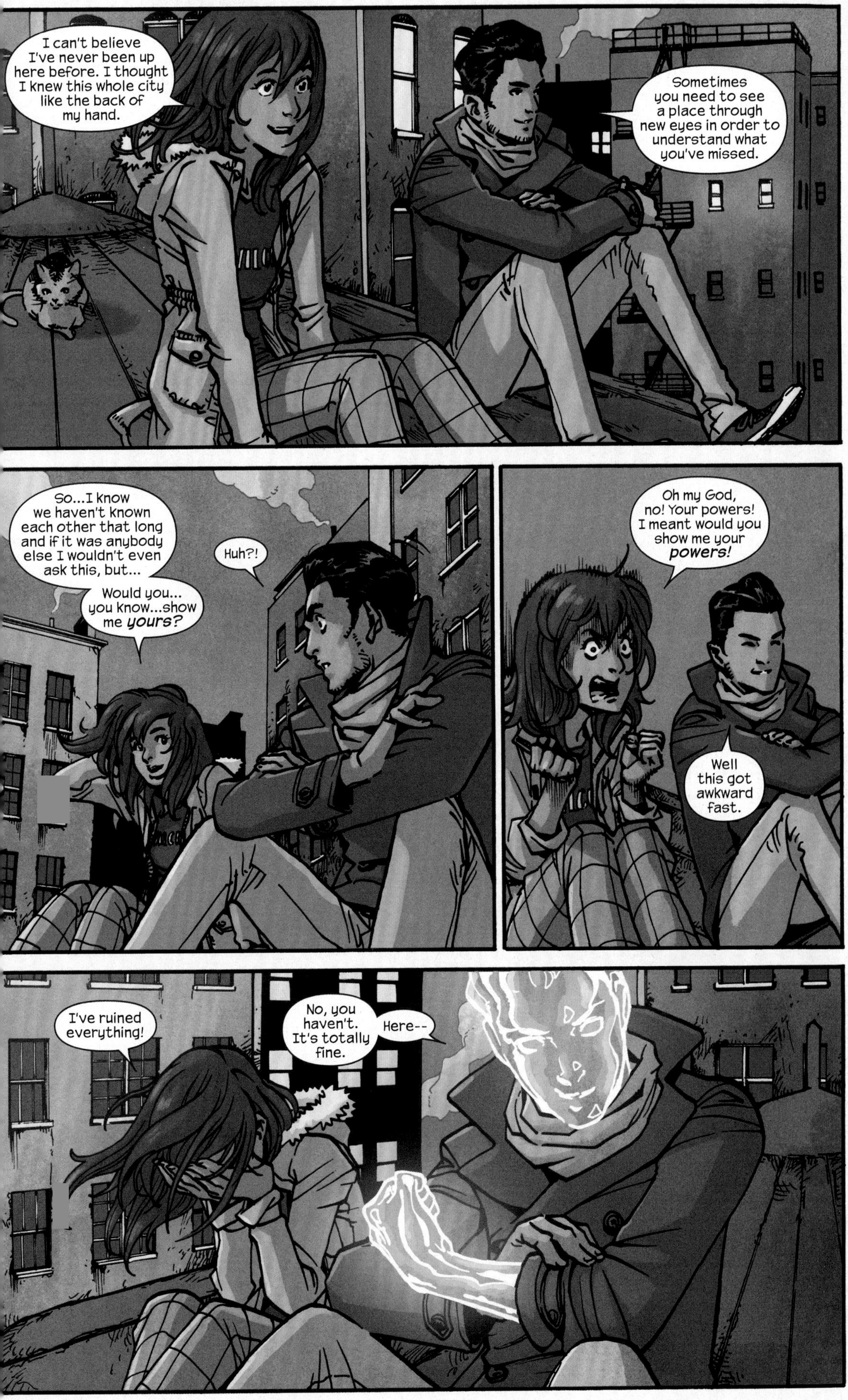
I can't believe I've never been up here before. I thought I knew this whole city like the back of my hand.
Sometimes you need to see a place through new eyes in order to understand what you've missed.
So...I know we haven't known each other that long and if it was anybody else I wouldn't even ask this, but...
Would you... you know...show me *yours?*
Huh?!
Oh my God, no! Your powers! I meant would you show me your *powers!*
Well this got awkward fast.
I've ruined everything!
No, you haven't. It's totally fine.
Here--

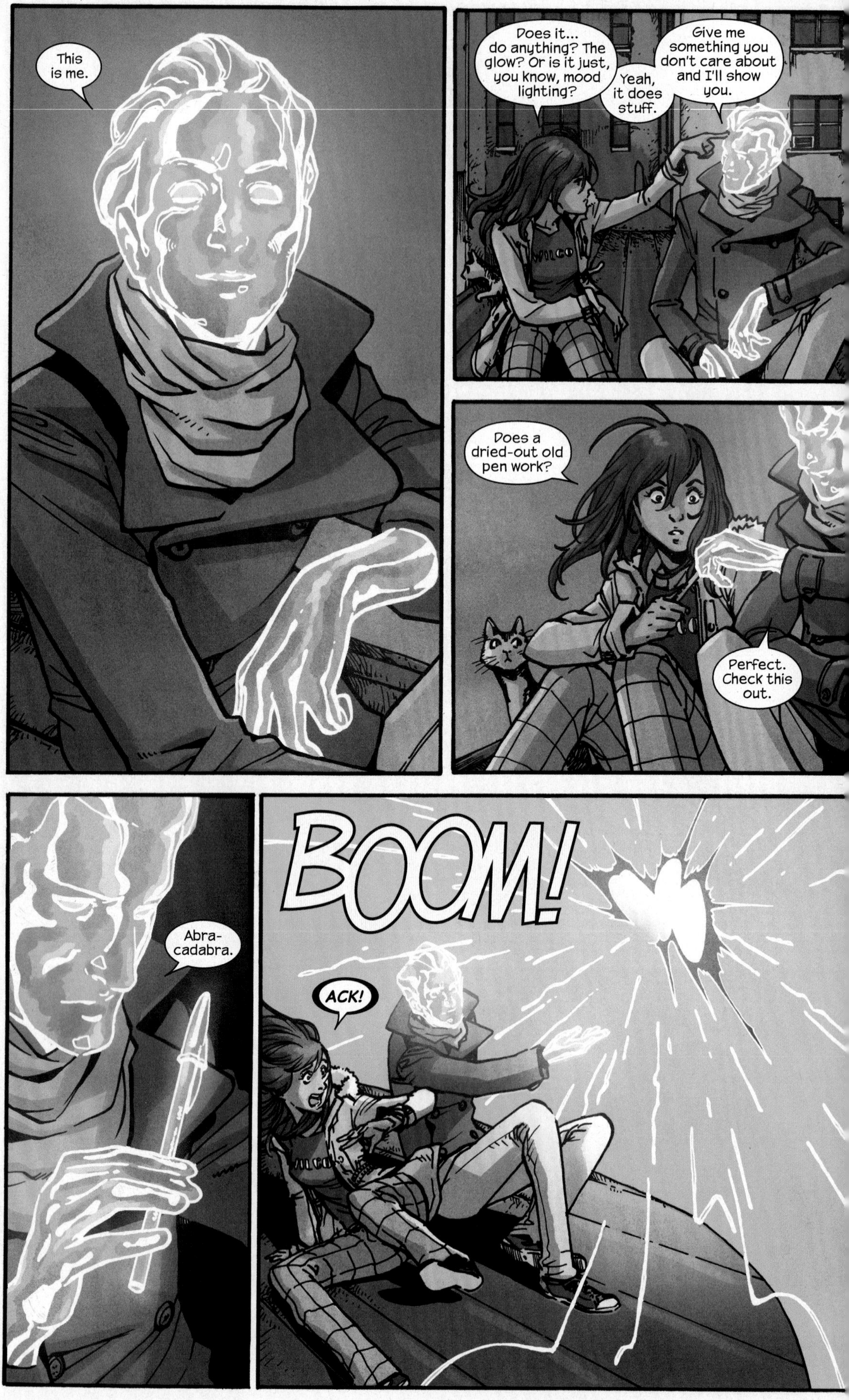
This is me.
Does it... do anything? The glow? Or is it just, you know, mood lighting?
Yeah, it does stuff.
Give me something you don't care about and I'll show you.
Does a dried-out old pen work?
Perfect. Check this out.
Abra-cadabra.
BOOM!
ACK!

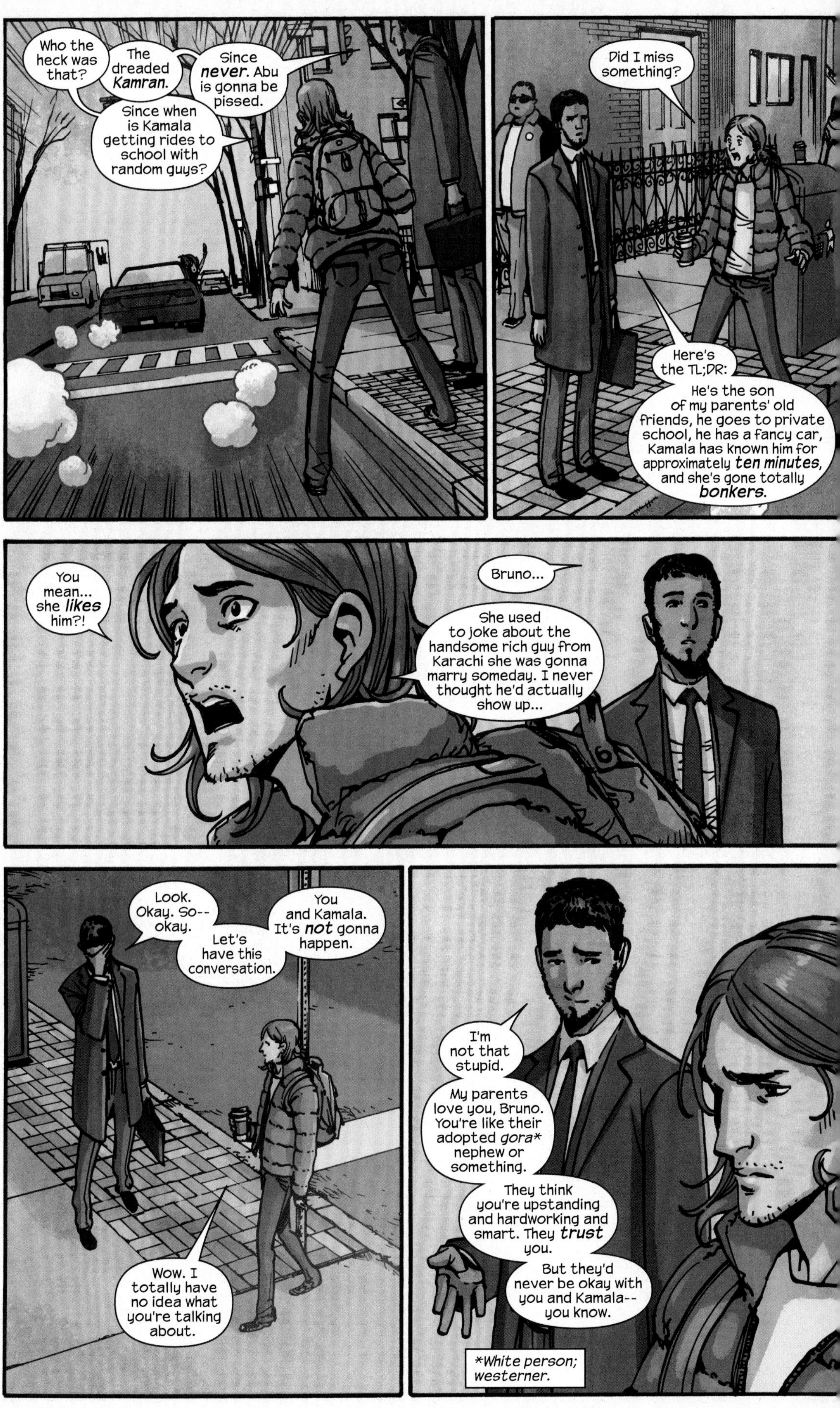
Who the heck was that?
The dreaded *Kamran*.
Since *never*. Abu is gonna be pissed.
Since when is Kamala getting rides to school with random guys?
Did I miss something?
Here's the TL;DR:
He's the son of my parents' old friends, he goes to private school, he has a fancy car, Kamala has known him for approximately *ten minutes*, and she's gone totally *bonkers*.
You mean... she *likes* him?!
Bruno...
She used to joke about the handsome rich guy from Karachi she was gonna marry someday. I never thought he'd actually show up...
Look. Okay. So-- okay.
Let's have this conversation.
You and Kamala. It's *not* gonna happen.
Wow. I totally have no idea what you're talking about.
I'm not that stupid.
My parents love you, Bruno. You're like their adopted *gora** nephew or something.
They think you're upstanding and hardworking and smart. They *trust* you.
But they'd never be okay with you and Kamala-- you know.
*White person; westerner.

ear sir or madam, thank you for considering me for assistant transponder of--

Hey, Kamala. Looking sharp, Aamir.

He's got a job interview.

Whoa, great. If I knew that, I'd have brought three coffees.

Where's the bus?

Late.

You look awful.

I was up til awful o'clock.

Doing what?

VROOM!

Oh great. It's *him.*

Who?!

Hey, Kamala. You guys want a ride?

Umm... Yes!

Hellooo? What? Abu and Ammi will have simultaneous coronary events if you get a lift from a dude you've known for like a day--

How about you guys? Want a lift to school?

Excelsior Academy doesn't start 'til 8:30, so I've got time.

I'll, uh, keep waiting for the bus.

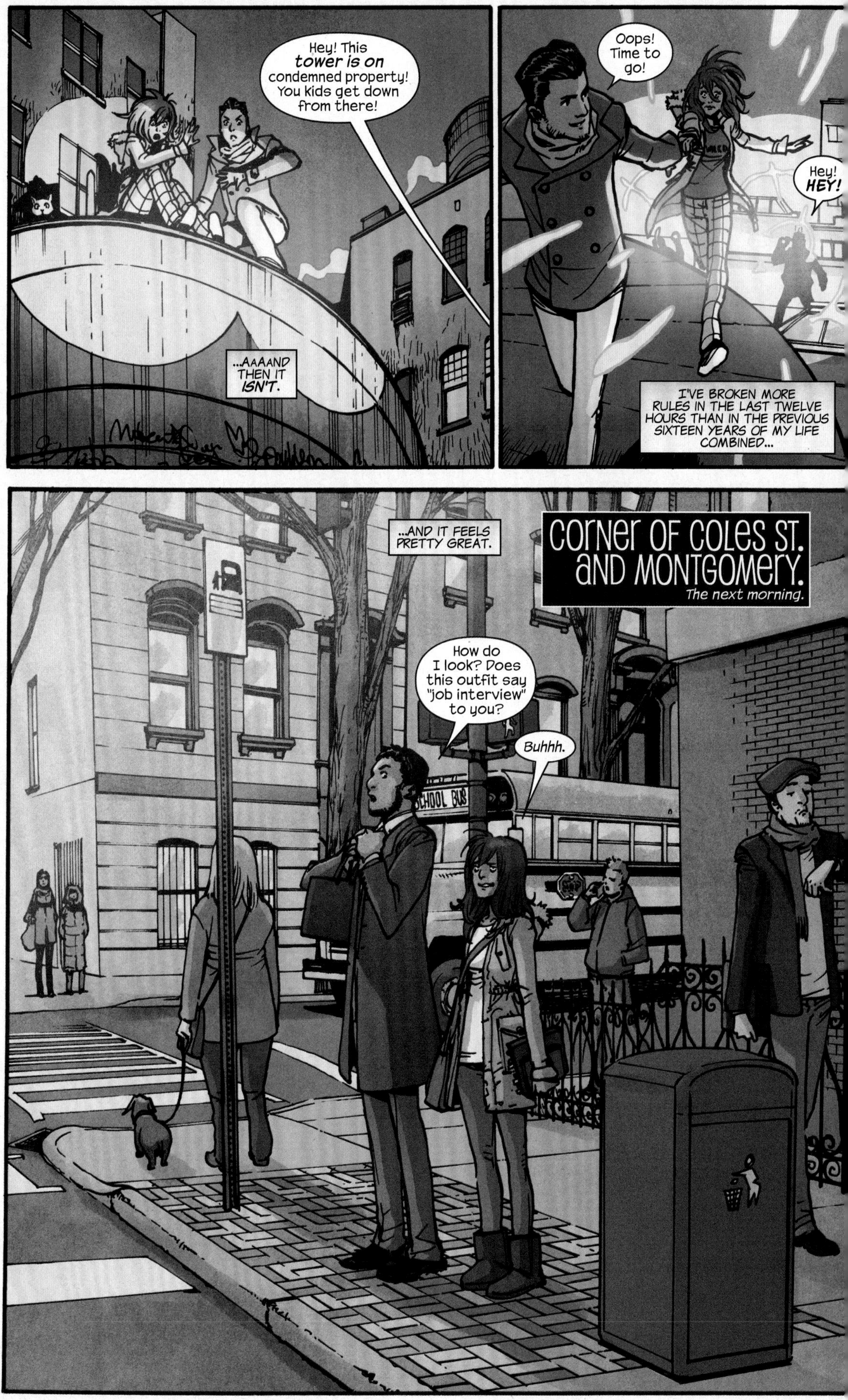
Hey! This tower is on condemned property! You kids get down from there!
...AAAAND THEN IT ISN'T.
Oops! Time to go!
Hey! HEY!
I'VE BROKEN MORE RULES IN THE LAST TWELVE HOURS THAN IN THE PREVIOUS SIXTEEN YEARS OF MY LIFE COMBINED...
...AND IT FEELS PRETTY GREAT.
CORNER OF COLES ST. AND MONTGOMERY.
The next morning.
How do I look? Does this outfit say "job interview" to you?
Buhhh.
SCHOOL BUS

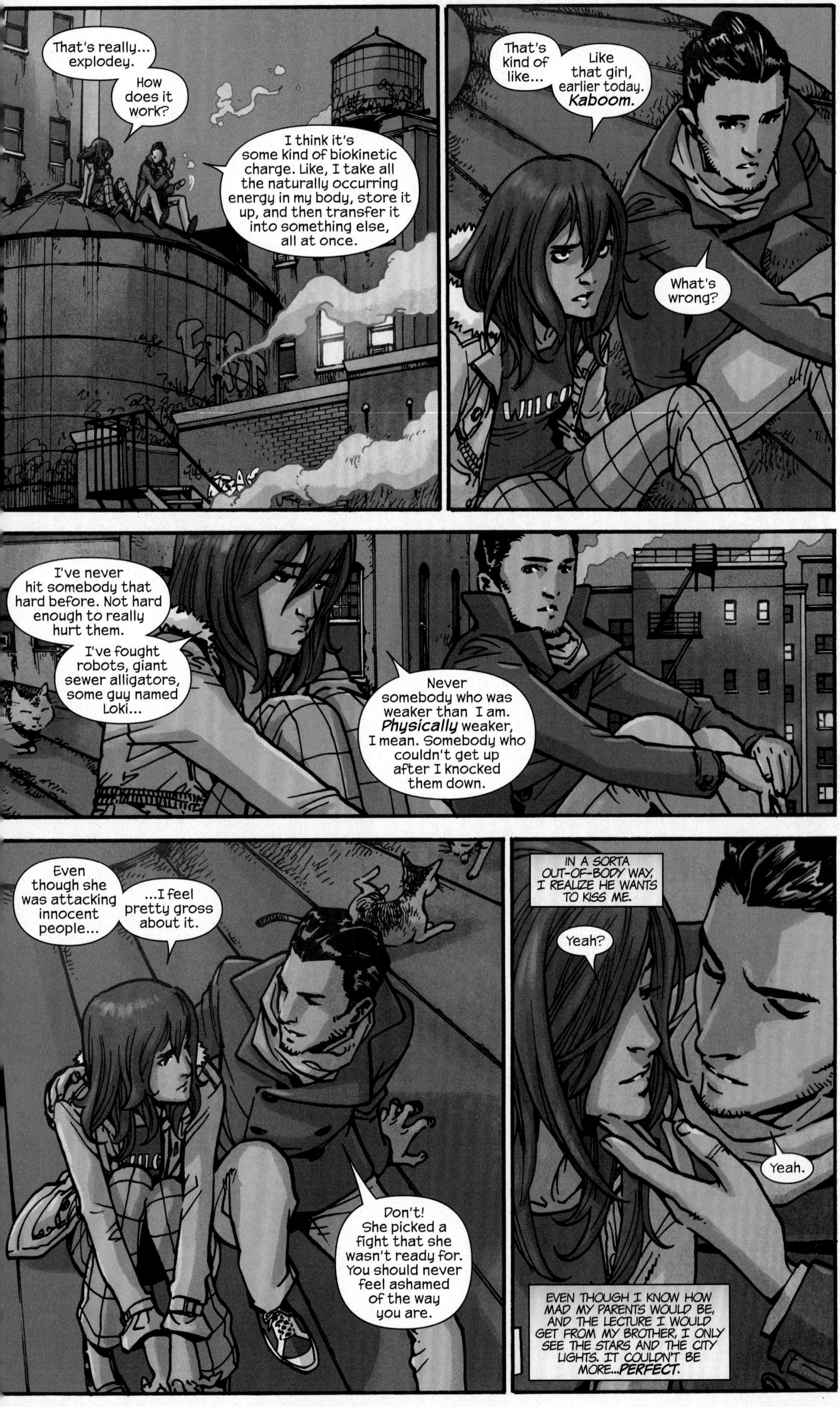

That's really... explodey.
How does it work?
I think it's some kind of biokinetic charge. Like, I take all the naturally occurring energy in my body, store it up, and then transfer it into something else, all at once.
That's kind of like...
Like that girl, earlier today. *Kaboom.*
What's wrong?
I've never hit somebody that hard before. Not hard enough to really hurt them.
I've fought robots, giant sewer alligators, some guy named Loki...
Never somebody who was weaker than I am. *Physically* weaker, I mean. Somebody who couldn't get up after I knocked them down.
Even though she was attacking innocent people...
...I feel pretty gross about it.
Don't! She picked a fight that she wasn't ready for. You should never feel ashamed of the way you are.
IN A SORTA OUT-OF-BODY WAY, I REALIZE HE WANTS TO KISS ME.
Yeah?
Yeah.
EVEN THOUGH I KNOW HOW MAD MY PARENTS WOULD BE, AND THE LECTURE I WOULD GET FROM MY BROTHER, I ONLY SEE THE STARS AND THE CITY LIGHTS. IT COULDN'T BE MORE...*PERFECT*.

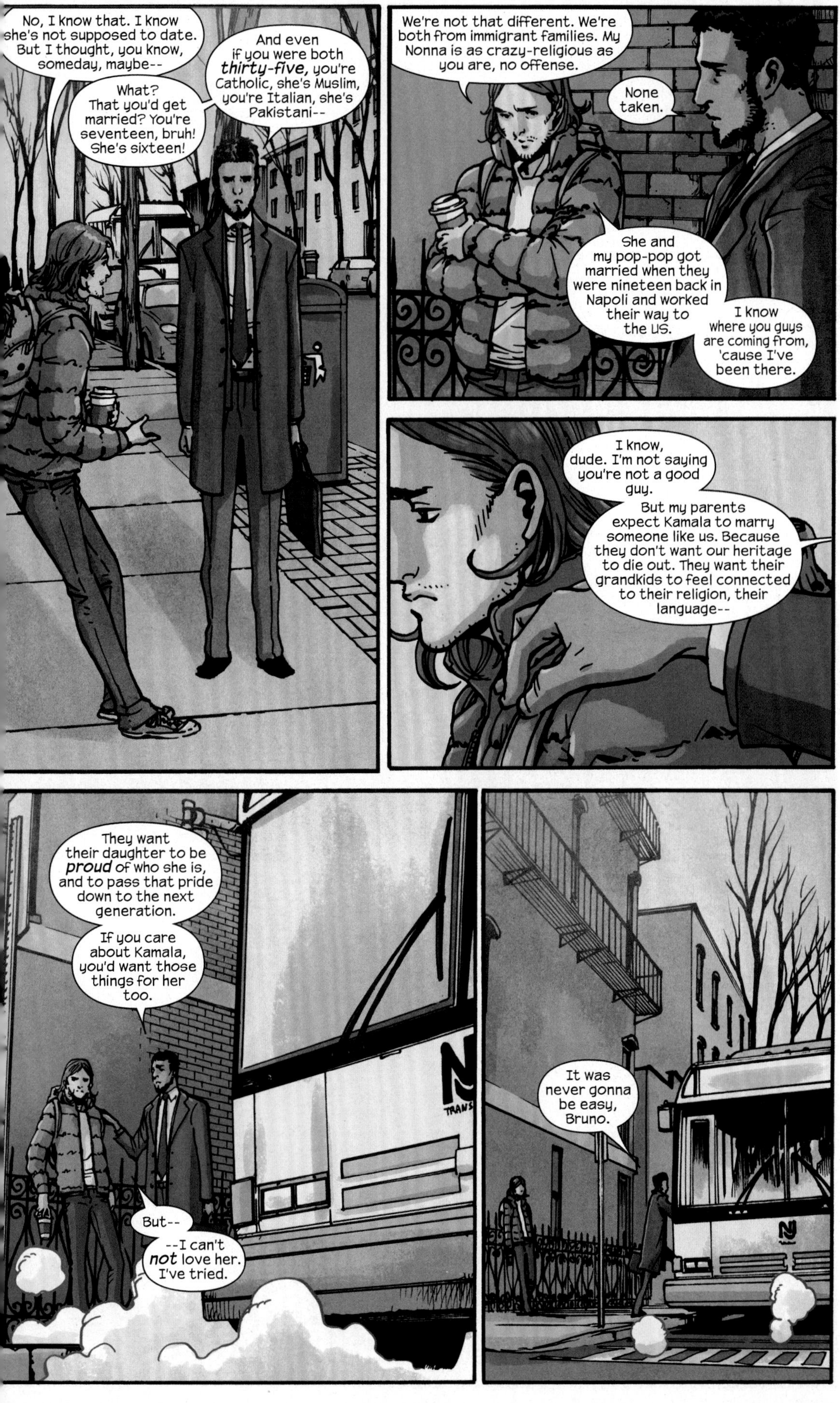
No, I know that. I know she's not supposed to date. But I thought, you know, someday, maybe--
What? That you'd get married? You're seventeen, bruh! She's sixteen!
And even if you were both *thirty-five,* you're Catholic, she's Muslim, you're Italian, she's Pakistani--
We're not that different. We're both from immigrant families. My Nonna is as crazy-religious as you are, no offense.
None taken.
She and my pop-pop got married when they were nineteen back in Napoli and worked their way to the US.
I know where you guys are coming from, 'cause I've been there.
I know, dude. I'm not saying you're not a good guy.
But my parents expect Kamala to marry someone like us. Because they don't want our heritage to die out. They want their grandkids to feel connected to their religion, their language--
They want their daughter to be *proud* of who she is, and to pass that pride down to the next generation.
If you care about Kamala, you'd want those things for her too.
But--
--I can't *not* love her. I've tried.
It was never gonna be easy, Bruno.

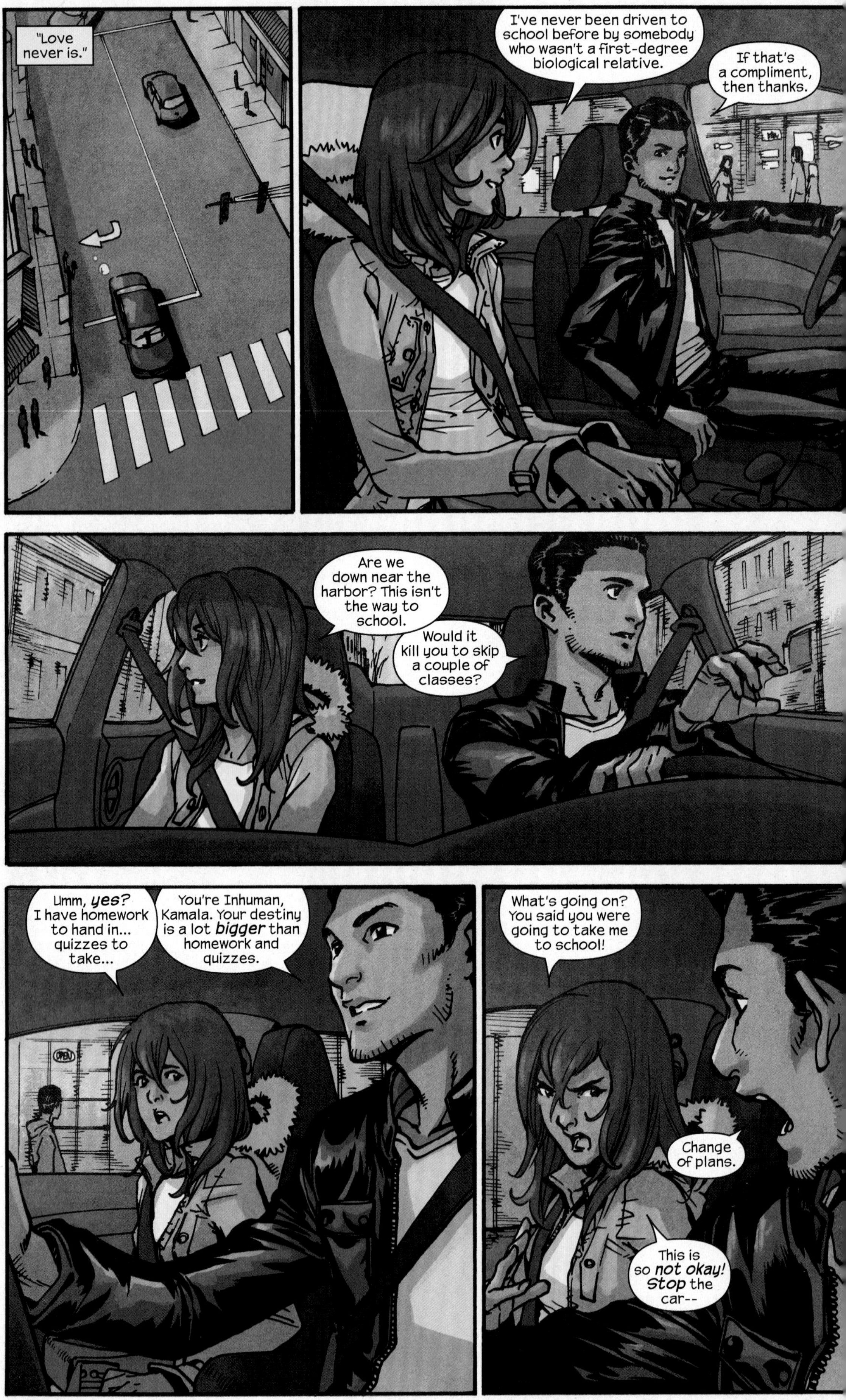
"Love never is."
I've never been driven to school before by somebody who wasn't a first-degree biological relative.
If that's a compliment, then thanks.
Are we down near the harbor? This isn't the way to school.
Would it kill you to skip a couple of classes?
Umm, *yes?* I have homework to hand in... quizzes to take...
You're Inhuman, Kamala. Your destiny is a lot *bigger* than homework and quizzes.
What's going on? You said you were going to take me to school!
Change of plans.
This is so *not okay! Stop* the car--

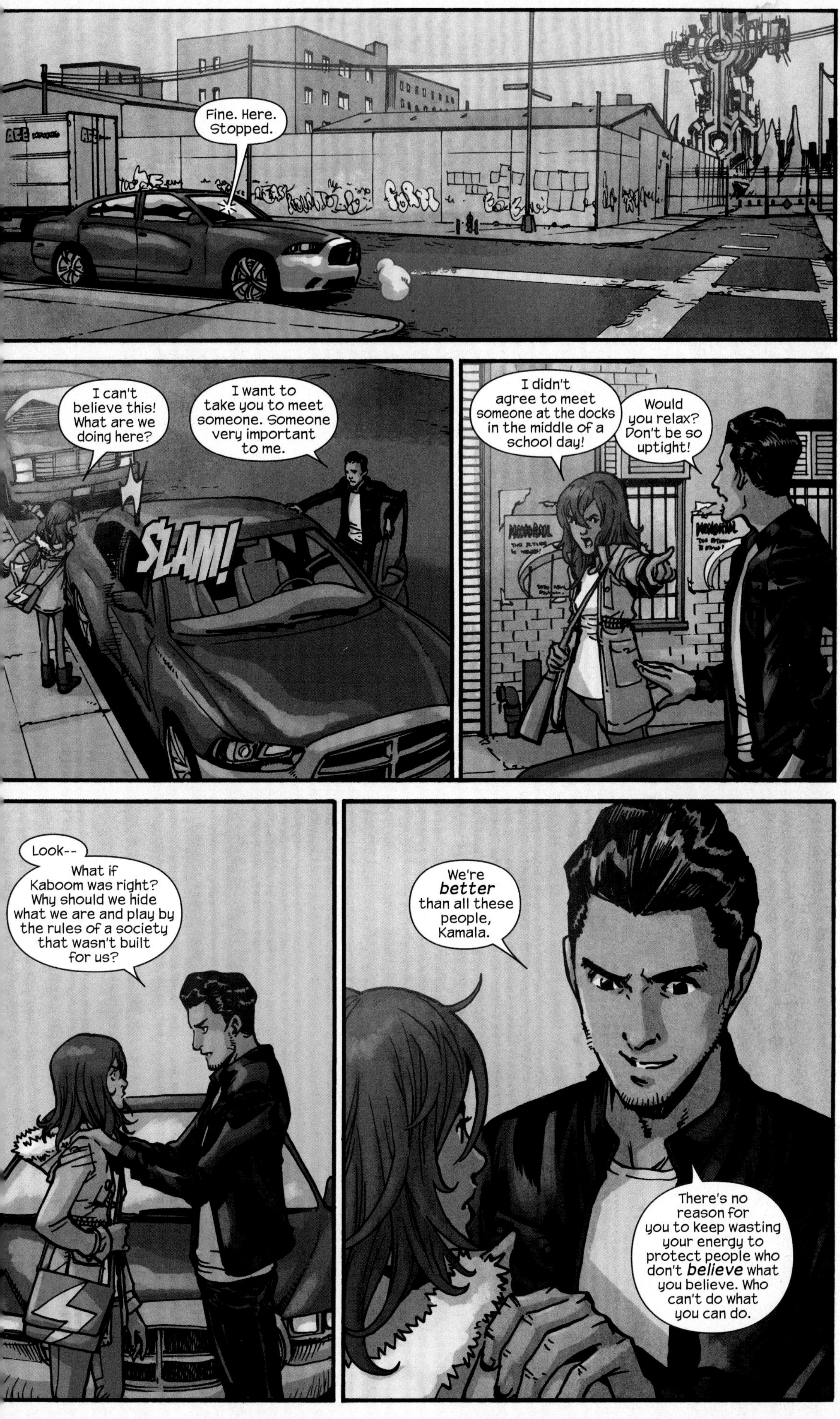
Fine. Here. Stopped.
I can't believe this! What are we doing here?
I want to take you to meet someone. Someone very important to me.
SLAM!
I didn't agree to meet someone at the docks in the middle of a school day!
Would you relax? Don't be so uptight!
Look--
What if Kaboom was right? Why should we hide what we are and play by the rules of a society that wasn't built for us?
We're **better** than all these people, Kamala.
There's no reason for you to keep wasting your energy to protect people who don't **believe** what you believe. Who can't do what you can do.

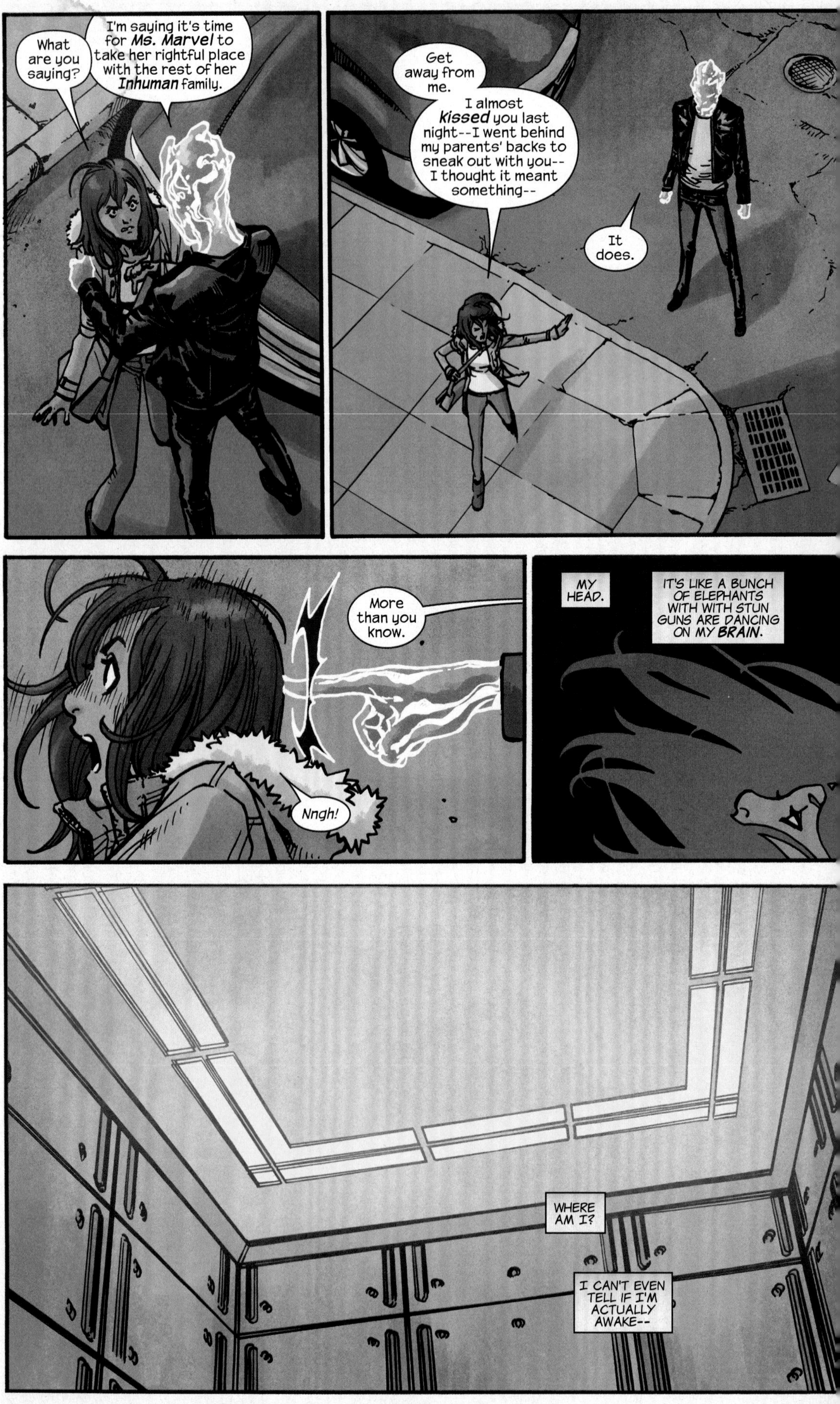
What are you saying?
I'm saying it's time for Ms. Marvel to take her rightful place with the rest of her Inhuman family.
Get away from me.
I almost kissed you last night--I went behind my parents' backs to sneak out with you-- I thought it meant something--
It does.
More than you know.
Nngh!
MY HEAD.
IT'S LIKE A BUNCH OF ELEPHANTS WITH WITH STUN GUNS ARE DANCING ON MY BRAIN.
WHERE AM I?
I CAN'T EVEN TELL IF I'M ACTUALLY AWAKE--

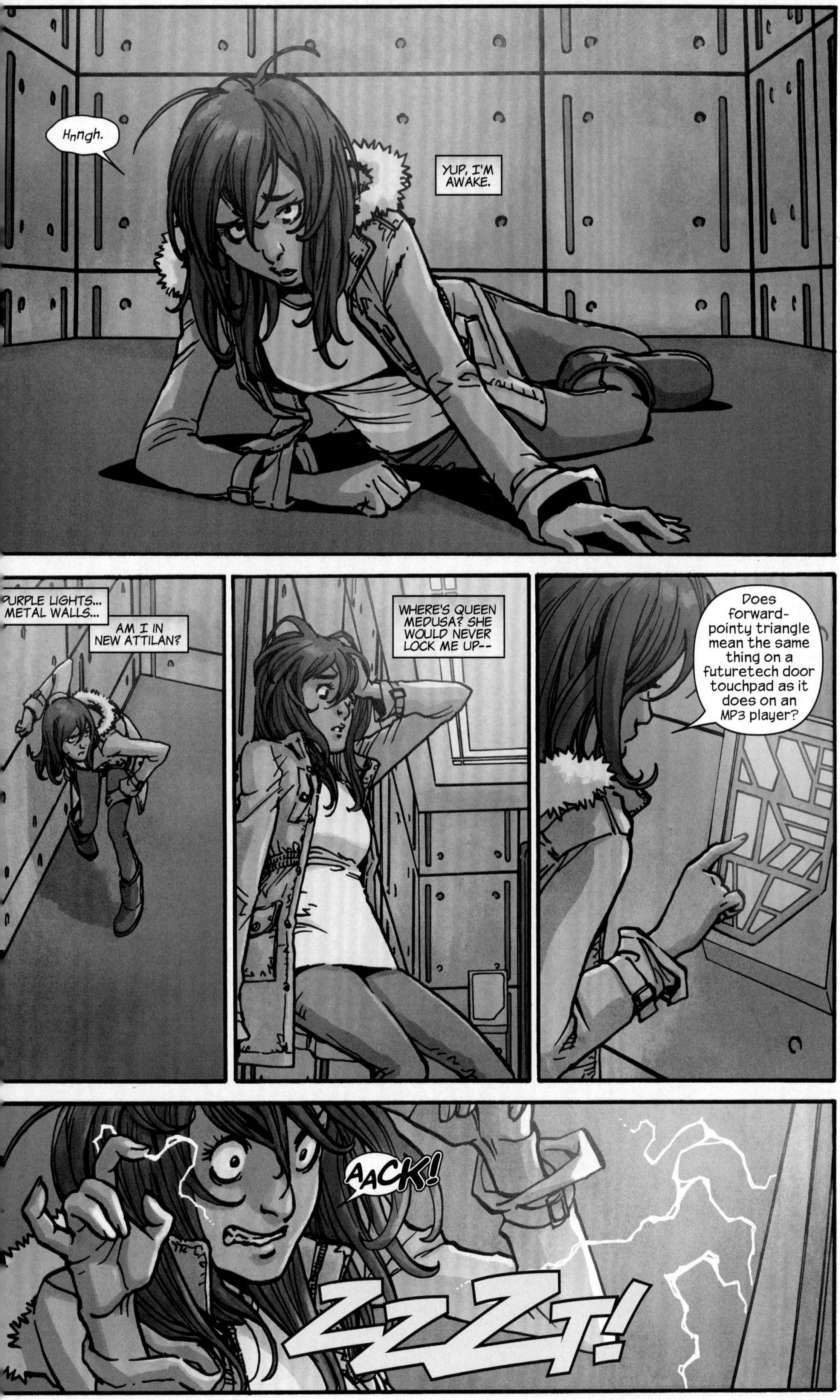
Hnngh.
YUP, I'M AWAKE.
PURPLE LIGHTS... METAL WALLS...
AM I IN NEW ATTILAN?
WHERE'S QUEEN MEDUSA? SHE WOULD NEVER LOCK ME UP--
Does forward-pointy triangle mean the same thing on a futuretech door touchpad as it does on an MP3 player?
AACK!
ZZZT!

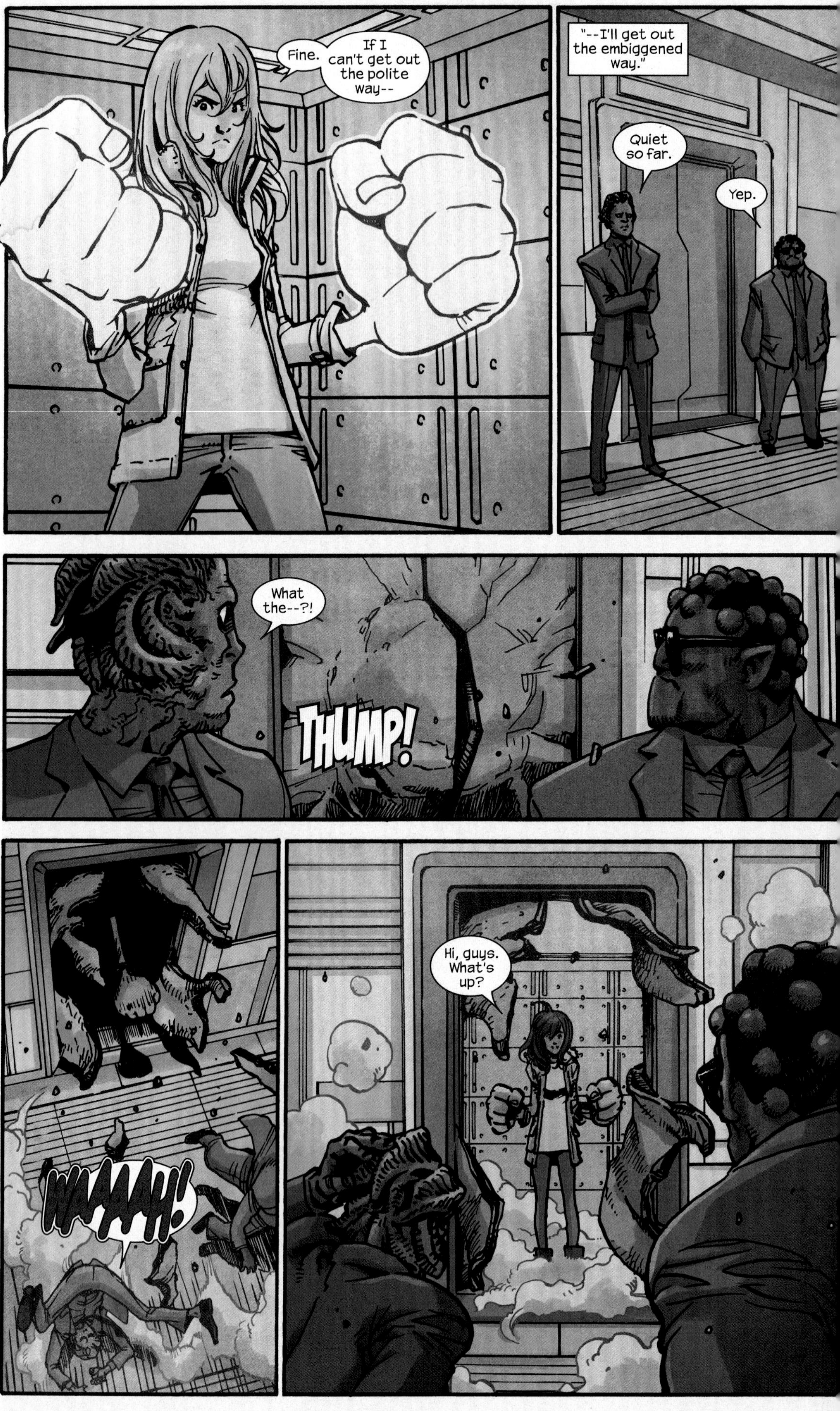
Fine.
If I can't get out the polite way--
"--I'll get out the embiggened way."
Quiet so far.
Yep.
What the--?!
THUMP!
WAAAAH!
Hi, guys. What's up?

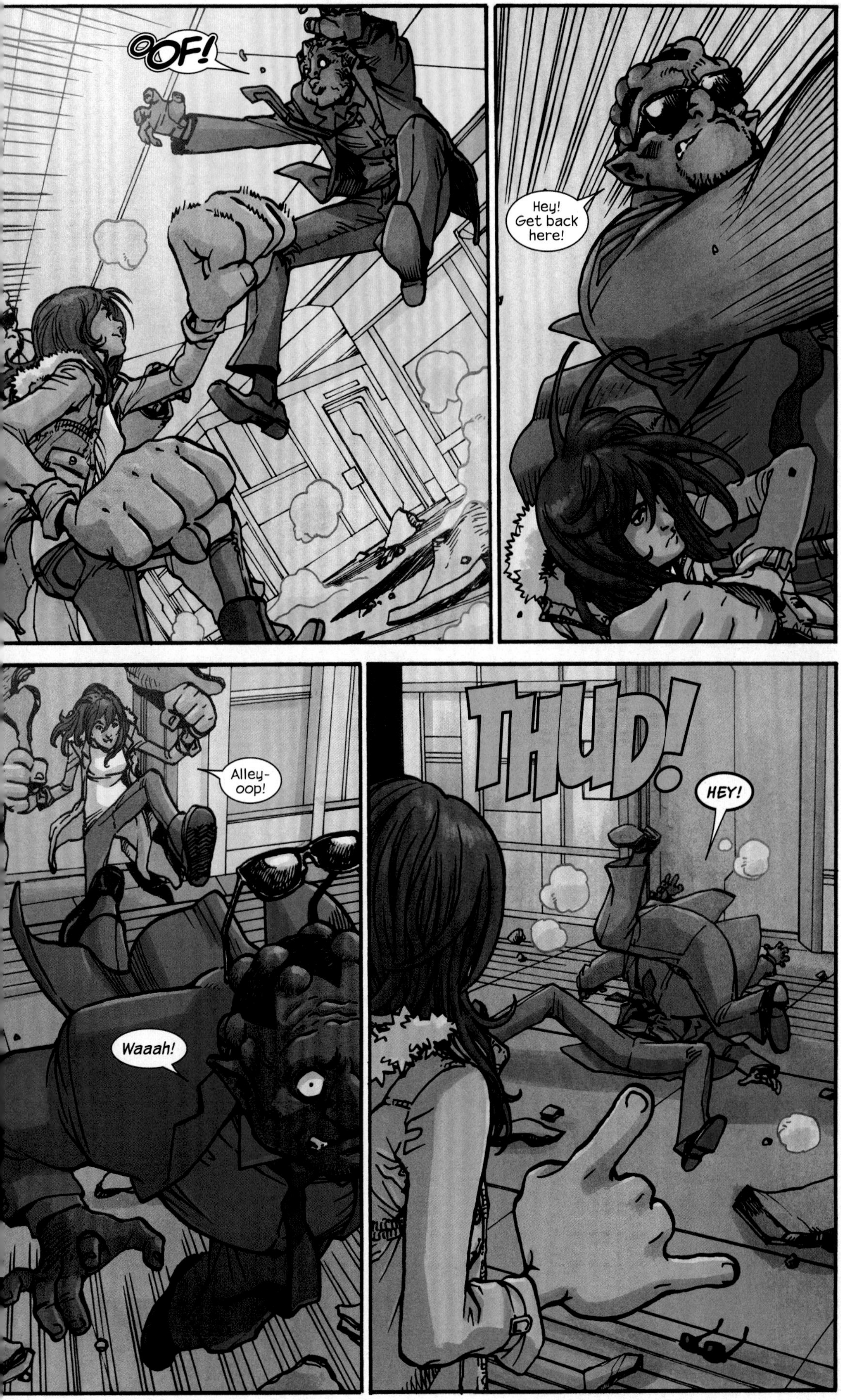
OOF!
Hey! Get back here!
Alley-oop!
Waaah!
THUD!
HEY!

Get back here, kid!
I DON'T GET IT. WHO ARE THESE PEOPLE? WHERE'S GORGON AND THE QUEEN AND EVERYBODY?
Hnngh!
IF I CAN JUST FIND SOMEBODY I KNOW, THERE MUST BE AN EXPLANATION FOR ALL OF THIS--
AARGH!
SO CLOSE.
UGH!
GET UP, KEEP GOING, GET UP, KEEP GOING--
You're right, Kamran. She's very persistent.

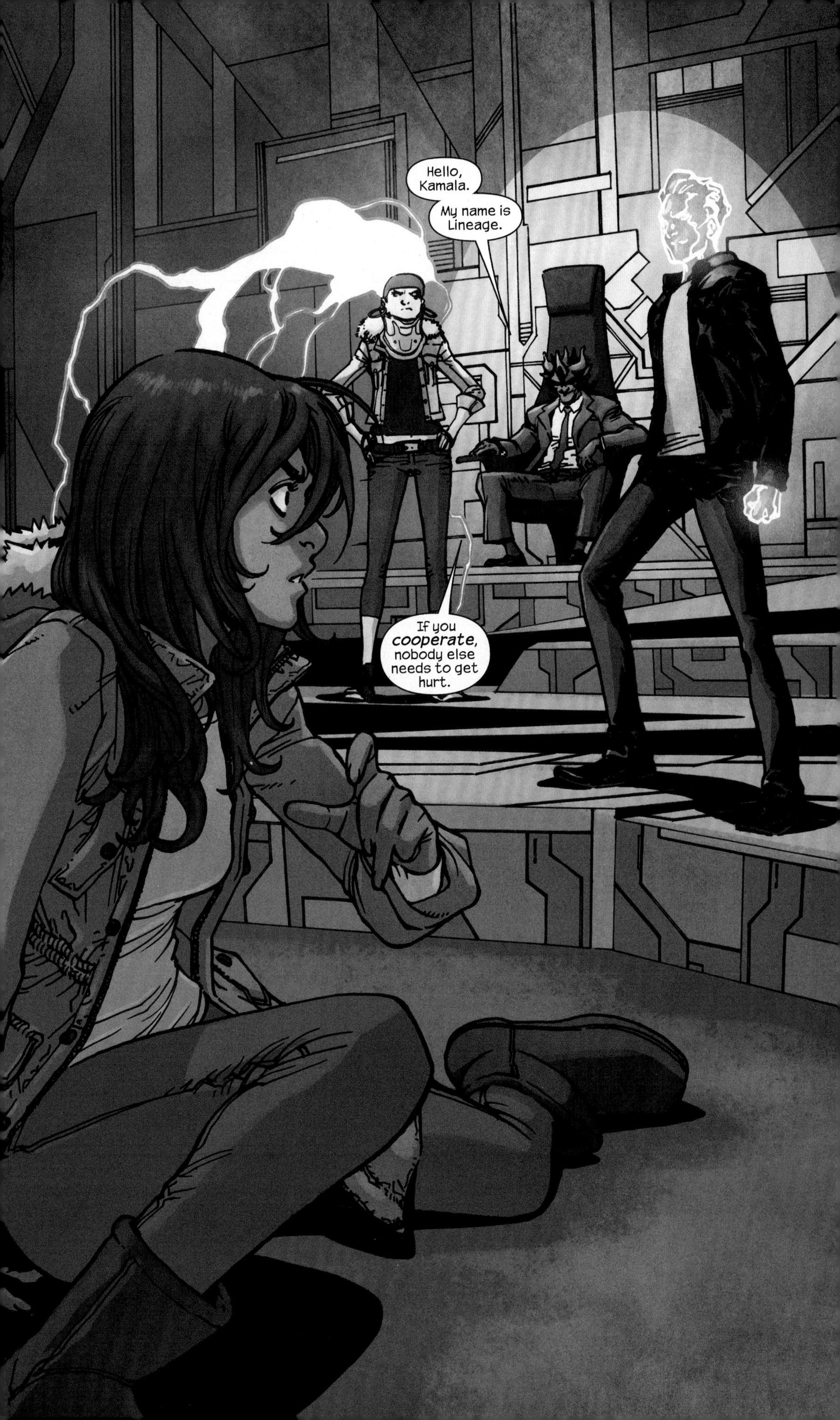
Hello, Kamala.
My name is Lineage.
If you *cooperate*, nobody else needs to get hurt.

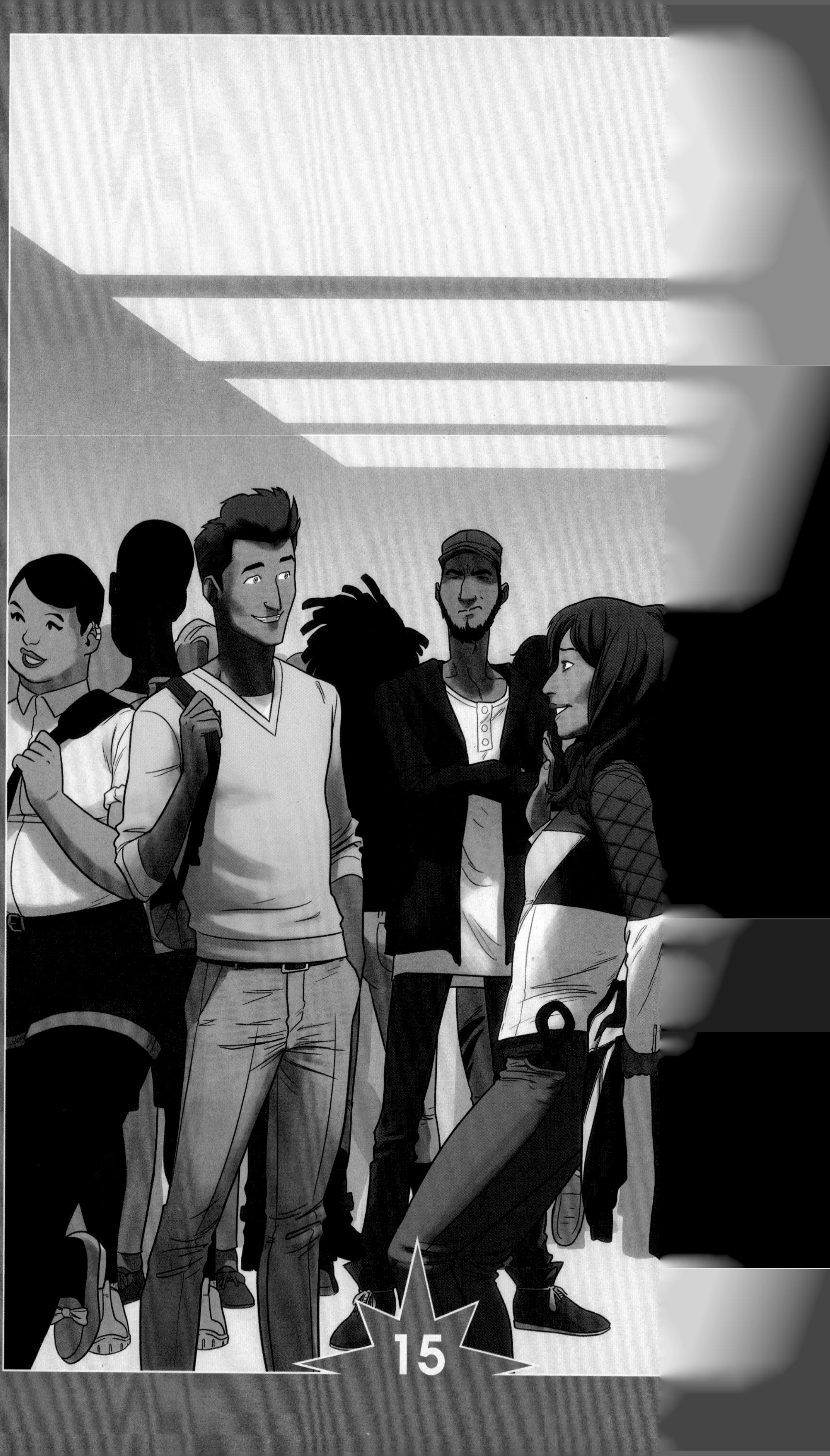

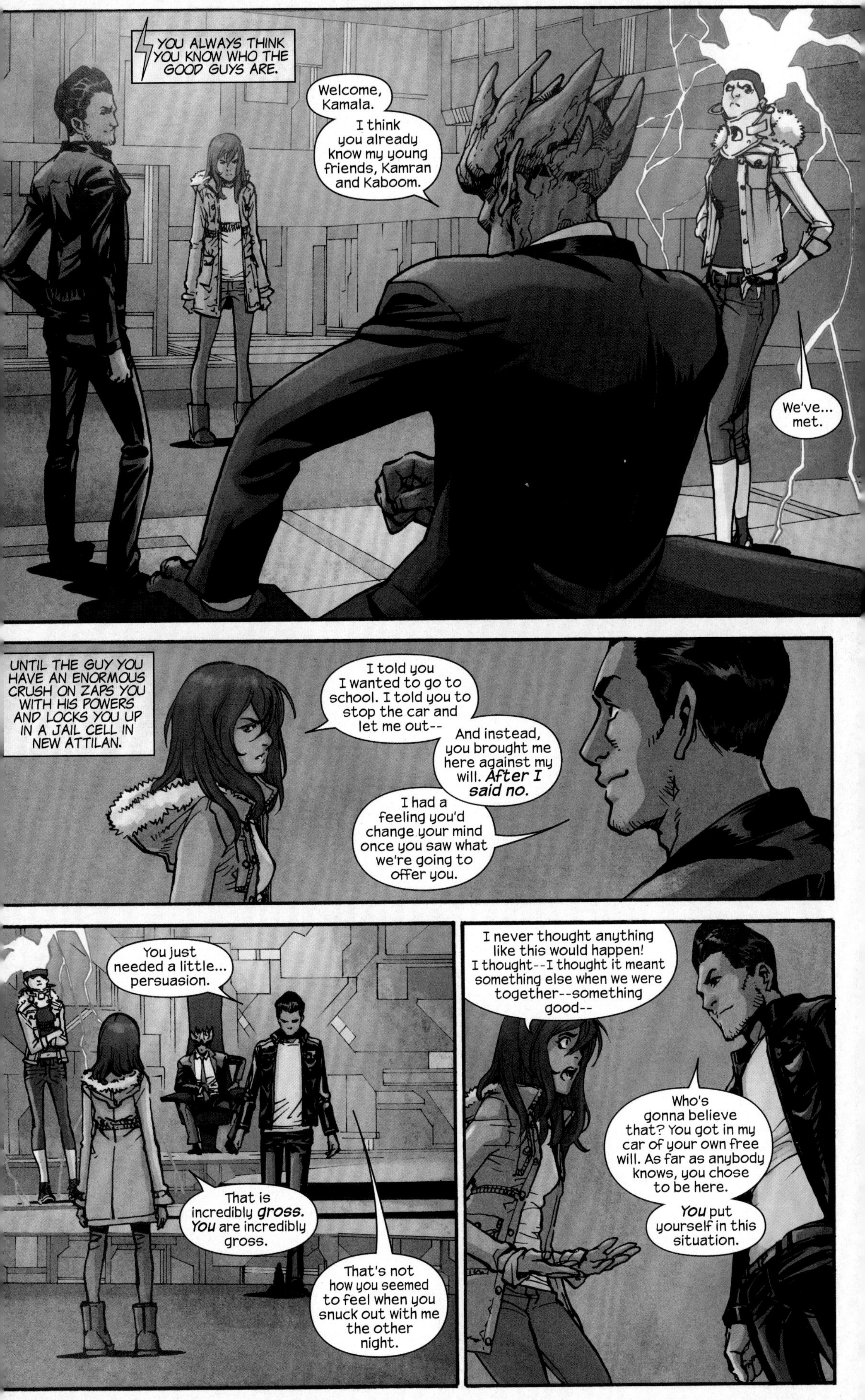
YOU ALWAYS THINK YOU KNOW WHO THE GOOD GUYS ARE.
Welcome, Kamala.
I think you already know my young friends, Kamran and Kaboom.
We've... met.
UNTIL THE GUY YOU HAVE AN ENORMOUS CRUSH ON ZAPS YOU WITH HIS POWERS AND LOCKS YOU UP IN A JAIL CELL IN NEW ATTILAN.
I told you I wanted to go to school. I told you to stop the car and let me out--
And instead, you brought me here against my will. *After I said no.*
I had a feeling you'd change your mind once you saw what we're going to offer you.
You just needed a little... persuasion.
That is incredibly *gross. You* are incredibly gross.
That's not how you seemed to feel when you snuck out with me the other night.
I never thought anything like this would happen! I thought--I thought it meant something else when we were together--something good--
Who's gonna believe that? You got in my car of your own free will. As far as anybody knows, you chose to be here.
You put yourself in this situation.

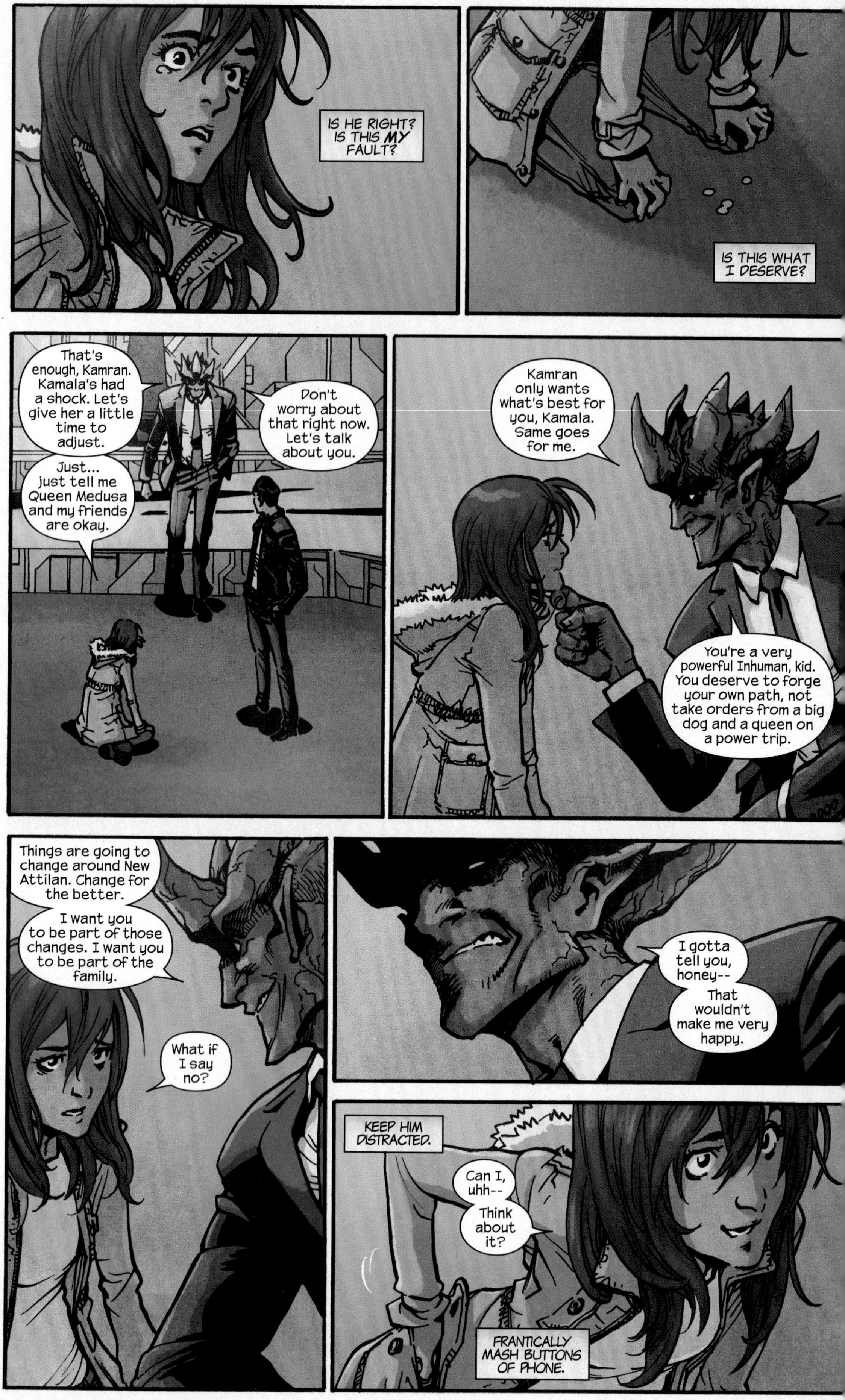
IS HE RIGHT? IS THIS MY FAULT?
IS THIS WHAT I DESERVE?
That's enough, Kamran. Kamala's had a shock. Let's give her a little time to adjust.
Just... just tell me Queen Medusa and my friends are okay.
Don't worry about that right now. Let's talk about you.
Kamran only wants what's best for you, Kamala. Same goes for me.
You're a very powerful Inhuman, kid. You deserve to forge your own path, not take orders from a big dog and a queen on a power trip.
Things are going to change around New Attilan. Change for the better.
I want you to be part of those changes. I want you to be part of the family.
What if I say no?
I gotta tell you, honey--
That wouldn't make me very happy.
KEEP HIM DISTRACTED.
Can I, uhh--
Think about it?
FRANTICALLY MASH BUTTONS OF PHONE.

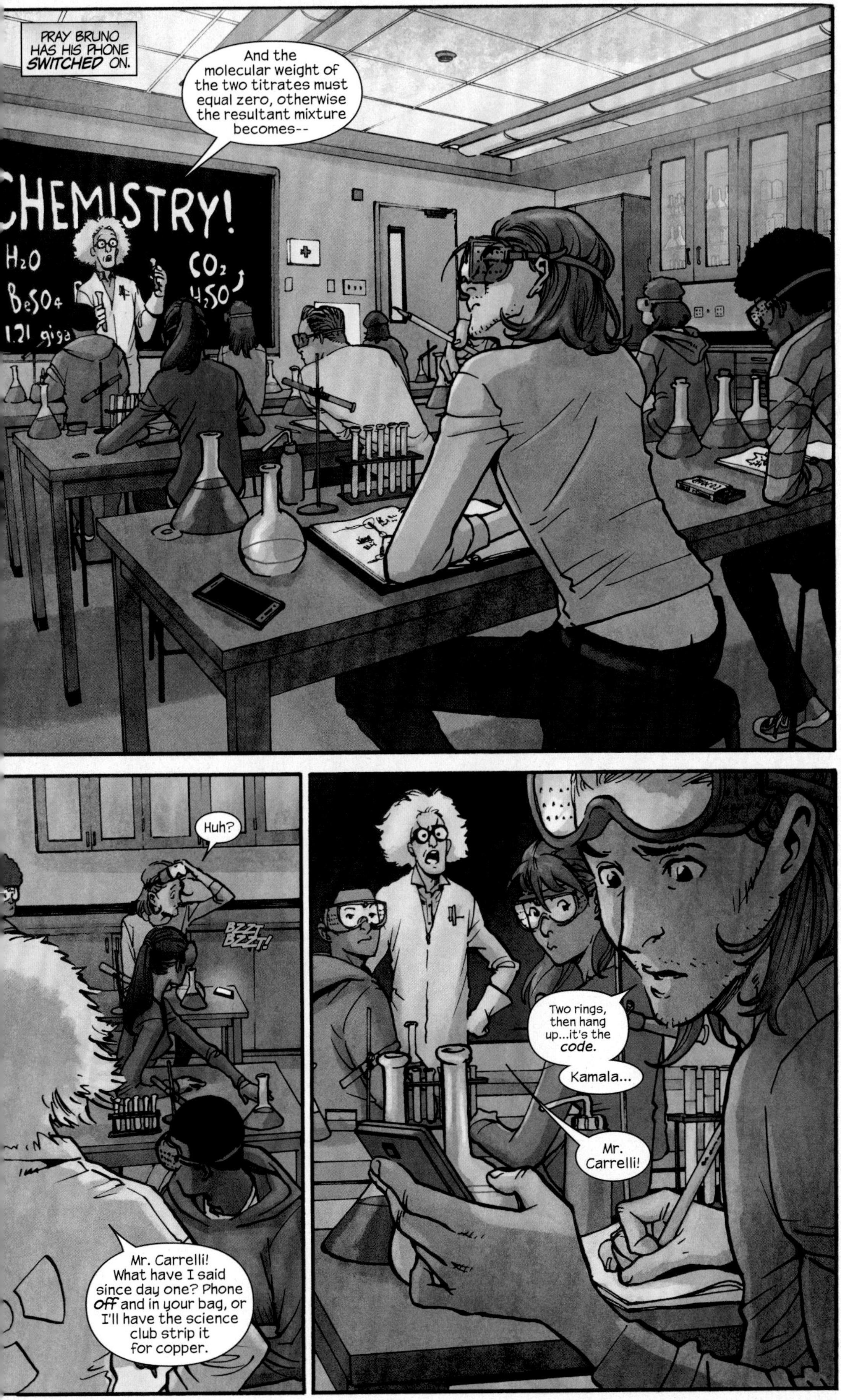
PRAY BRUNO HAS HIS PHONE *SWITCHED* ON.
And the molecular weight of the two titrates must equal zero, otherwise the resultant mixture becomes--
CHEMISTRY!
H_2O
CO_2
$BeSO_4$
H_2SO
1.21 giga
Huh?
BZZT! BZZT!
Mr. Carrelli! What have I said since day one? Phone *off* and in your bag, or I'll have the science club strip it for copper.
Two rings, then hang up...it's the *code*.
Kamala...
Mr. Carrelli!

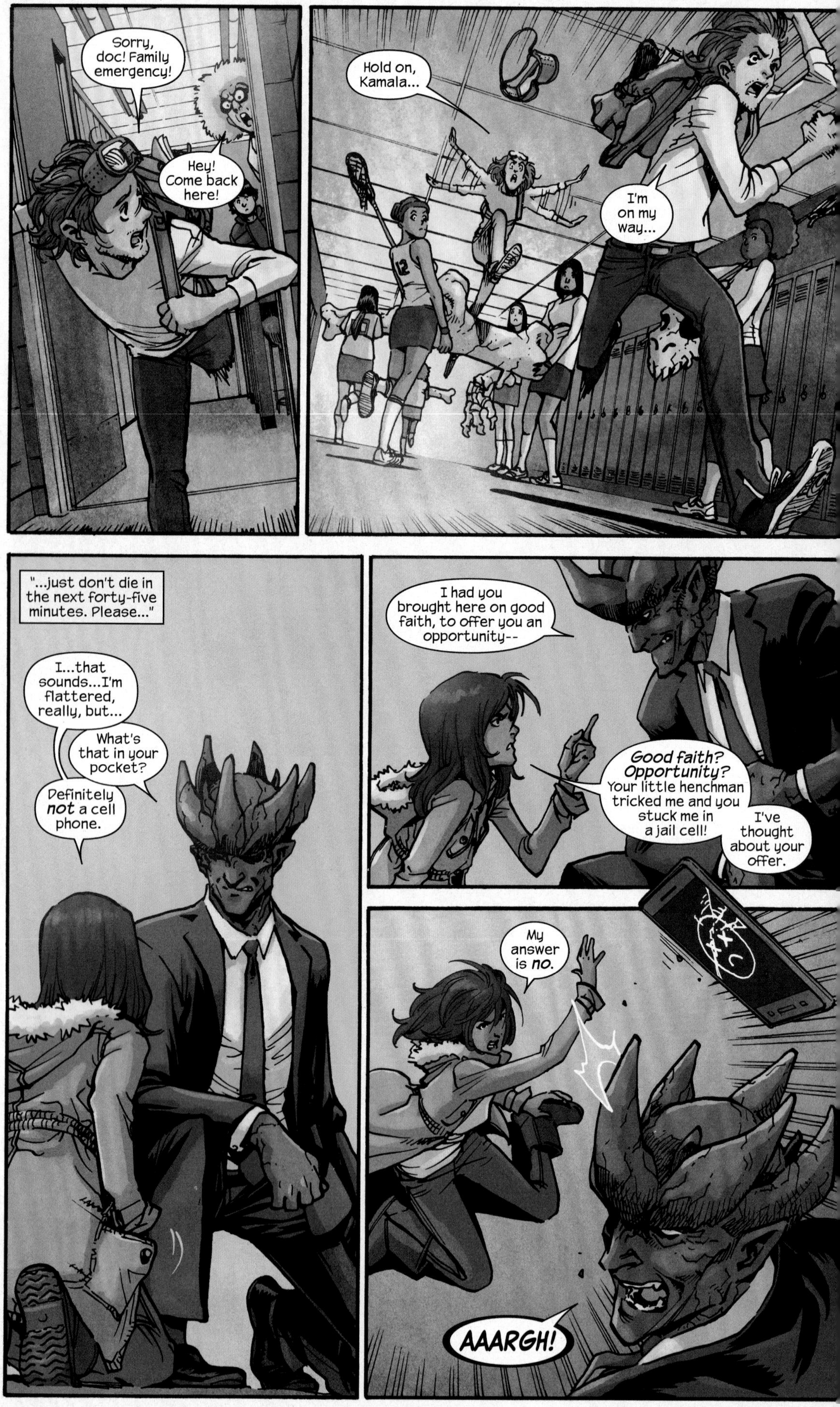
Sorry, doc! Family emergency!
Hey! Come back here!
Hold on, Kamala...
I'm on my way...
"...just don't die in the next forty-five minutes. Please..."
I...that sounds...I'm flattered, really, but...
What's that in your pocket?
Definitely *not* a cell phone.
I had you brought here on good faith, to offer you an opportunity--
Good faith? Opportunity? Your little henchman tricked me and you stuck me in a jail cell!
I've thought about your offer.
My answer is *no*.
AAARGH!

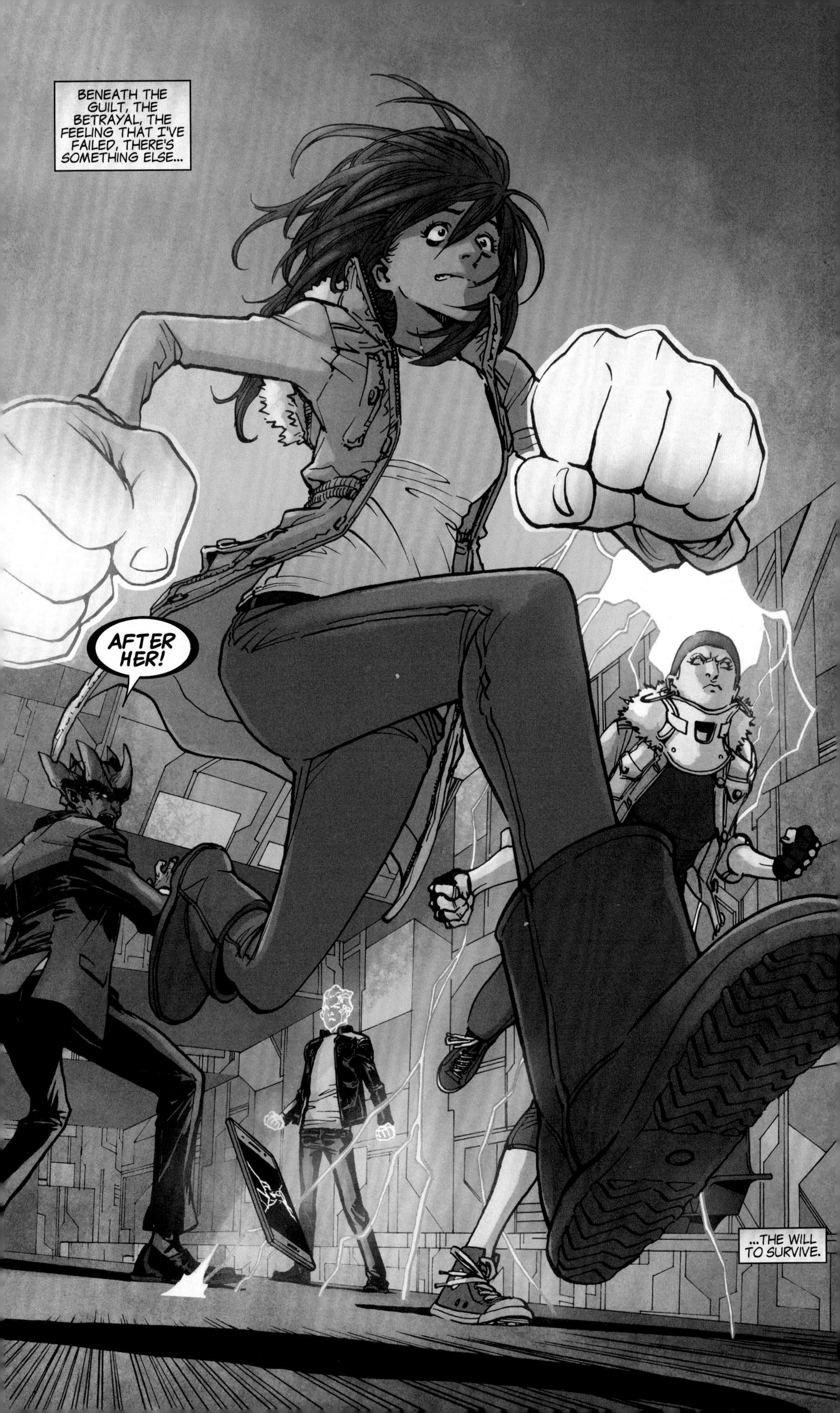
BENEATH THE GUILT, THE BETRAYAL, THE FEELING THAT I'VE FAILED, THERE'S SOMETHING ELSE...
AFTER HER!
...THE WILL TO SURVIVE.

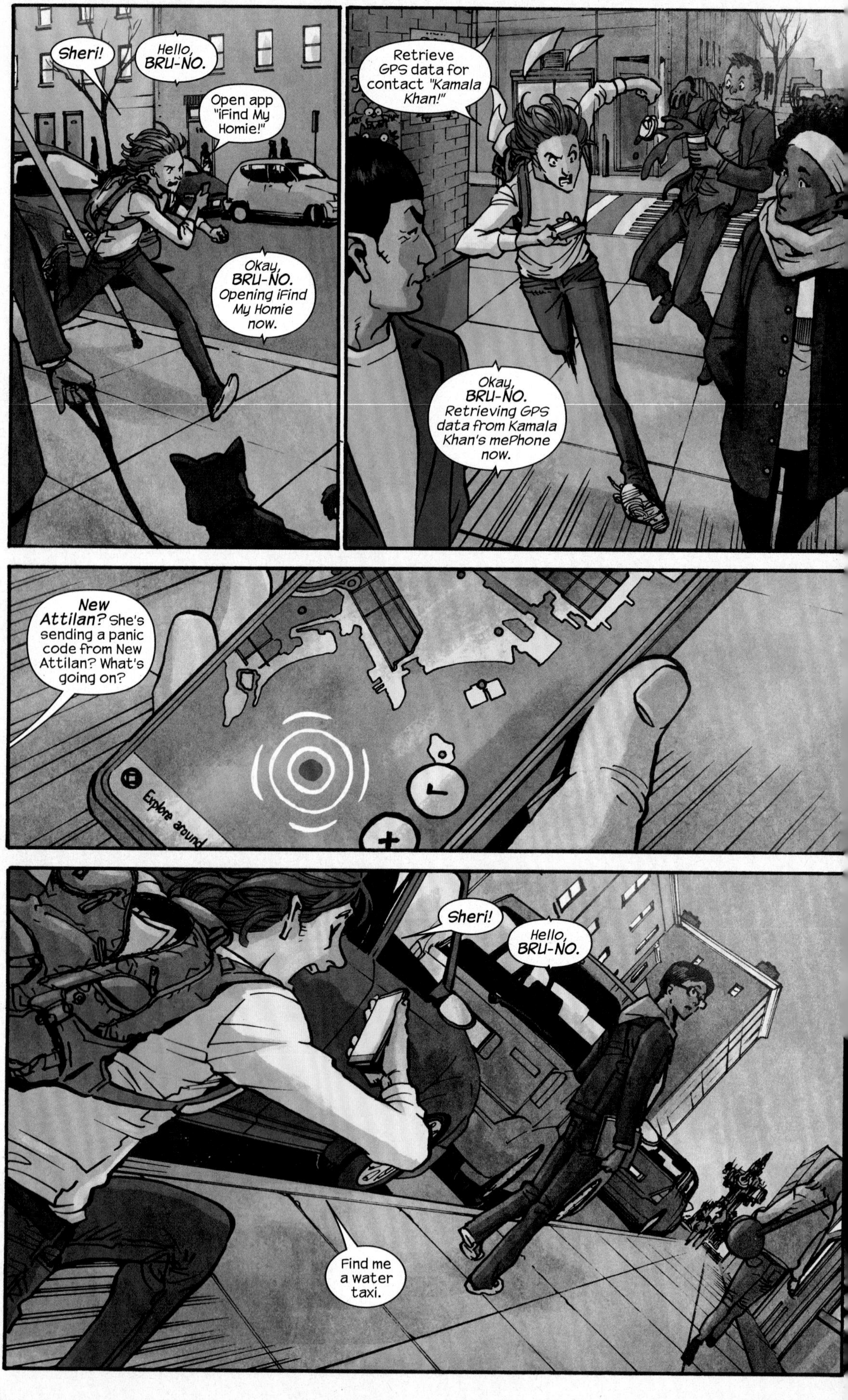
Sheri!
Hello, BRU-NO.
Open app "iFind My Homie!"
Okay, BRU-NO. Opening iFind My Homie now.
Retrieve GPS data for contact "Kamala Khan!"
Okay, BRU-NO. Retrieving GPS data from Kamala Khan's mePhone now.
New Attilan? She's sending a panic code from New Attilan? What's going on?
Explore around
Sheri!
Hello, BRU-NO.
Find me a water taxi.

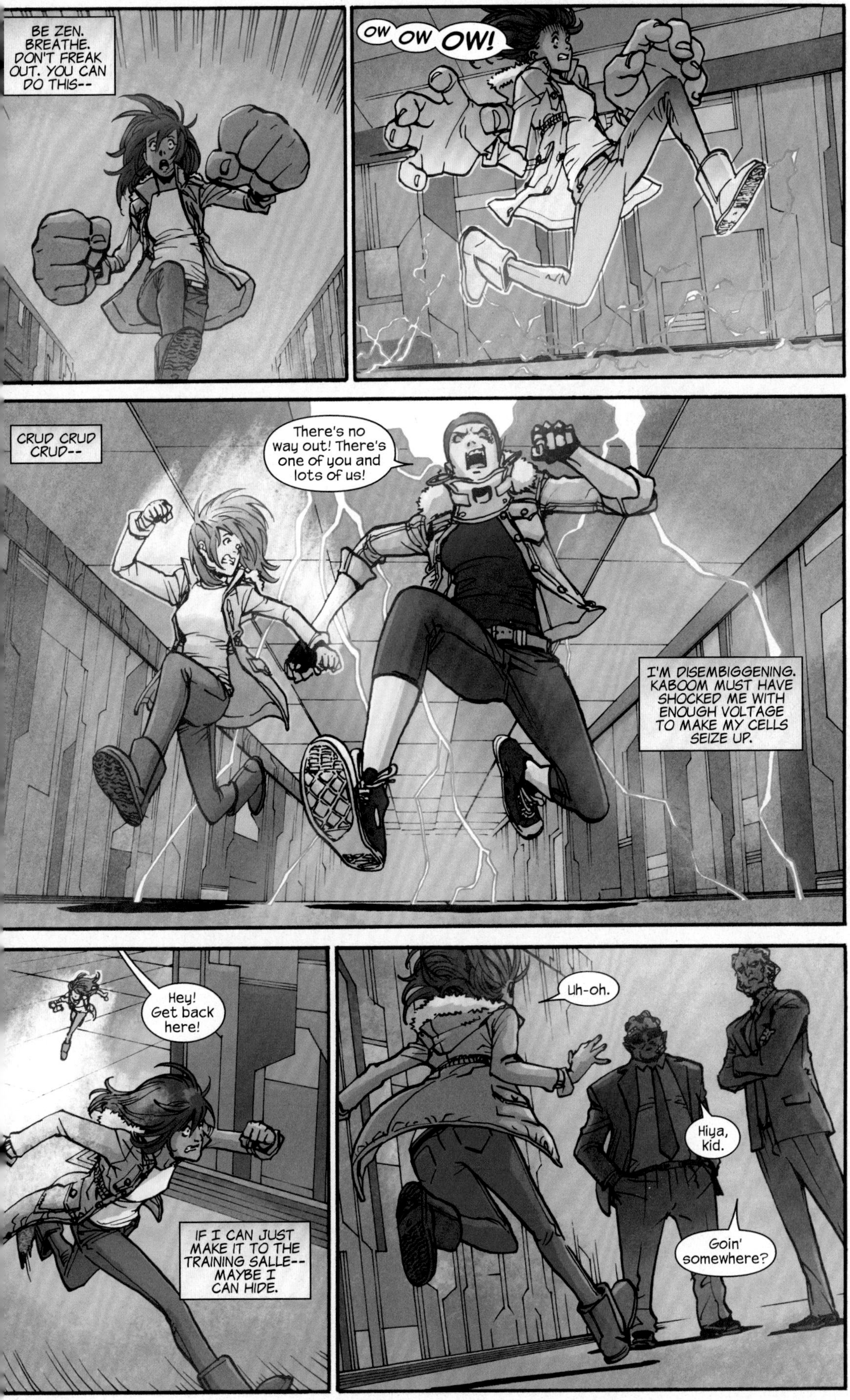
BE ZEN. BREATHE. DON'T FREAK OUT. YOU CAN DO THIS--
OW OW OW!
CRUD CRUD CRUD--
There's no way out! There's one of you and lots of us!
I'M DISEMBIGGENING. KABOOM MUST HAVE SHOCKED ME WITH ENOUGH VOLTAGE TO MAKE MY CELLS SEIZE UP.
Hey! Get back here!
IF I CAN JUST MAKE IT TO THE TRAINING SALLE-- MAYBE I CAN HIDE.
Uh-oh.
Hiya, kid.
Goin' somewhere?

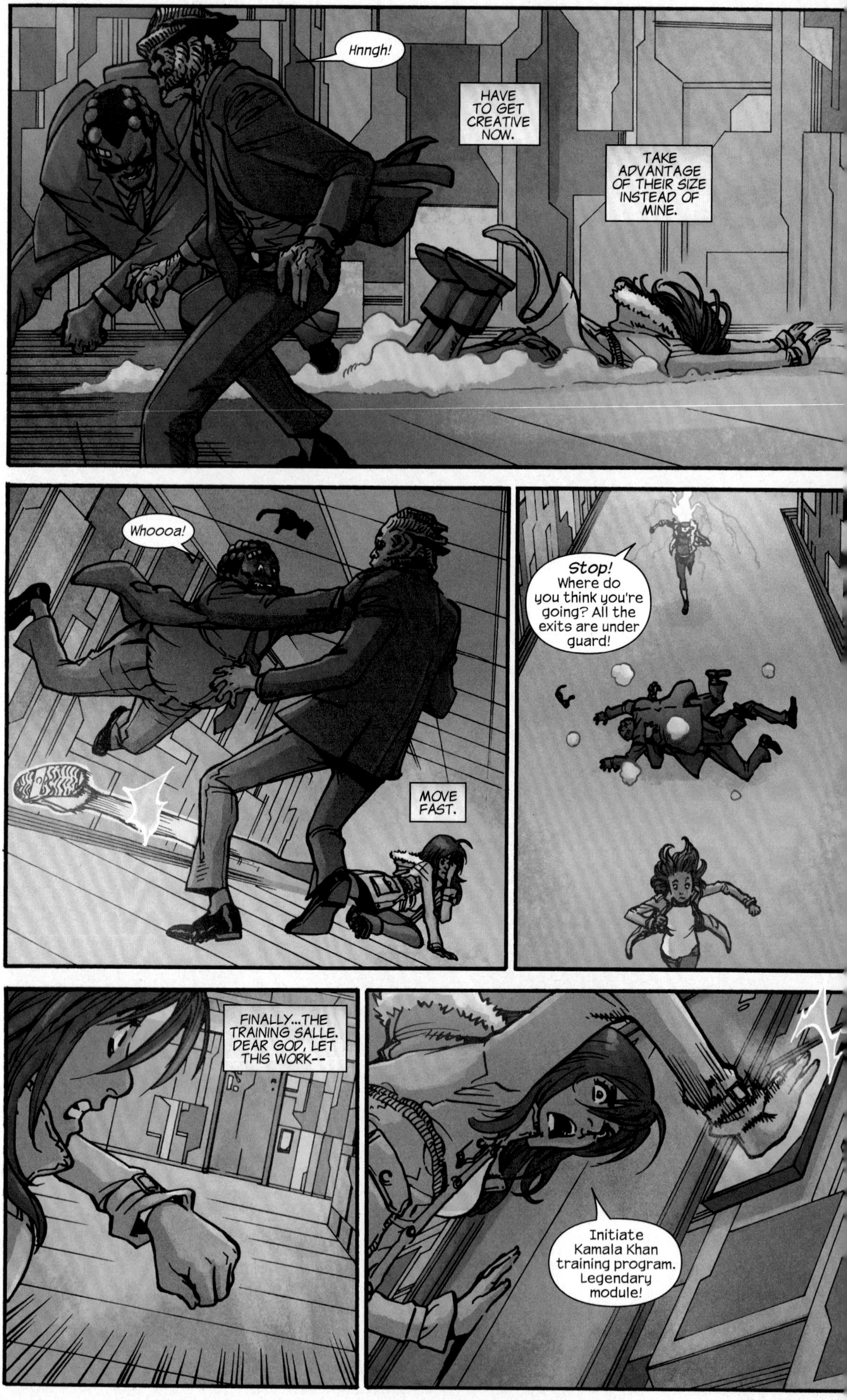
Hnngh!
HAVE TO GET CREATIVE NOW.
TAKE ADVANTAGE OF THEIR SIZE INSTEAD OF MINE.
Whoooa!
MOVE FAST.
Stop! Where do you think you're going? All the exits are under guard!
FINALLY...THE TRAINING SALLE. DEAR GOD, LET THIS WORK--
Initiate Kamala Khan training program. Legendary module!

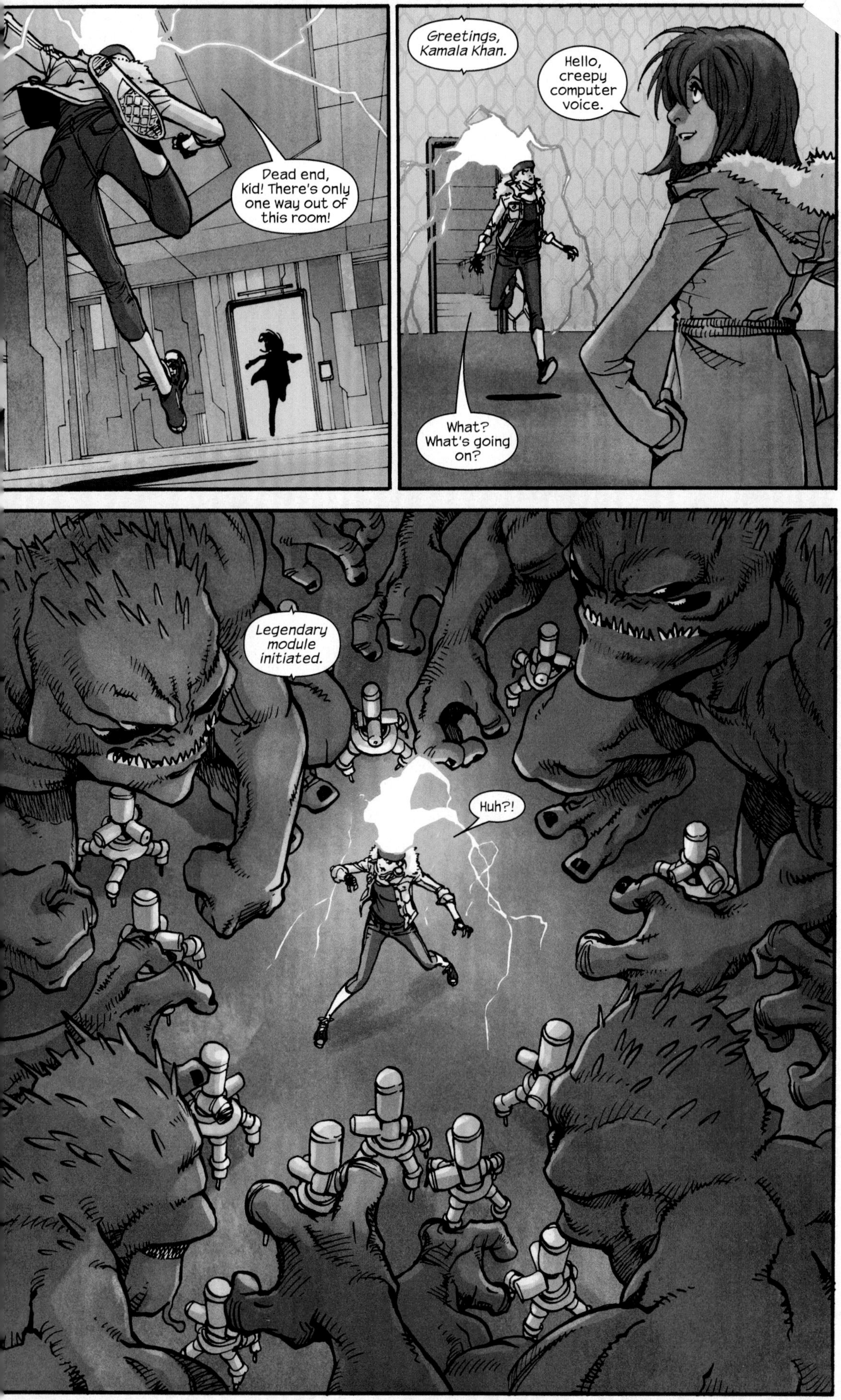
Dead end, kid! There's only one way out of this room!
Greetings, Kamala Khan.
Hello, creepy computer voice.
What? What's going on?
Legendary module initiated.
Huh?!

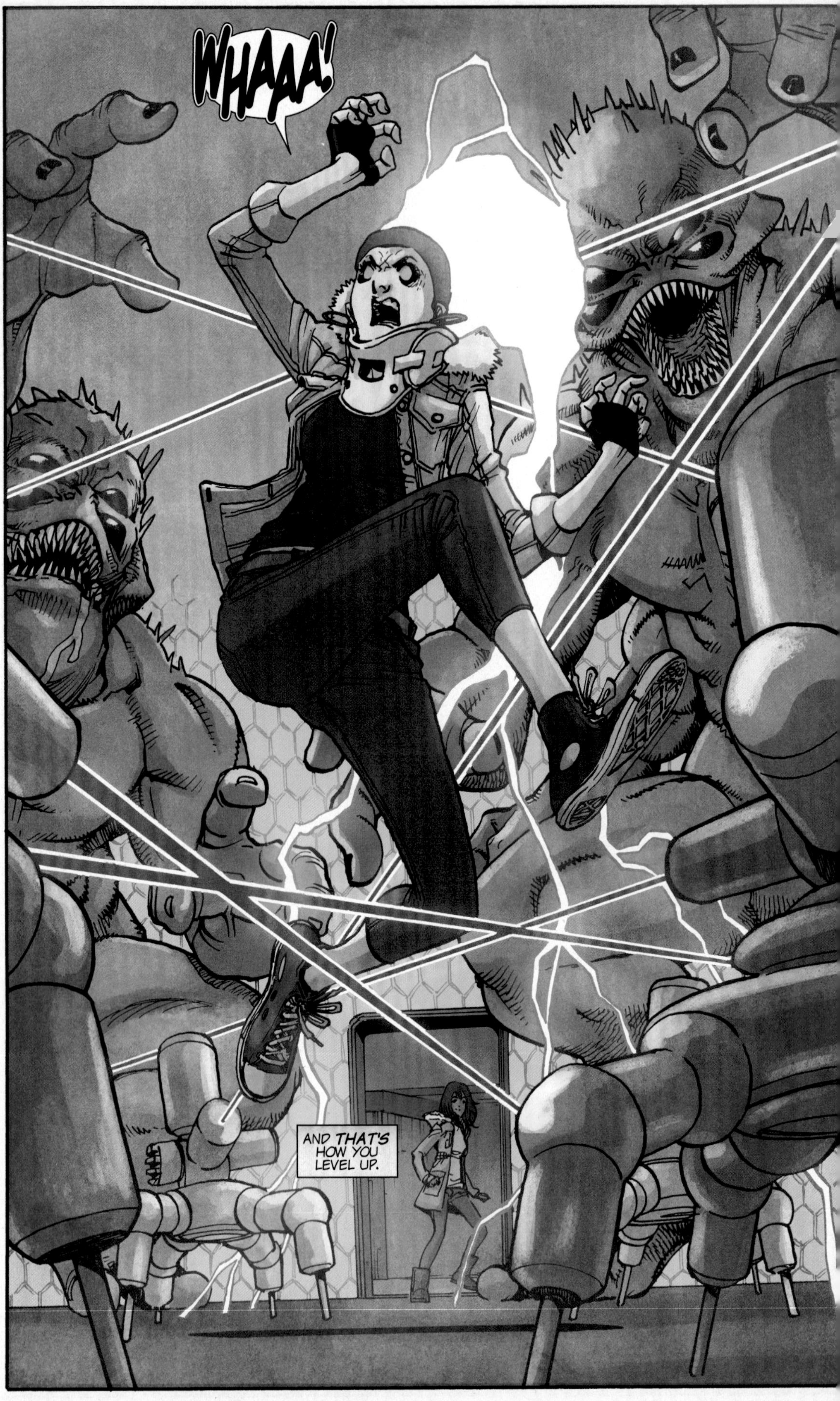
WHAAA!
AND THAT'S HOW YOU LEVEL UP.

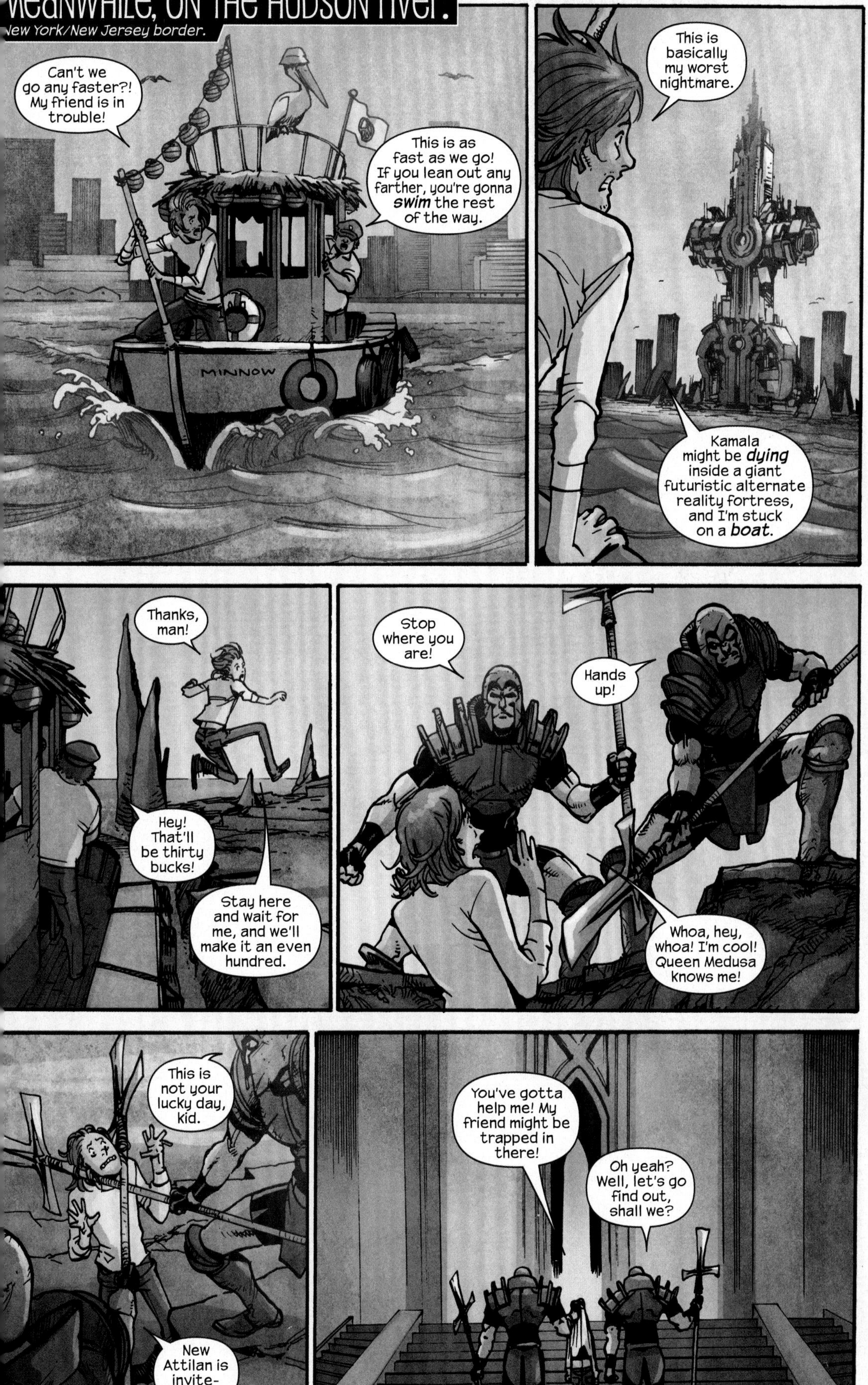
MEANWHILE, ON THE HUDSON RIVER.
New York/New Jersey border.
Can't we go any faster?! My friend is in trouble!
This is as fast as we go! If you lean out any farther, you're gonna swim the rest of the way.
MINNOW
This is basically my worst nightmare.
Kamala might be dying inside a giant futuristic alternate reality fortress, and I'm stuck on a boat.
Thanks, man!
Hey! That'll be thirty bucks!
Stay here and wait for me, and we'll make it an even hundred.
Stop where you are!
Hands up!
Whoa, hey, whoa! I'm cool! Queen Medusa knows me!
This is not your lucky day, kid.
New Attilan is invite-only.
You've gotta help me! My friend might be trapped in there!
Oh yeah? Well, let's go find out, shall we?

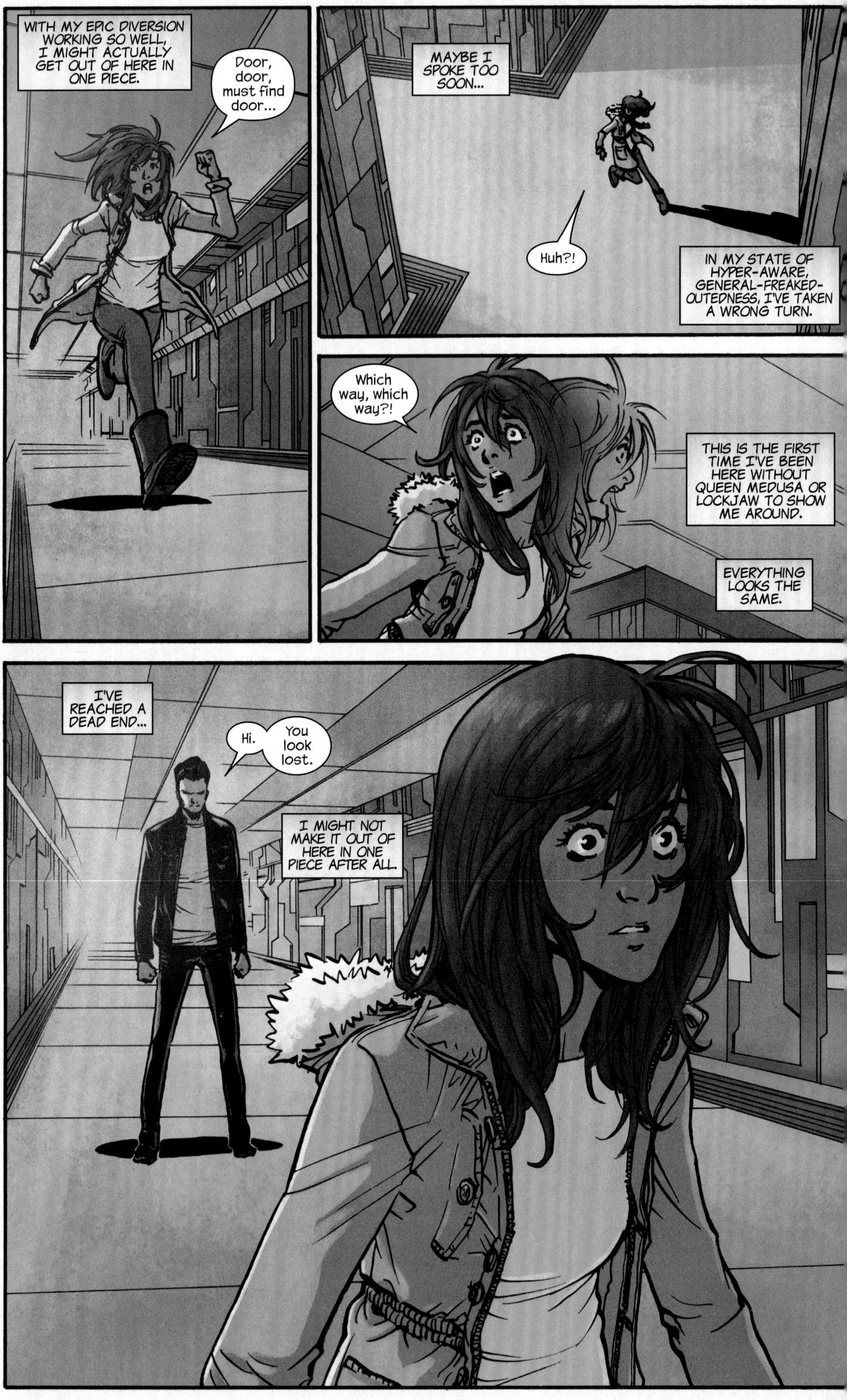

WITH MY EPIC DIVERSION WORKING SO WELL, I MIGHT ACTUALLY GET OUT OF HERE IN ONE PIECE.
Door, door, must find door...
MAYBE I SPOKE TOO SOON...
Huh?!
IN MY STATE OF HYPER-AWARE, GENERAL-FREAKED-OUTEDNESS, I'VE TAKEN A WRONG TURN.
Which way, which way?!
THIS IS THE FIRST TIME I'VE BEEN HERE WITHOUT QUEEN MEDUSA OR LOCKJAW TO SHOW ME AROUND.
EVERYTHING LOOKS THE SAME.
I'VE REACHED A DEAD END...
Hi.
You look lost.
I MIGHT NOT MAKE IT OUT OF HERE IN ONE PIECE AFTER ALL.

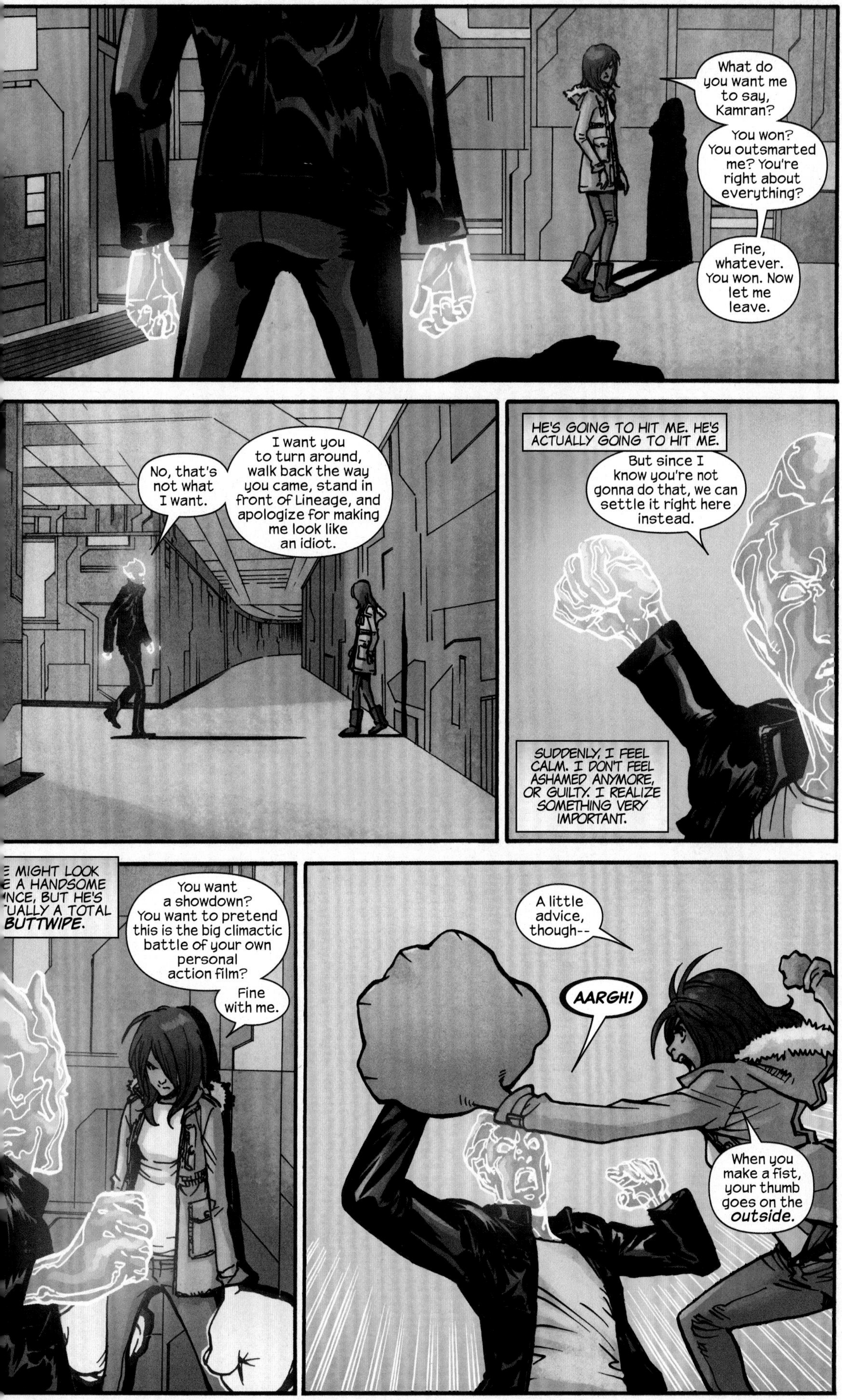

What do you want me to say, Kamran?
You won? You outsmarted me? You're right about everything?
Fine, whatever. You won. Now let me leave.
No, that's not what I want.
I want you to turn around, walk back the way you came, stand in front of Lineage, and apologize for making me look like an idiot.
HE'S GOING TO HIT ME. HE'S ACTUALLY GOING TO HIT ME.
But since I know you're not gonna do that, we can settle it right here instead.
SUDDENLY, I FEEL CALM. I DON'T FEEL ASHAMED ANYMORE, OR GUILTY. I REALIZE SOMETHING VERY IMPORTANT.
E MIGHT LOOK E A HANDSOME NCE, BUT HE'S TUALLY A TOTAL BUTTWIPE.
You want a showdown? You want to pretend this is the big climactic battle of your own personal action film?
Fine with me.
A little advice, though--
AARGH!
When you make a fist, your thumb goes on the outside.

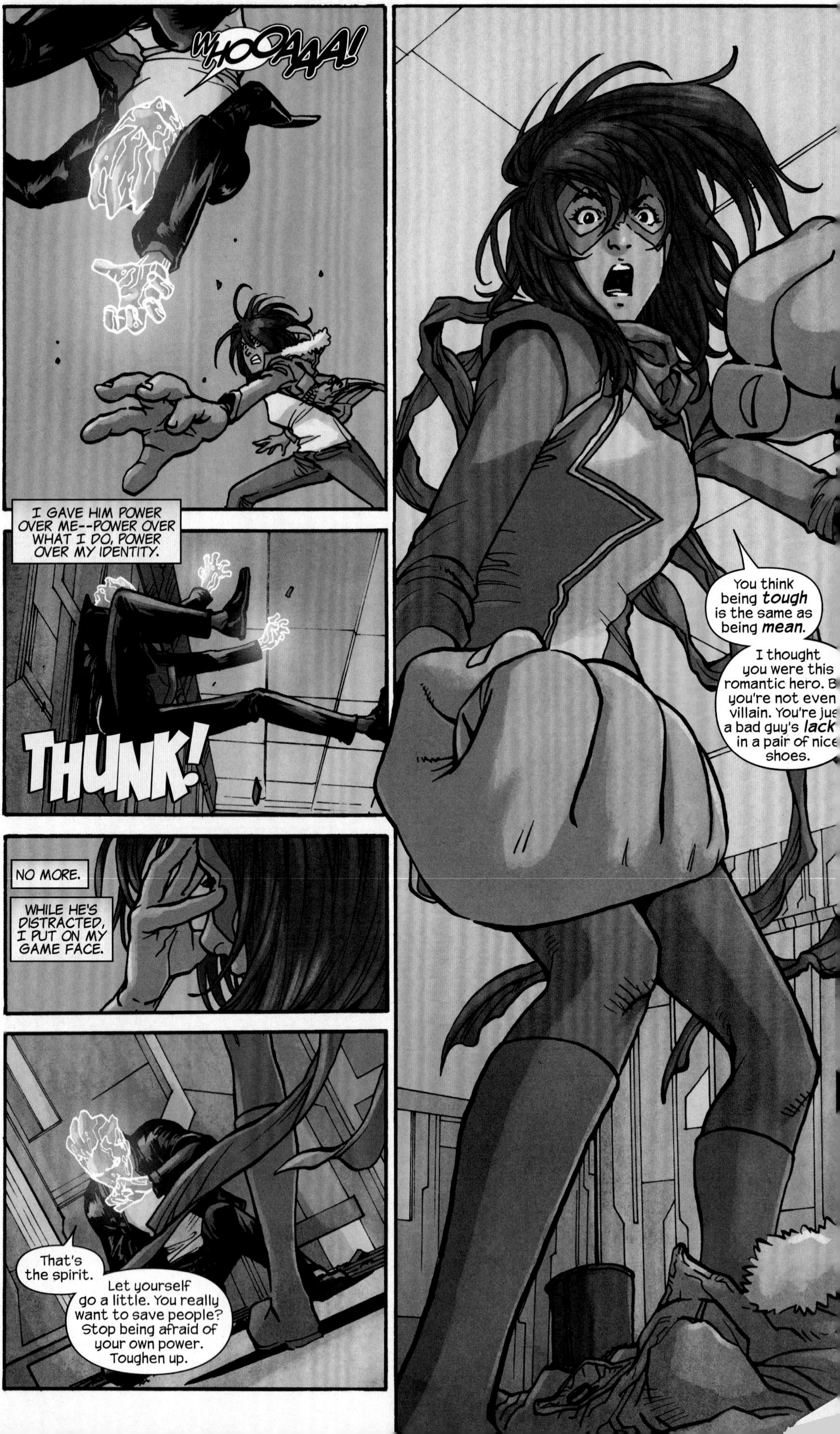
WHOOAAA!
I GAVE HIM POWER OVER ME--POWER OVER WHAT I DO, POWER OVER MY IDENTITY.
THUNK!
NO MORE.
WHILE HE'S DISTRACTED, I PUT ON MY GAME FACE.
That's the spirit.
Let yourself go a little. You really want to save people? Stop being afraid of your own power. Toughen up.
You think being *tough* is the same as being *mean*.
I thought you were this romantic hero. B you're not even villain. You're jus a bad guy's *lack* in a pair of nice shoes.

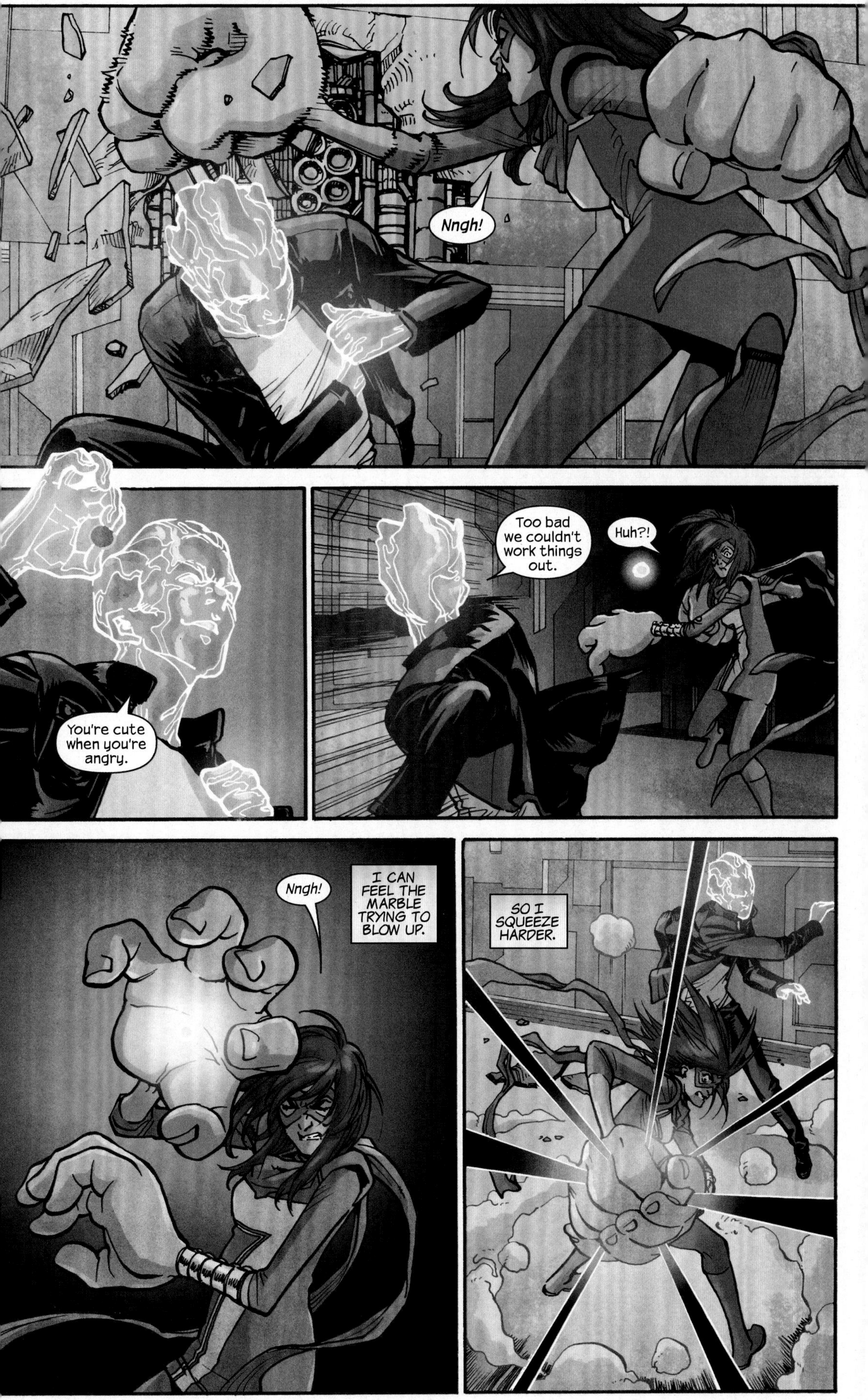
Nngh!
You're cute when you're angry.
Too bad we couldn't work things out.
Huh?!
Nngh!
I CAN FEEL THE MARBLE TRYING TO BLOW UP.
SO I SQUEEZE HARDER.

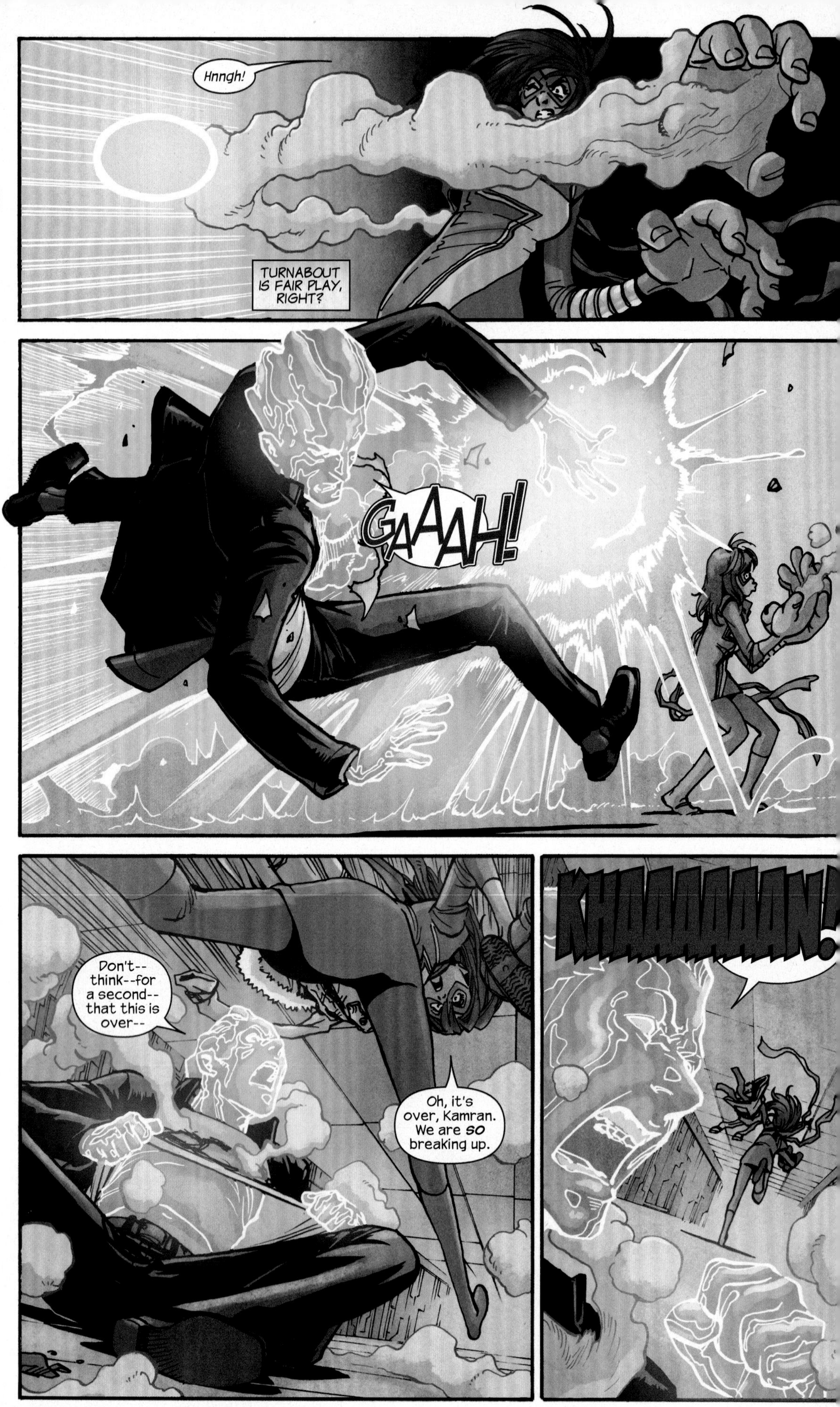

Hnngh!
TURNABOUT IS FAIR PLAY, RIGHT?
GAAAH!
Don't--think--for a second--that this is over--
Oh, it's over, Kamran. We are *SO* breaking up.
KHAAAAAAN!

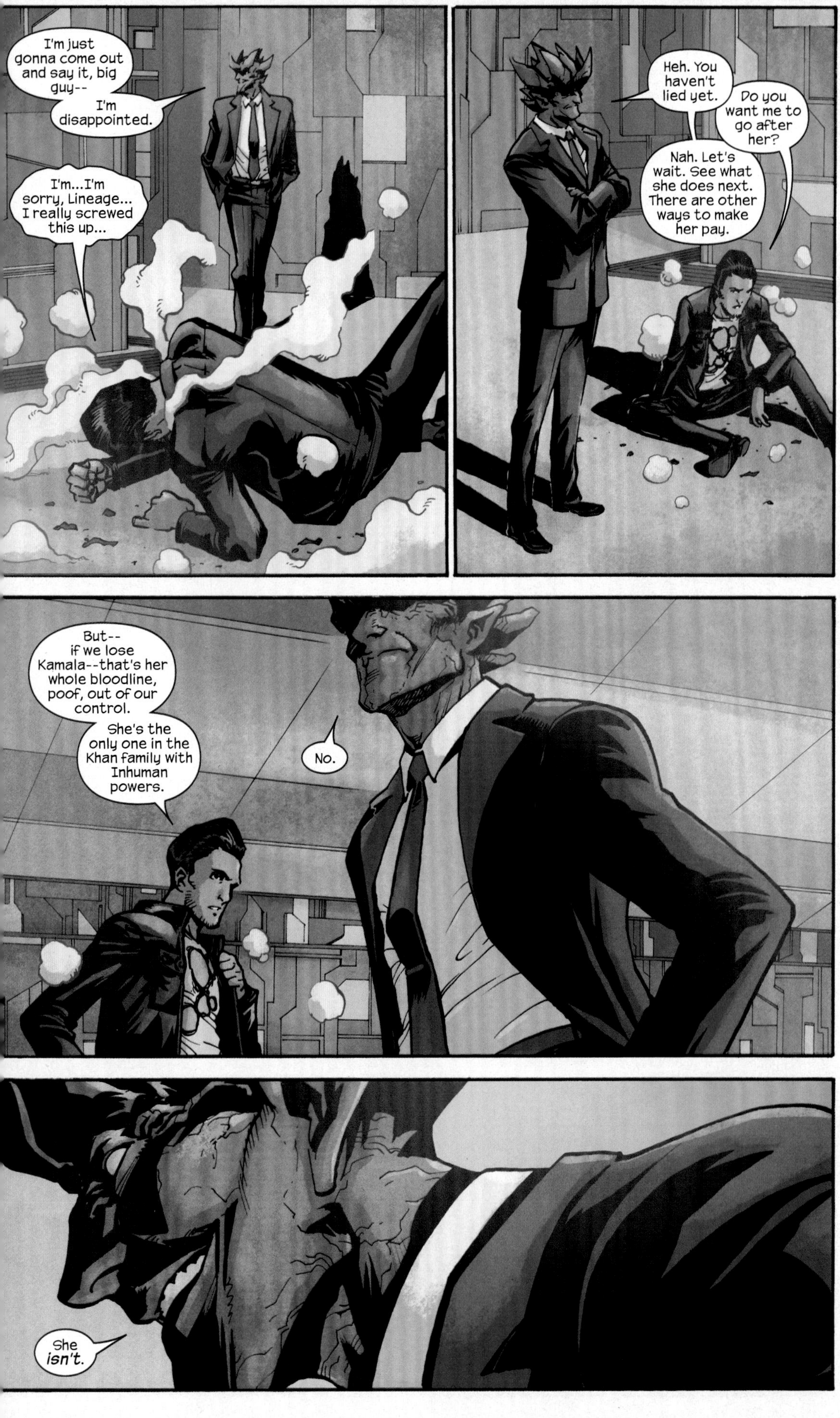
I'm just gonna come out and say it, big guy--
I'm disappointed.
I'm...I'm sorry, Lineage... I really screwed this up...
Heh. You haven't lied yet.
Do you want me to go after her?
Nah. Let's wait. See what she does next. There are other ways to make her pay.
But-- if we lose Kamala--that's her whole bloodline, poof, out of our control.
She's the only one in the Khan family with Inhuman powers.
No.
She *isn't*.

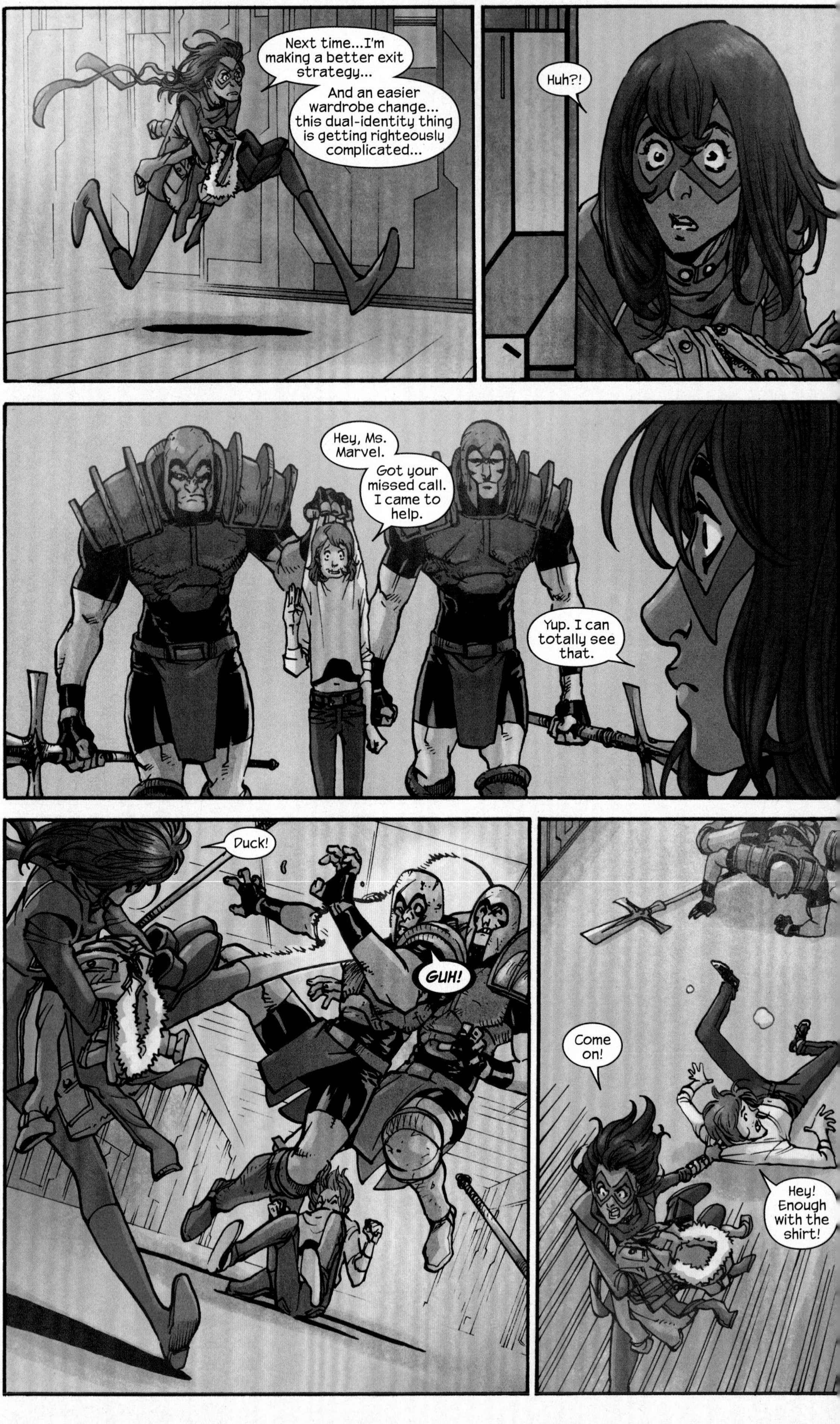

Next time...I'm making a better exit strategy...
And an easier wardrobe change... this dual-identity thing is getting righteously complicated...
Huh?!
Hey, Ms. Marvel.
Got your missed call. I came to help.
Yup. I can totally see that.
Duck!
GUH!
Come on!
Hey! Enough with the shirt!

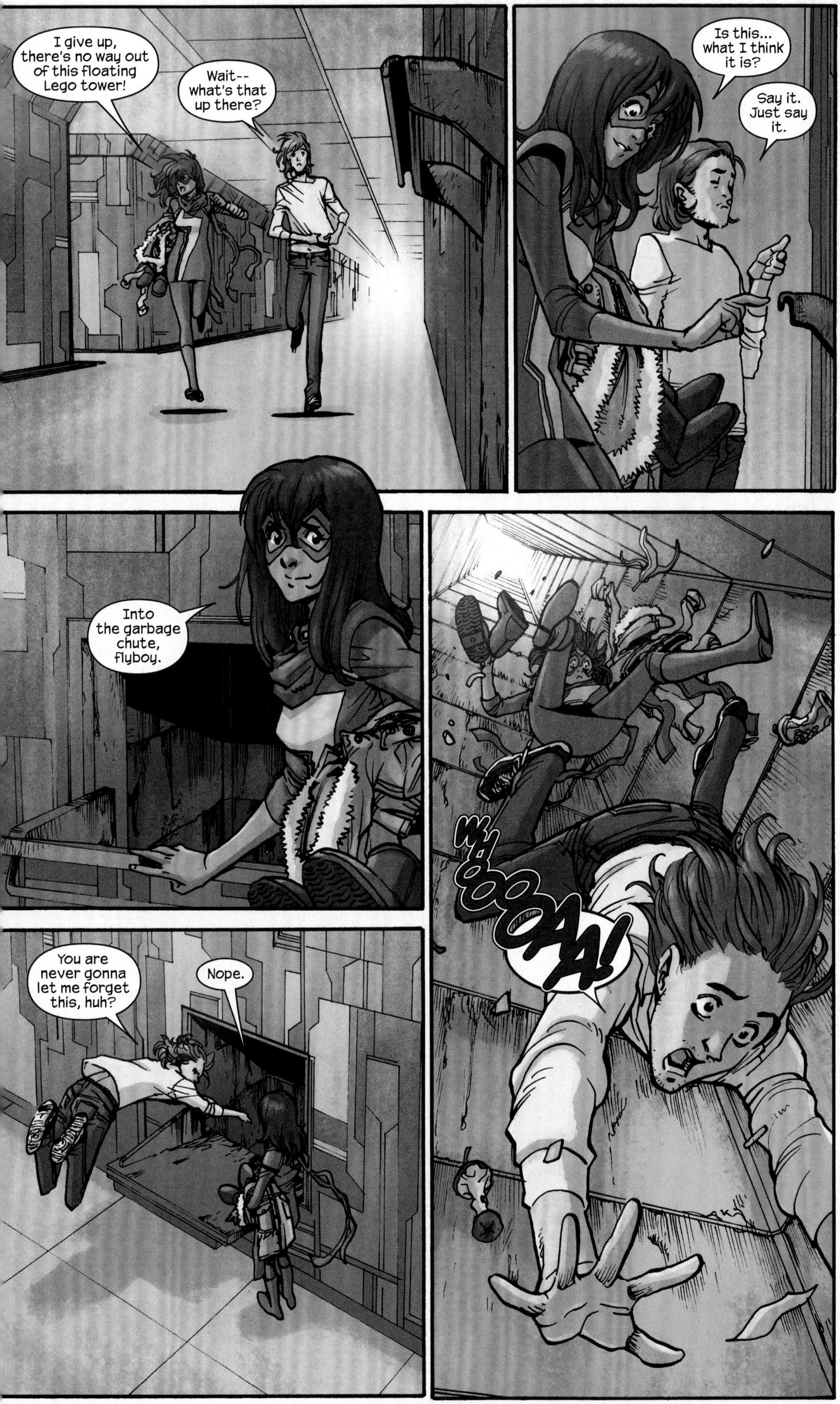
I give up, there's no way out of this floating Lego tower!
Wait-- what's that up there?
Is this... what I think it is?
Say it. Just say it.
Into the garbage chute, flyboy.
WHOOOOAA!
You are never gonna let me forget this, huh?
Nope.

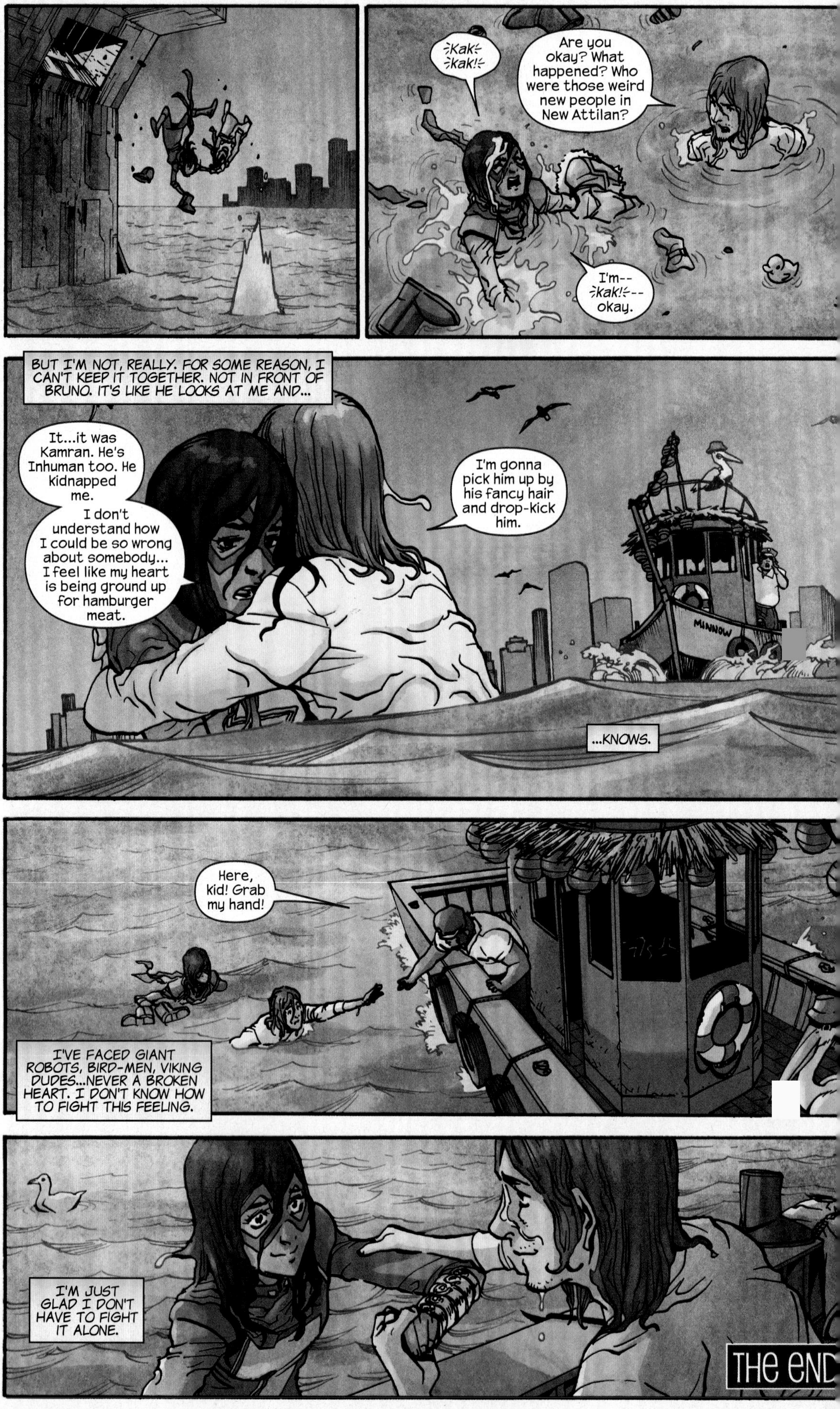

-Kak-
-kak!-
Are you okay? What happened? Who were those weird new people in New Attilan?
I'm-- -kak!- -- okay.
BUT I'M NOT, REALLY. FOR SOME REASON, I CAN'T KEEP IT TOGETHER. NOT IN FRONT OF BRUNO. IT'S LIKE HE LOOKS AT ME AND...
It...it was Kamran. He's Inhuman too. He kidnapped me.
I don't understand how I could be so wrong about somebody... I feel like my heart is being ground up for hamburger meat.
I'm gonna pick him up by his fancy hair and drop-kick him.
MINNOW
...KNOWS.
Here, kid! Grab my hand!
I'VE FACED GIANT ROBOTS, BIRD-MEN, VIKING DUDES...NEVER A BROKEN HEART. I DON'T KNOW HOW TO FIGHT THIS FEELING.
I'M JUST GLAD I DON'T HAVE TO FIGHT IT ALONE.
THE END

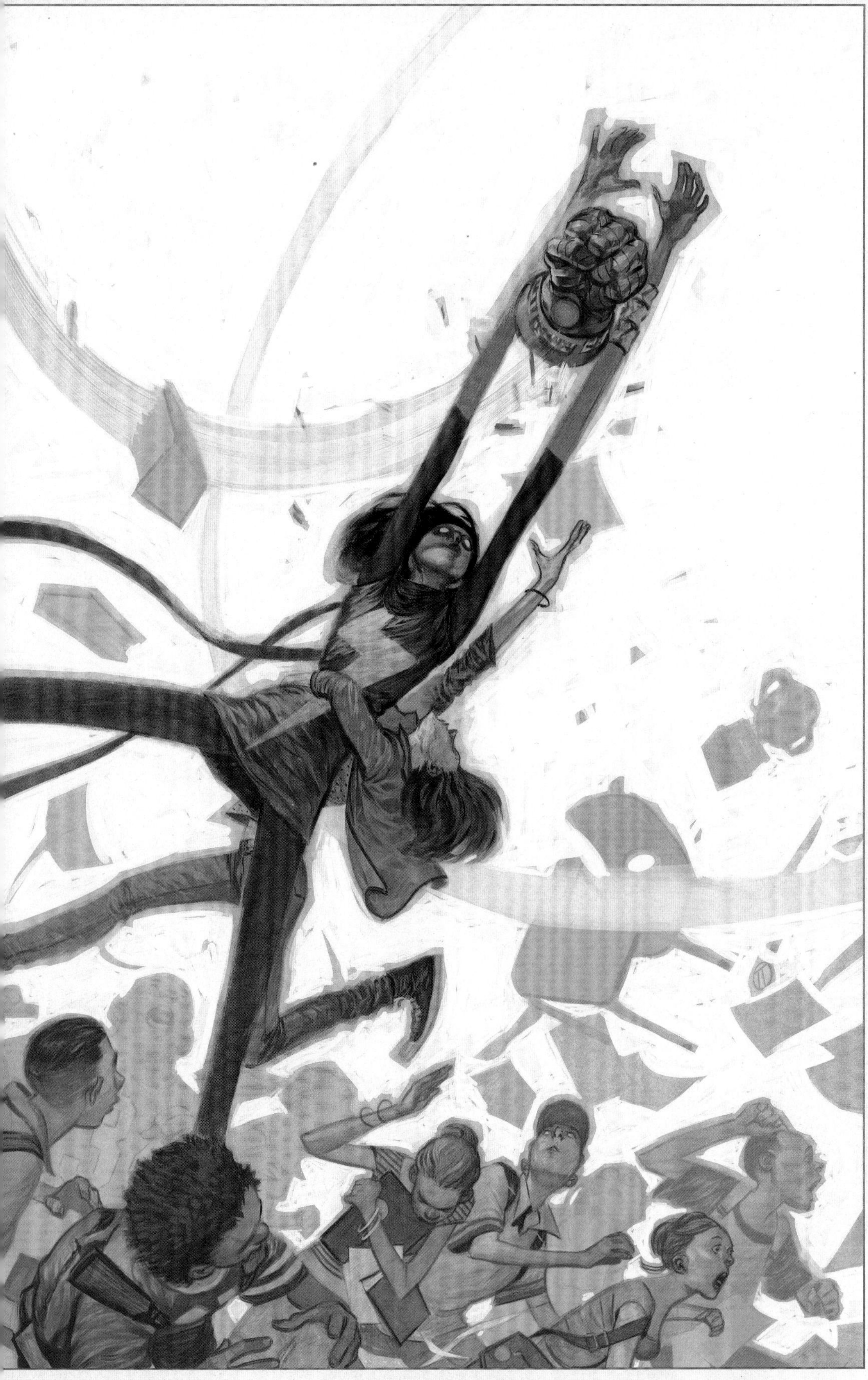

S.H.I.E.L.D. #2

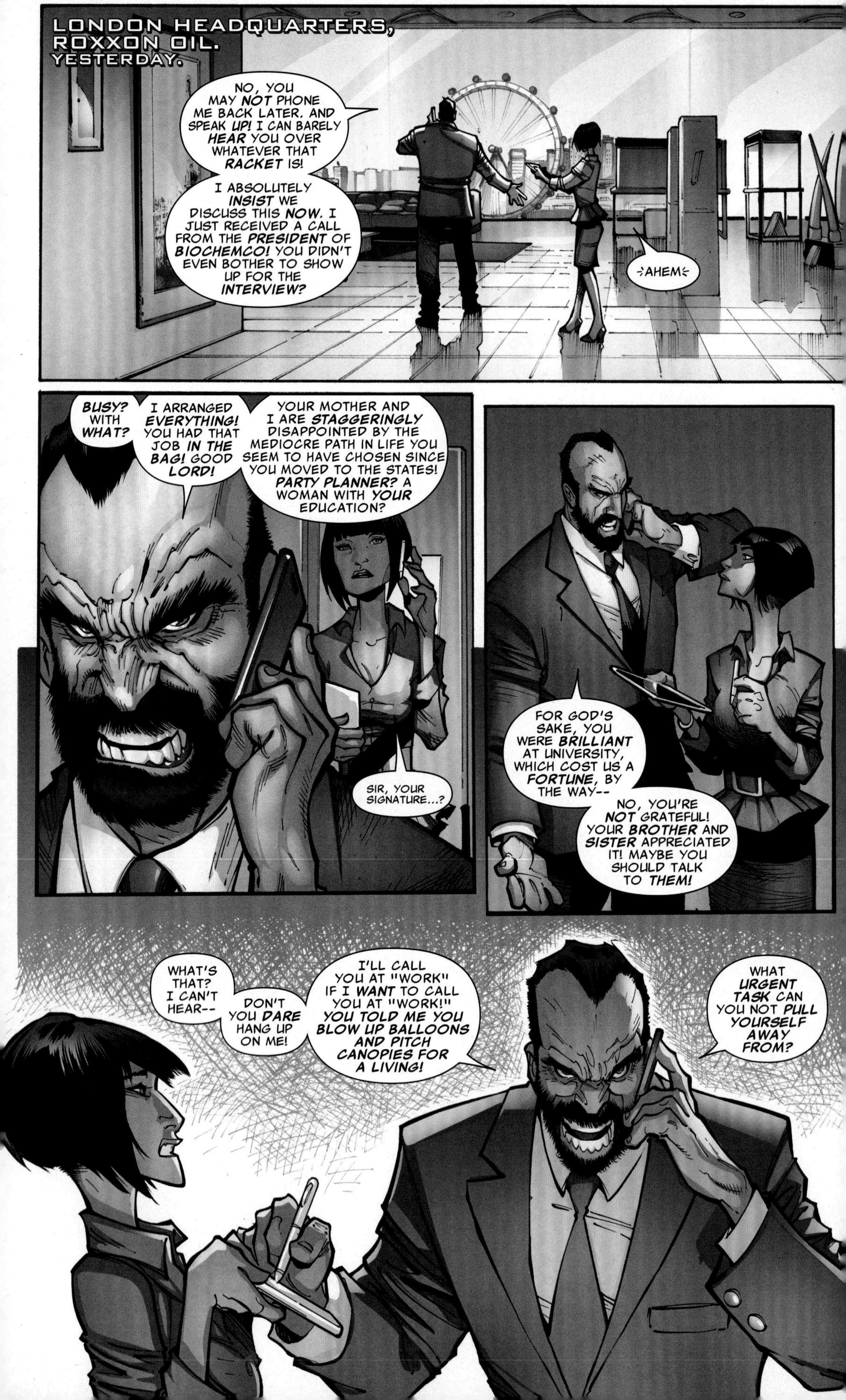
LONDON HEADQUARTERS, ROXXON OIL. YESTERDAY.
NO, YOU MAY NOT PHONE ME BACK LATER. AND SPEAK UP! I CAN BARELY HEAR YOU OVER WHATEVER THAT RACKET IS!
I ABSOLUTELY INSIST WE DISCUSS THIS NOW. I JUST RECEIVED A CALL FROM THE PRESIDENT OF BIOCHEMCO! YOU DIDN'T EVEN BOTHER TO SHOW UP FOR THE INTERVIEW?
AHEM
BUSY? WITH WHAT?
I ARRANGED EVERYTHING! YOU HAD THAT JOB IN THE BAG! GOOD LORD!
YOUR MOTHER AND I ARE STAGGERINGLY DISAPPOINTED BY THE MEDIOCRE PATH IN LIFE YOU SEEM TO HAVE CHOSEN SINCE YOU MOVED TO THE STATES! PARTY PLANNER? A WOMAN WITH YOUR EDUCATION?
SIR, YOUR SIGNATURE...?
FOR GOD'S SAKE, YOU WERE BRILLIANT AT UNIVERSITY, WHICH COST US A FORTUNE, BY THE WAY--
NO, YOU'RE NOT GRATEFUL! YOUR BROTHER AND SISTER APPRECIATED IT! MAYBE YOU SHOULD TALK TO THEM!
WHAT'S THAT? I CAN'T HEAR--
DON'T YOU DARE HANG UP ON ME!
I'LL CALL YOU AT "WORK" IF I WANT TO CALL YOU AT "WORK!" YOU TOLD ME YOU BLOW UP BALLOONS AND PITCH CANOPIES FOR A LIVING!
WHAT URGENT TASK CAN YOU NOT PULL YOURSELF AWAY FROM?

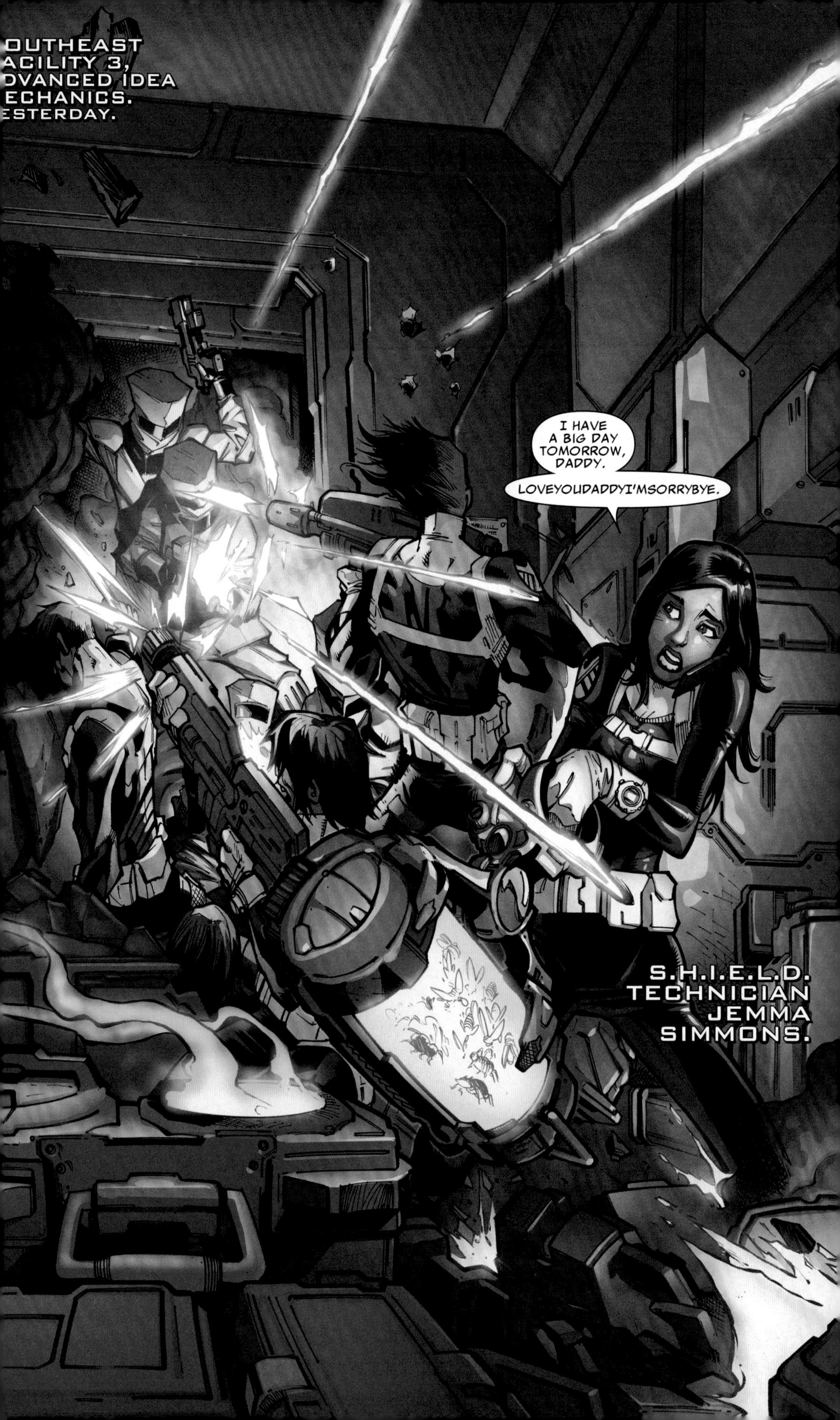
OUTHEAST
ACILITY 3,
DVANCED IDEA
ECHANICS.
ESTERDAY.
I HAVE A BIG DAY TOMORROW, DADDY.
LOVEYOUDADDYI'MSORRYBYE.
S.H.I.E.L.D. TECHNICIAN JEMMA SIMMONS.

ACCESS GRANTED...

STRATEGIC HOMELAND INTERVENTION ENFORCEMENT LOGISTICS DIVISION

S.H.I.E.L.D.

ACTIVE MISSION:
THE ANIMATOR

PAST MISSION:

S.H.I.E.L.D., the Strategic Homeland Intervention, Enforcement and Logistics Division, mitigates and confronts threats to the security of the Earth and its people. Its highly trained agents detect and defend against any menace that might rear its ugly head against us. Among these agents are Phil Coulson—cool-headed, mild-mannered, and singularly dedicated to his work—and xenobiologist Jemma Simmons, calmly collected, wildly intelligent, and surprisingly sentimental. Coulson, Simmons, and their fellow S.H.I.E.L.D. agents encounter mutants, monsters, villains, gods, an[redacted]the best and worst of humanity on a daily basis as they endeavor to carry out S.H.I.E.L.D.'s mission.

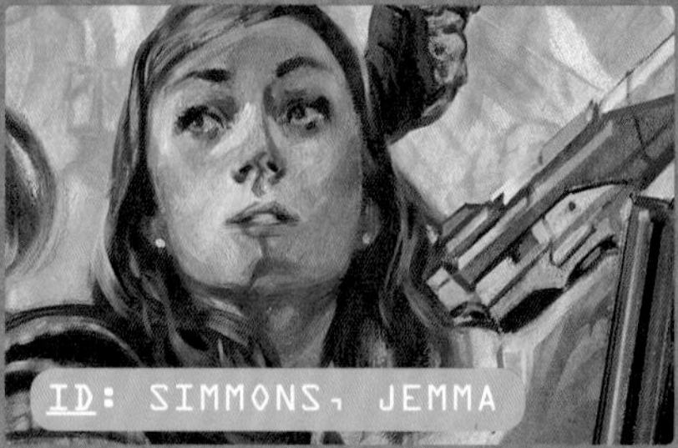
ID: SIMMONS, JEMMA

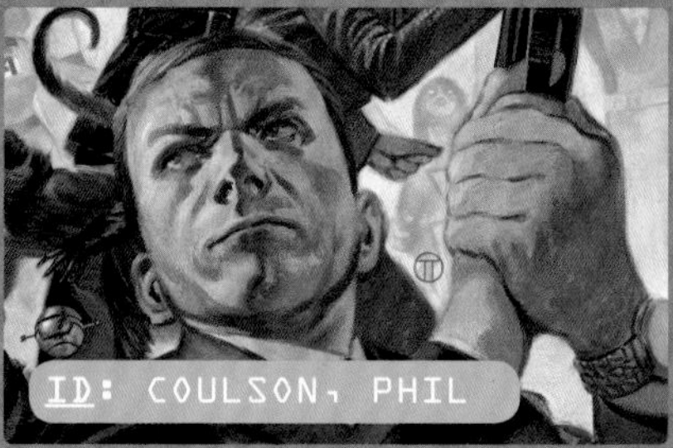
ID: COULSON, PHIL

KNOWN AGENTS:

MARK WAID
WRITER
HUMBERTO RAMOS
PENCILER
VICTOR OLAZABA
INKER
EDGAR DELGADO
COLORIST
VC'[redacted]OE CARAMAGNA
LETTERER
JESSICA PIZARRO
DESIGNER

JULIAN TOTINO TEDESCO
COVER ARTIST
HUMBERTO RAMOS & EDGAR DELGADO;
SALVADOR LARROCA & ISRAEL SILVA
VARIANT COVER ARTISTS

JON MOISAN
ASSISTANT EDITOR
TOM BREVOORT
WITH ELLIE PYLE
(K.I.A.)
EDITORS
AXEL ALONSO
EDITOR IN CHIEF

JOE QUESADA
CHIEF CREATIVE OFFICER
DAN BUCKLEY
PUBLISHER
ALAN FINE
EXECUTIVE PRODUCER

FITZ AND H.E.N.R.Y. STRIPS BY JOE QUESADA
S.H.I.E.L.D. CREATED BY STAN LEE AND JACK KIRBY

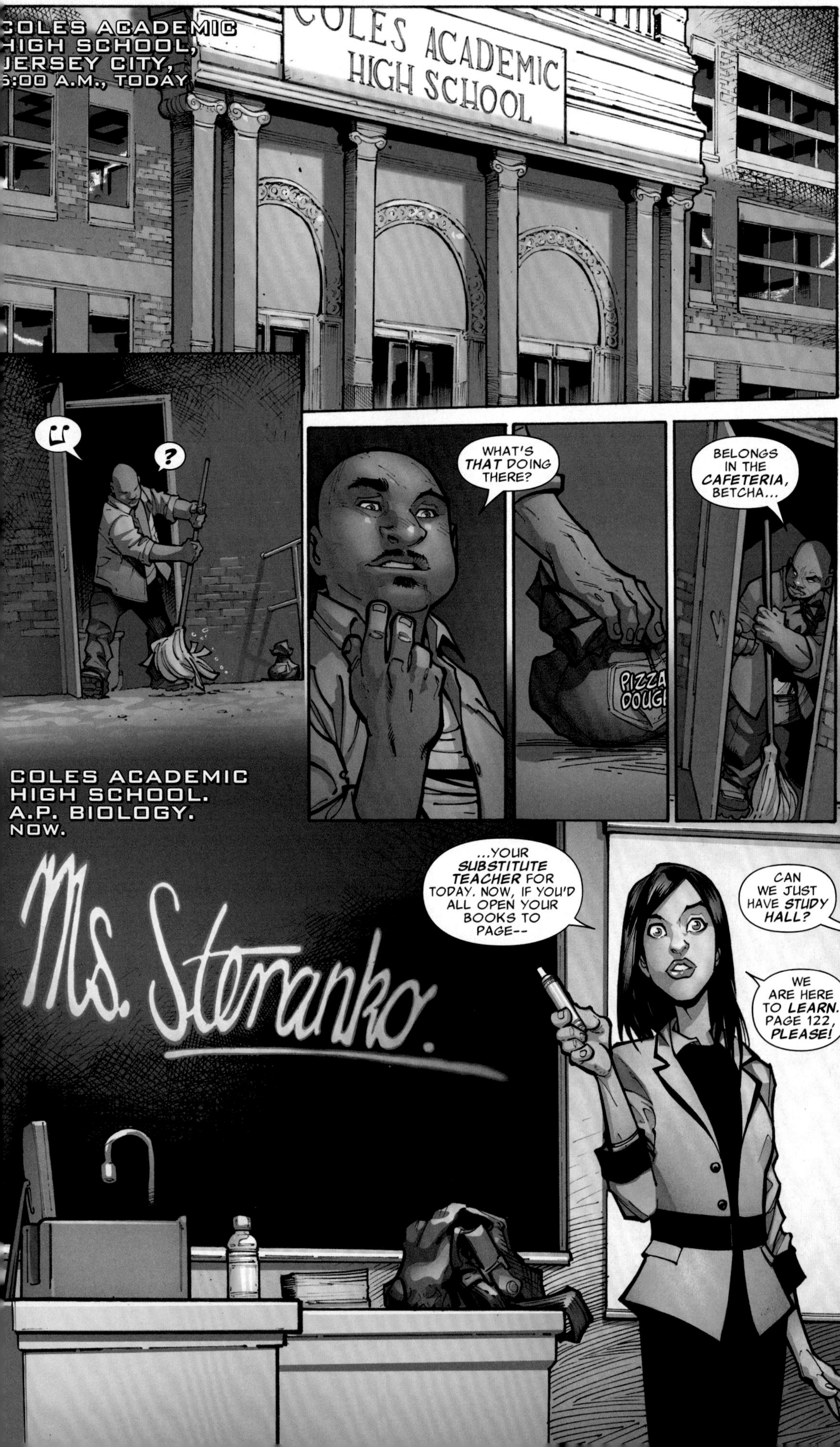
COLES ACADEMIC HIGH SCHOOL, JERSEY CITY, :00 A.M., TODAY
COLES ACADEMIC HIGH SCHOOL
?
WHAT'S *THAT* DOING THERE?
PIZZA DOUGH
BELONGS IN THE *CAFETERIA*, BETCHA...
COLES ACADEMIC HIGH SCHOOL. A.P. BIOLOGY. NOW.
Ms. Steranko.
...YOUR *SUBSTITUTE TEACHER* FOR TODAY. NOW, IF YOU'D ALL OPEN YOUR BOOKS TO PAGE--
CAN WE JUST HAVE *STUDY HALL*?
WE ARE HERE TO *LEARN*. PAGE 122, *PLEASE!*

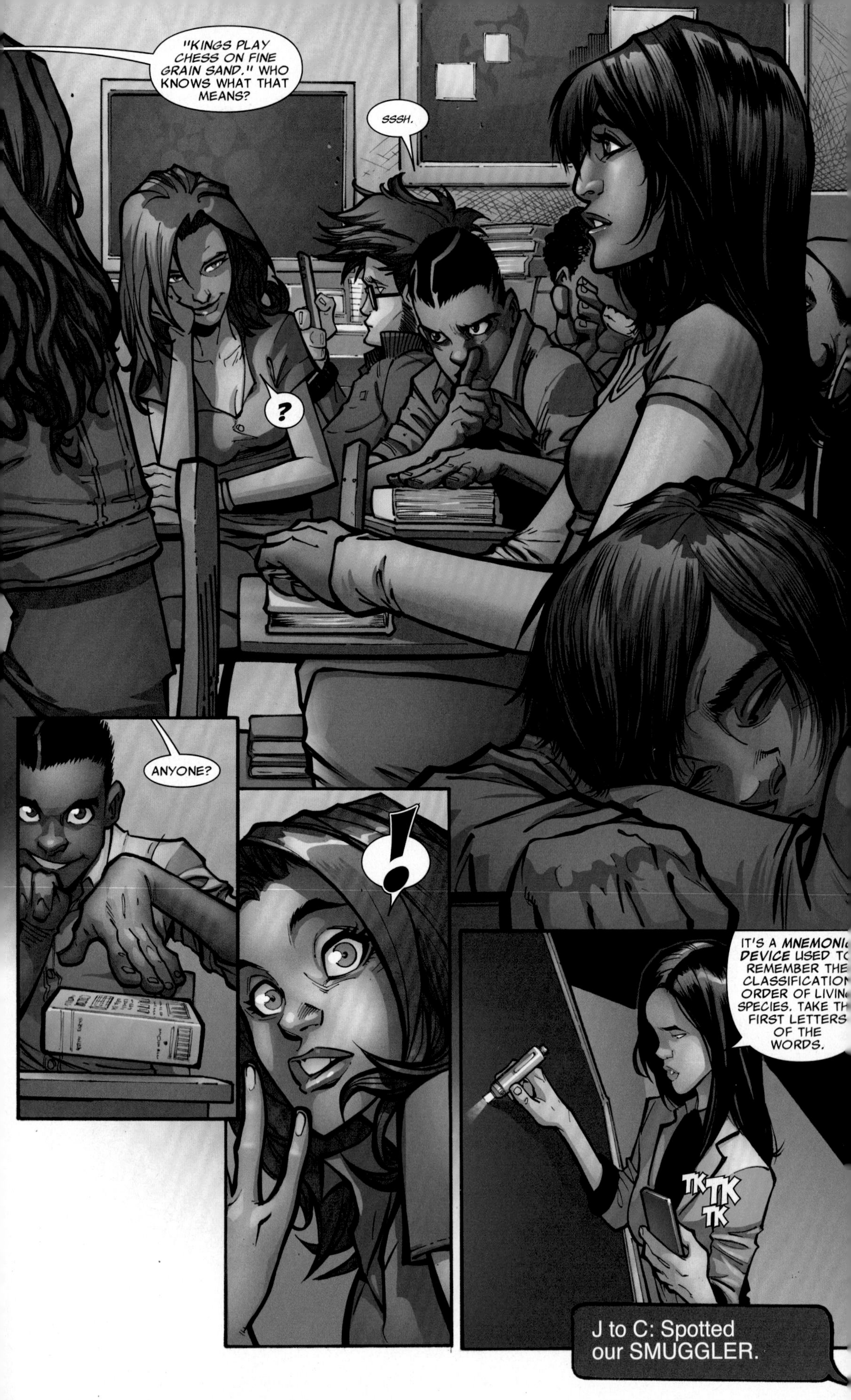
"KINGS PLAY CHESS ON FINE GRAIN SAND." WHO KNOWS WHAT THAT MEANS?
SSSH.
?
ANYONE?
!
IT'S A MNEMONIC DEVICE USED TO REMEMBER THE CLASSIFICATION ORDER OF LIVING SPECIES. TAKE THE FIRST LETTERS OF THE WORDS.
TK TK TK TK
J to C: Spotted our SMUGGLER.

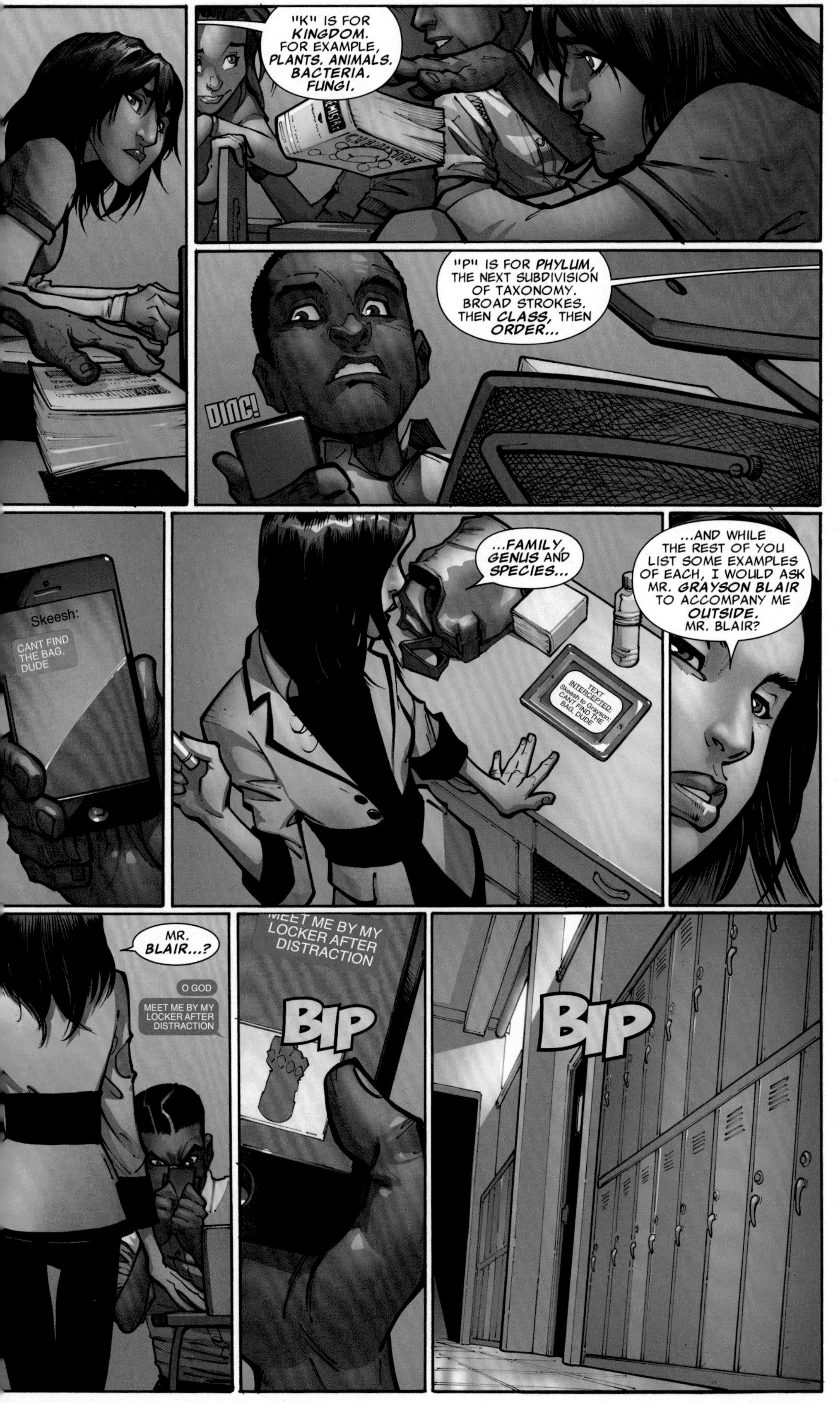
"K" IS FOR KINGDOM. FOR EXAMPLE, PLANTS. ANIMALS. BACTERIA. FUNGI.
CHEMISTRY
"P" IS FOR PHYLUM, THE NEXT SUBDIVISION OF TAXONOMY. BROAD STROKES. THEN CLASS, THEN ORDER...
DING!
Skeesh:
CANT FIND THE BAG, DUDE
...FAMILY, GENUS AND SPECIES...
TEXT INTERCEPTED: Skeesh to Grayson: CANT FIND THE BAG, DUDE
...AND WHILE THE REST OF YOU LIST SOME EXAMPLES OF EACH, I WOULD ASK MR. GRAYSON BLAIR TO ACCOMPANY ME OUTSIDE. MR. BLAIR?
MR. BLAIR...?
O GOD
MEET ME BY MY LOCKER AFTER DISTRACTION
MEET ME BY MY LOCKER AFTER DISTRACTION
BIP
BIP

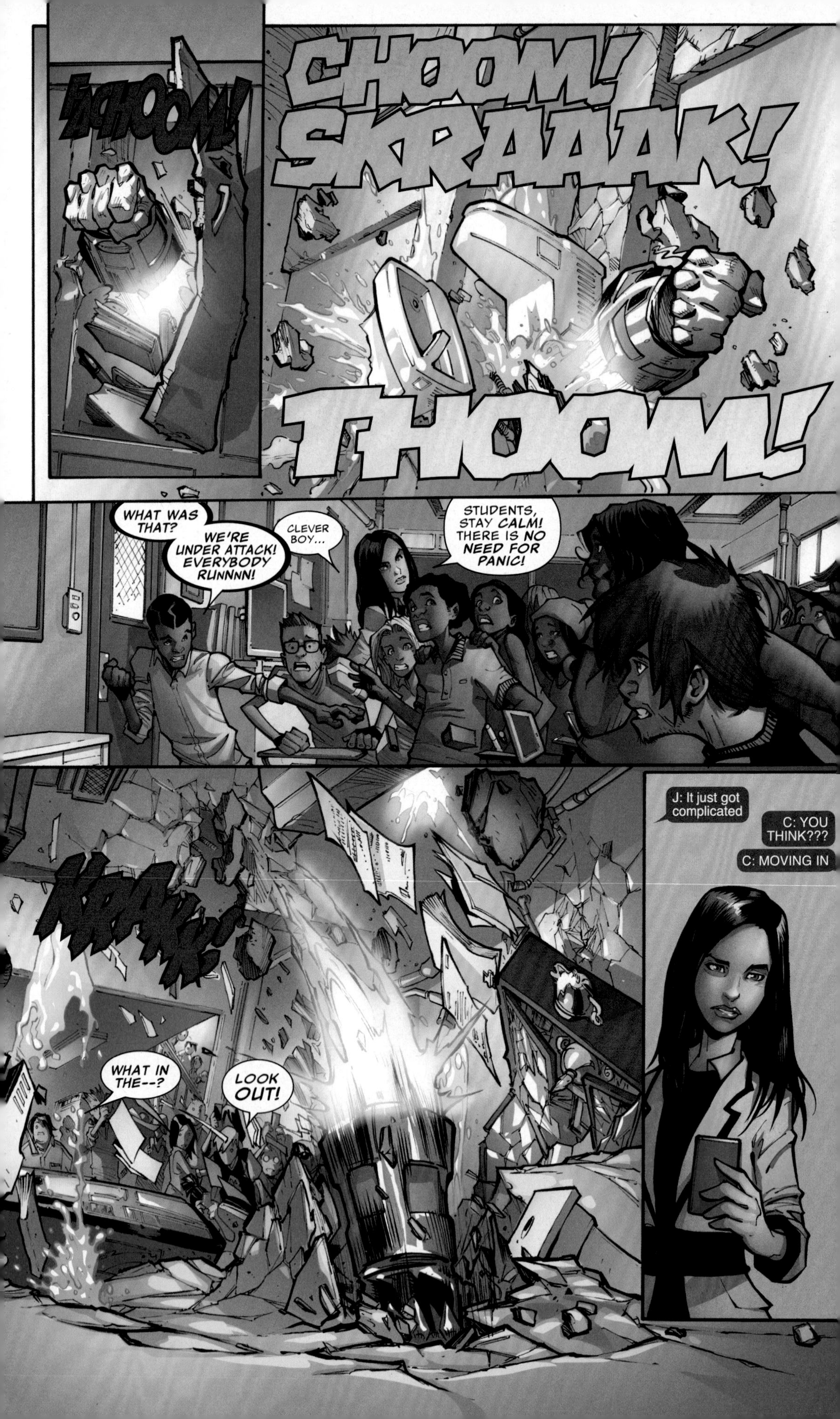
CHOOM!
SKRAAAK!
THOOM!
WHAT WAS THAT?
WE'RE UNDER ATTACK! EVERYBODY RUNNNN!
CLEVER BOY...
STUDENTS, STAY CALM! THERE IS NO NEED FOR PANIC!
WHAT IN THE--?
LOOK OUT!
J: It just got complicated
C: YOU THINK???
C: MOVING IN

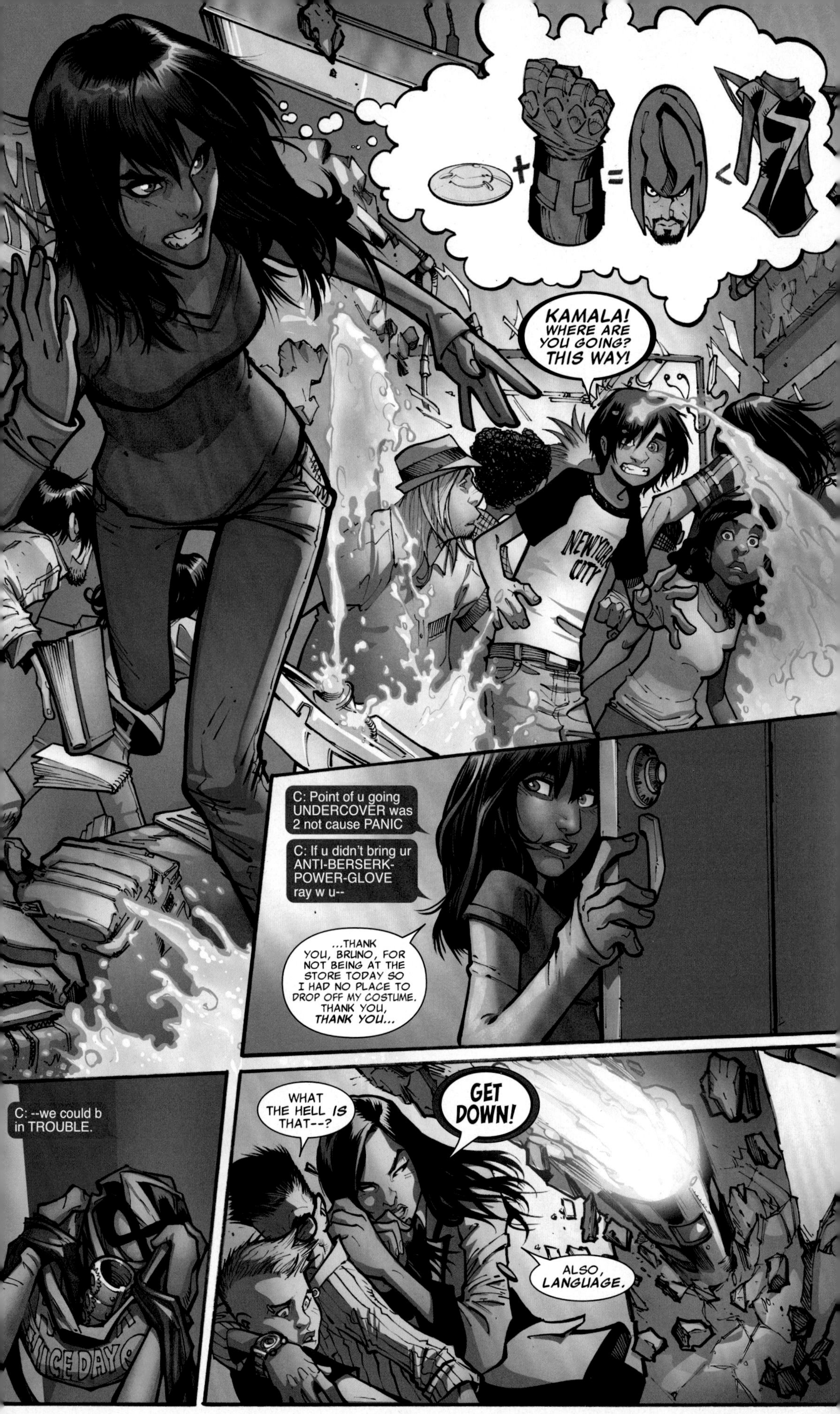
KAMALA! WHERE ARE YOU GOING? THIS WAY!
C: Point of u going UNDERCOVER was 2 not cause PANIC
C: If u didn't bring ur ANTI-BERSERK-POWER-GLOVE ray w u--
...THANK YOU, BRUNO, FOR NOT BEING AT THE STORE TODAY SO I HAD NO PLACE TO DROP OFF MY COSTUME. THANK YOU, THANK YOU...
C: --we could b in TROUBLE.
WHAT THE HELL IS THAT--?
GET DOWN!
ALSO, LANGUAGE.

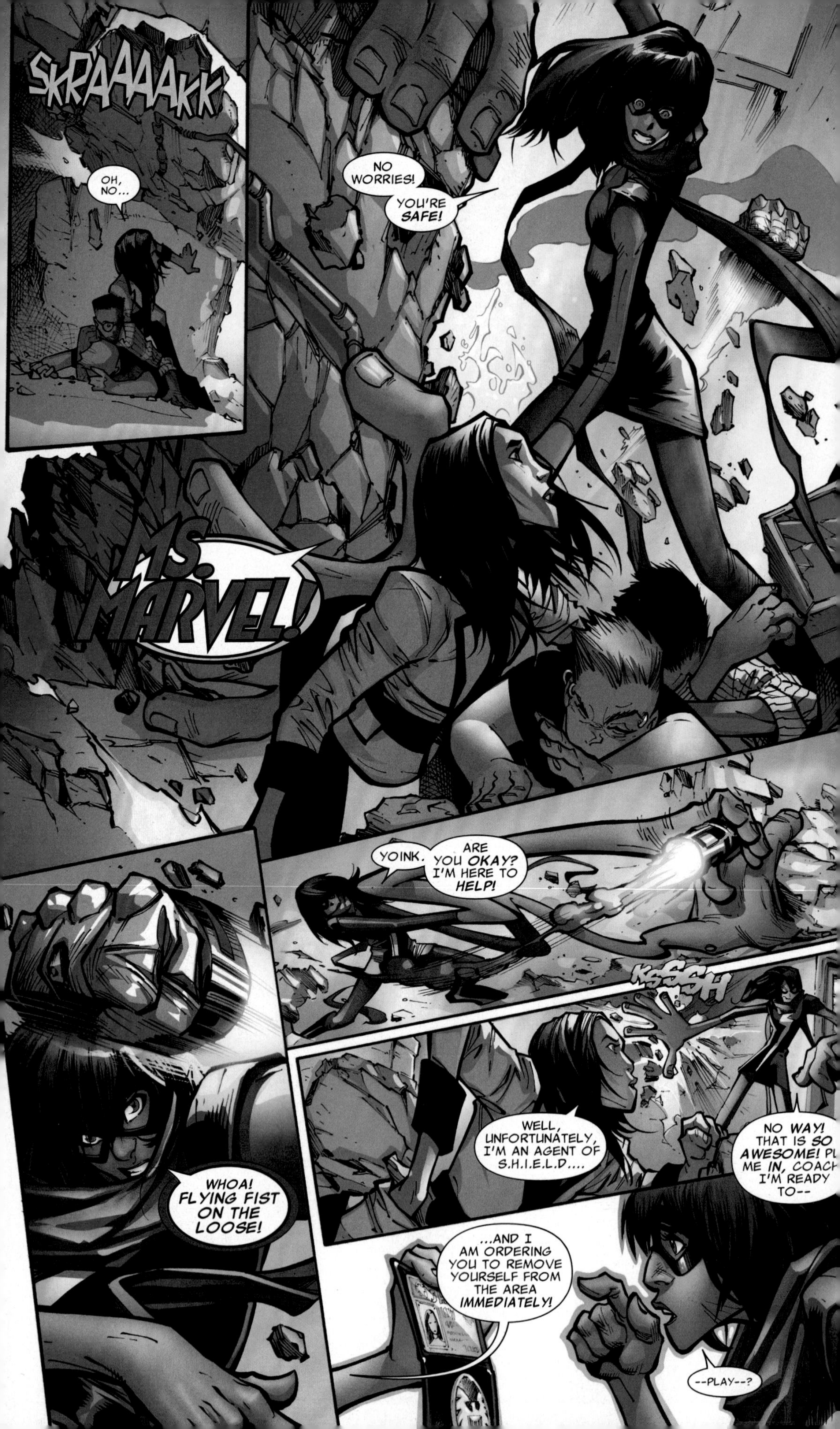
SKRAAAAKK
OH, NO...
NO WORRIES!
YOU'RE SAFE!
MS. MARVEL!
YOINK.
ARE YOU OKAY? I'M HERE TO HELP!
WHOA! FLYING FIST ON THE LOOSE!
KSSSH
WELL, UNFORTUNATELY, I'M AN AGENT OF S.H.I.E.L.D....
NO WAY! THAT IS SO AWESOME! PL ME IN, COACH I'M READY TO--
...AND I AM ORDERING YOU TO REMOVE YOURSELF FROM THE AREA IMMEDIATELY!
--PLAY--?

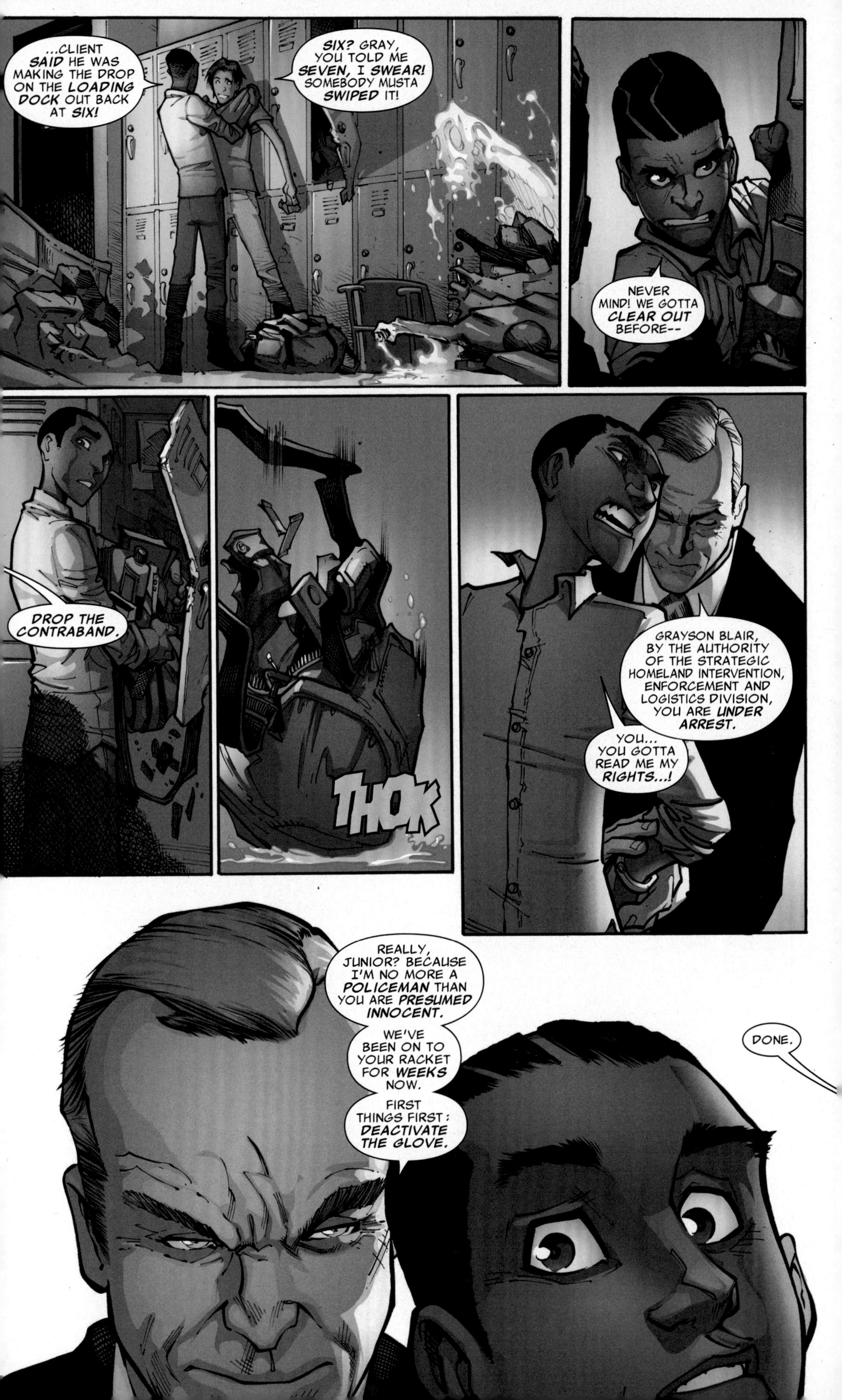
...CLIENT SAID HE WAS MAKING THE DROP ON THE LOADING DOCK OUT BACK AT SIX!
SIX? GRAY, YOU TOLD ME SEVEN, I SWEAR! SOMEBODY MUSTA SWIPED IT!
NEVER MIND! WE GOTTA CLEAR OUT BEFORE--
DROP THE CONTRABAND.
THOK
GRAYSON BLAIR, BY THE AUTHORITY OF THE STRATEGIC HOMELAND INTERVENTION, ENFORCEMENT AND LOGISTICS DIVISION, YOU ARE UNDER ARREST.
YOU... YOU GOTTA READ ME MY RIGHTS...!
REALLY, JUNIOR? BECAUSE I'M NO MORE A POLICEMAN THAN YOU ARE PRESUMED INNOCENT.
WE'VE BEEN ON TO YOUR RACKET FOR WEEKS NOW.
FIRST THINGS FIRST: DEACTIVATE THE GLOVE.
DONE.

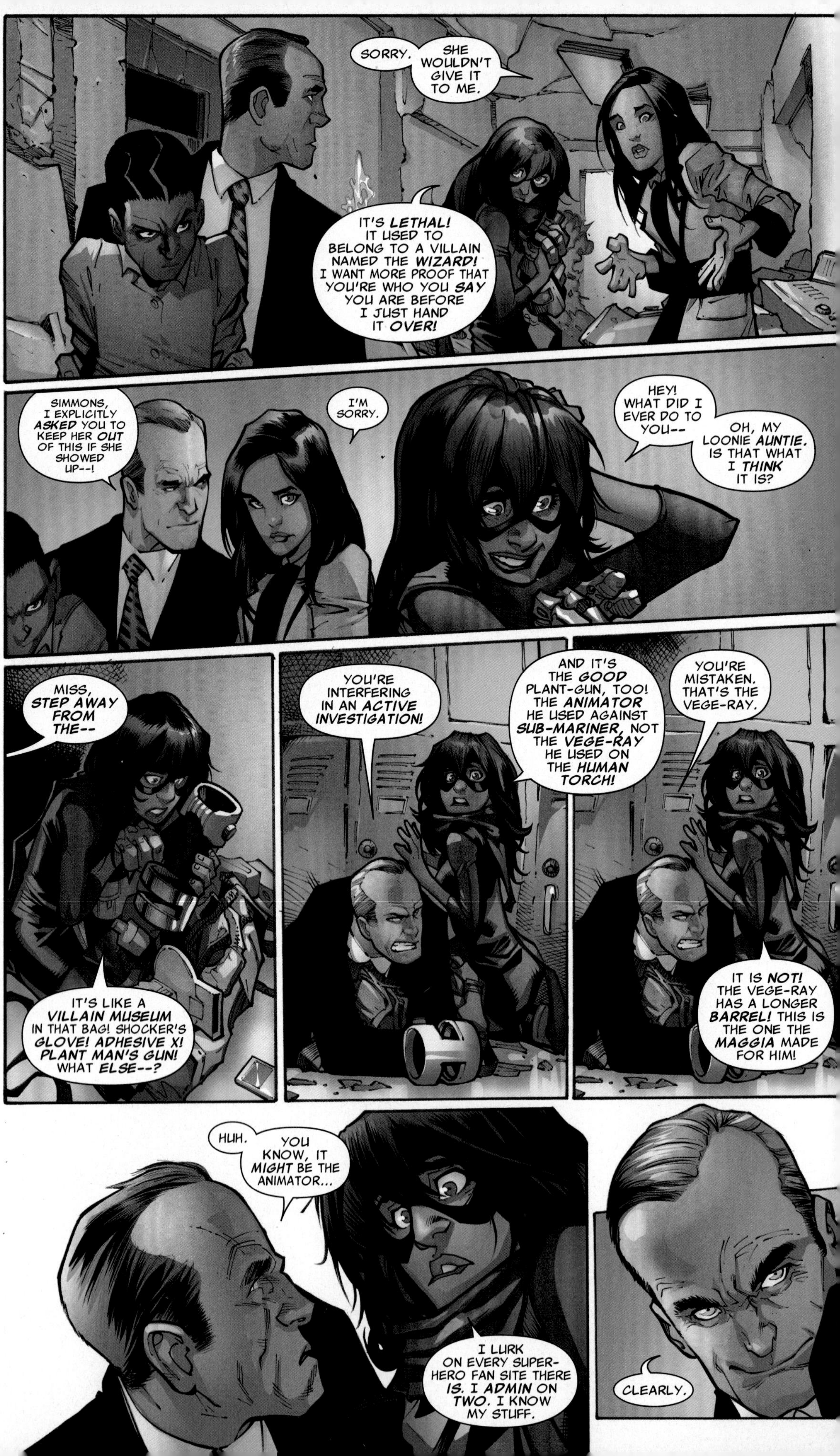
SORRY.
SHE WOULDN'T GIVE IT TO ME.
IT'S LETHAL! IT USED TO BELONG TO A VILLAIN NAMED THE WIZARD! I WANT MORE PROOF THAT YOU'RE WHO YOU SAY YOU ARE BEFORE I JUST HAND IT OVER!
SIMMONS, I EXPLICITLY ASKED YOU TO KEEP HER OUT OF THIS IF SHE SHOWED UP--!
I'M SORRY.
HEY! WHAT DID I EVER DO TO YOU--
OH, MY LOONIE AUNTIE. IS THAT WHAT I THINK IT IS?
MISS, STEP AWAY FROM THE--
IT'S LIKE A VILLAIN MUSEUM IN THAT BAG! SHOCKER'S GLOVE! ADHESIVE X! PLANT MAN'S GUN! WHAT ELSE--?
YOU'RE INTERFERING IN AN ACTIVE INVESTIGATION!
AND IT'S THE GOOD PLANT-GUN, TOO! THE ANIMATOR HE USED AGAINST SUB-MARINER, NOT THE VEGE-RAY HE USED ON THE HUMAN TORCH!
YOU'RE MISTAKEN. THAT'S THE VEGE-RAY.
IT IS NOT! THE VEGE-RAY HAS A LONGER BARREL! THIS IS THE ONE THE MAGGIA MADE FOR HIM!
HUH.
YOU KNOW, IT MIGHT BE THE ANIMATOR...
I LURK ON EVERY SUPER-HERO FAN SITE THERE IS. I ADMIN ON TWO. I KNOW MY STUFF.
CLEARLY.

BUT WHY DOES SOME **STUDENT** HAVE ALL **THIS?**

HE'S BEEN RUNNING A BLACK MARKET SITE THAT DEALS IN DATED **VILLAIN SURPLUS.** SOLD A **BEETLE** GLOVE TO A GUY WHO KIDNAPPED FORMER **MAYOR JAMESON** LAST YEAR.

THE THINGS KIDS DO FOR **MONEY** THESE DAYS, RIGHT? WHEN I WAS A BOY, I SOLD **GRIT.**

WHAT'S **GRIT?**

A **NEWSPAPER.** FOR **FARMERS.**

HOW **OLD** ARE YOU?

GET HER **OUT** OF HERE.

YESSIR. COME ALONG, MS. MARVEL.

WAIT! WHY? I JUST WANT TO **HELP!**

NOT. NOW.

ALL RIGHT, KID. WHERE'S THE DOUGH?

I DON'T HAVE IT. IT'S IN BITCOIN.

WE **BOTH** KNOW I'M NOT TALKING ABOUT MONEY, SO I'M ONLY GOING TO ASK YOU ONE MORE TIME--

--WHERE IS THE **DOUGH?**

SOMEONE SWIPED IT, I SWEAR!

PIZZA DAY.

MS. MARVEL!

STOP!

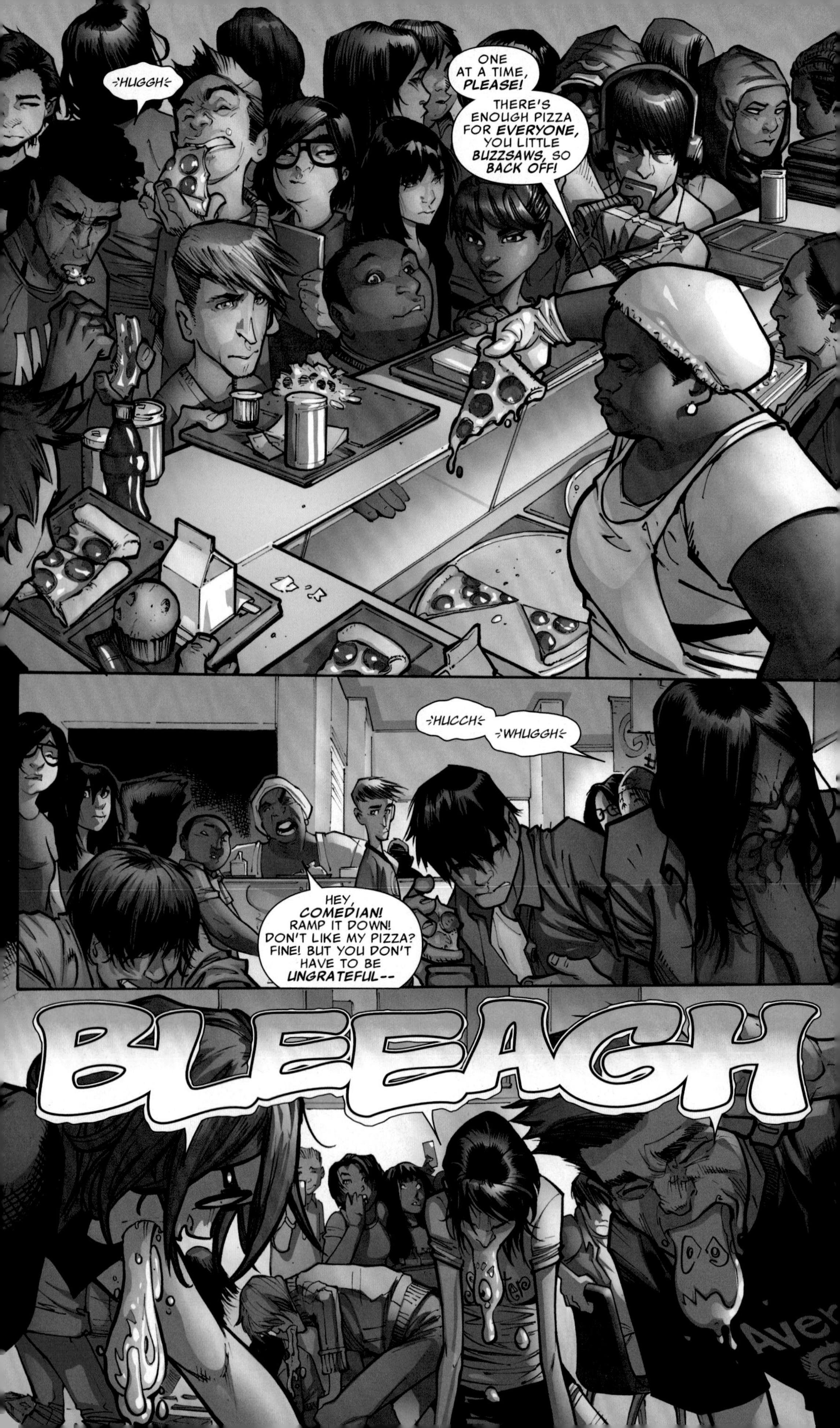
HUGGH
ONE AT A TIME, PLEASE!
THERE'S ENOUGH PIZZA FOR EVERYONE, YOU LITTLE BUZZSAWS, SO BACK OFF!
HUCCH
WHUGGH
HEY, COMEDIAN! RAMP IT DOWN! DON'T LIKE MY PIZZA? FINE! BUT YOU DON'T HAVE TO BE UNGRATEFUL--
BLEEACH

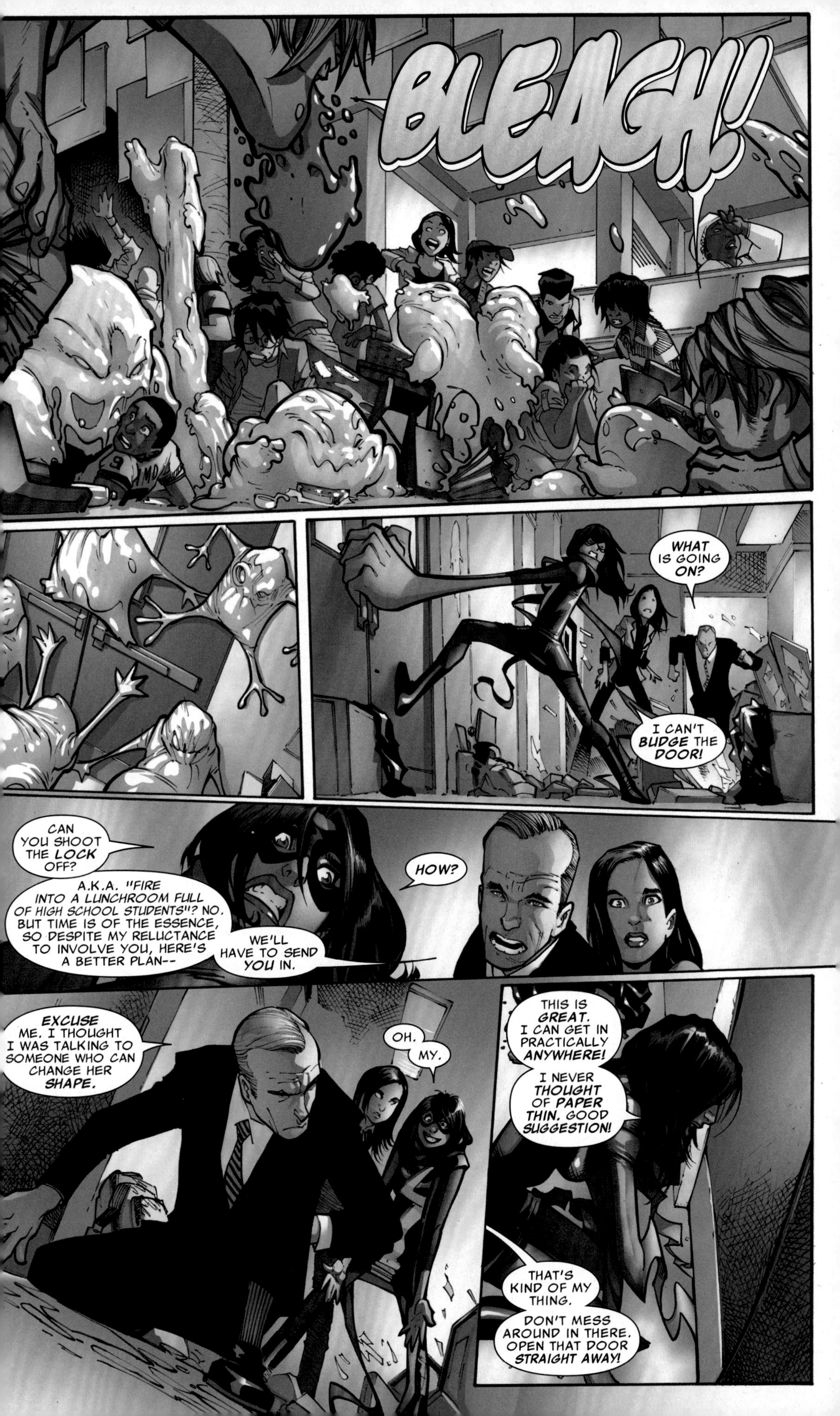
BLEACH!
WHAT IS GOING ON?
I CAN'T BUDGE THE DOOR!
CAN YOU SHOOT THE LOCK OFF?
HOW?
A.K.A. "FIRE INTO A LUNCHROOM FULL OF HIGH SCHOOL STUDENTS"? NO. BUT TIME IS OF THE ESSENCE, SO DESPITE MY RELUCTANCE TO INVOLVE YOU, HERE'S A BETTER PLAN--
WE'LL HAVE TO SEND YOU IN.
EXCUSE ME. I THOUGHT I WAS TALKING TO SOMEONE WHO CAN CHANGE HER SHAPE.
OH.
MY.
THIS IS GREAT. I CAN GET IN PRACTICALLY ANYWHERE!
I NEVER THOUGHT OF PAPER THIN. GOOD SUGGESTION!
THAT'S KIND OF MY THING.
DON'T MESS AROUND IN THERE. OPEN THAT DOOR STRAIGHT AWAY!

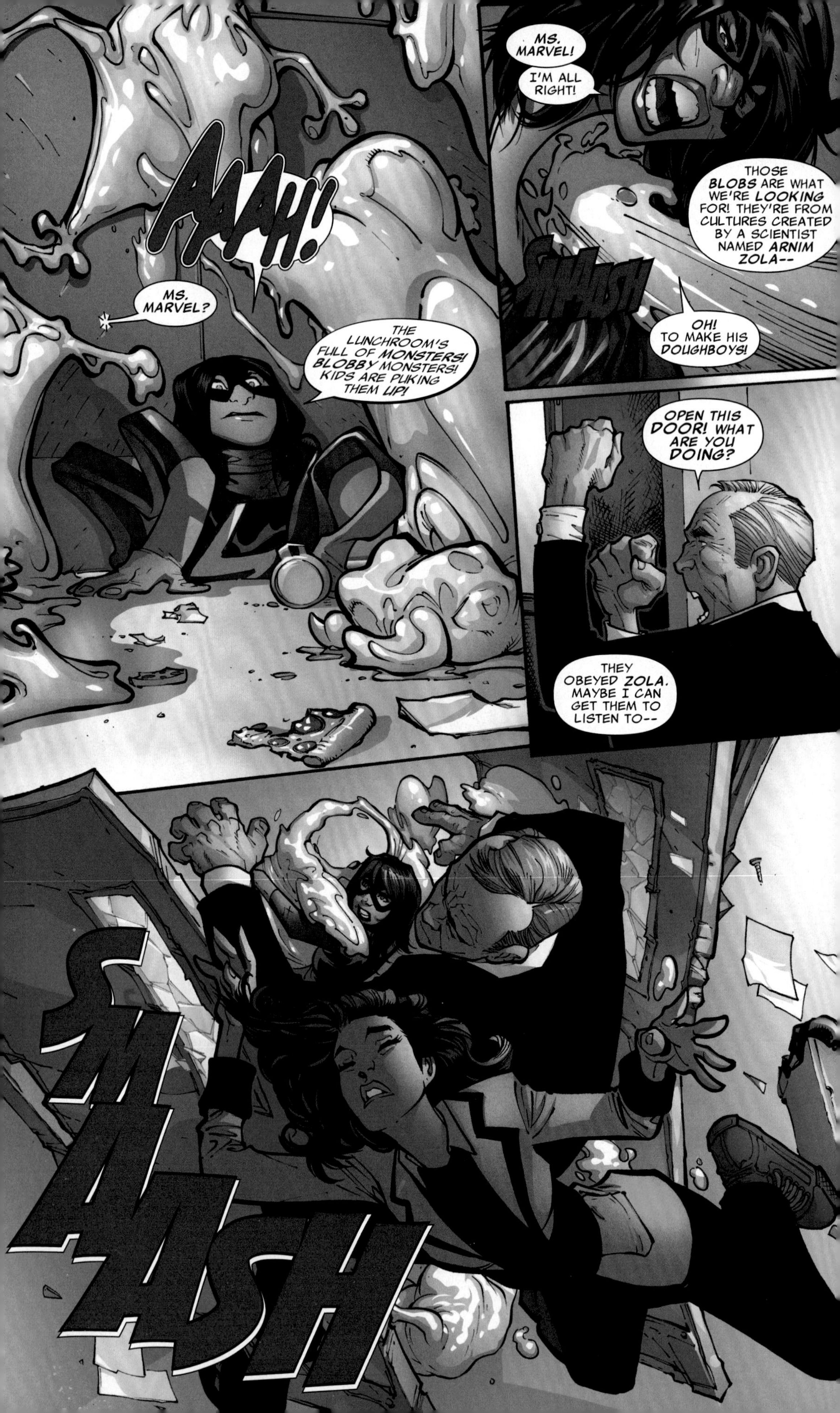

AAAH!
MS. MARVEL?
THE LUNCHROOM'S FULL OF MONSTERS! BLOBBY MONSTERS! KIDS ARE PUKING THEM UP!
MS. MARVEL!
I'M ALL RIGHT!
THOSE BLOBS ARE WHAT WE'RE LOOKING FOR! THEY'RE FROM CULTURES CREATED BY A SCIENTIST NAMED ARNIM ZOLA--
OH! TO MAKE HIS DOUGHBOYS!
OPEN THIS DOOR! WHAT ARE YOU DOING?
THEY OBEYED ZOLA. MAYBE I CAN GET THEM TO LISTEN TO--
SMASH

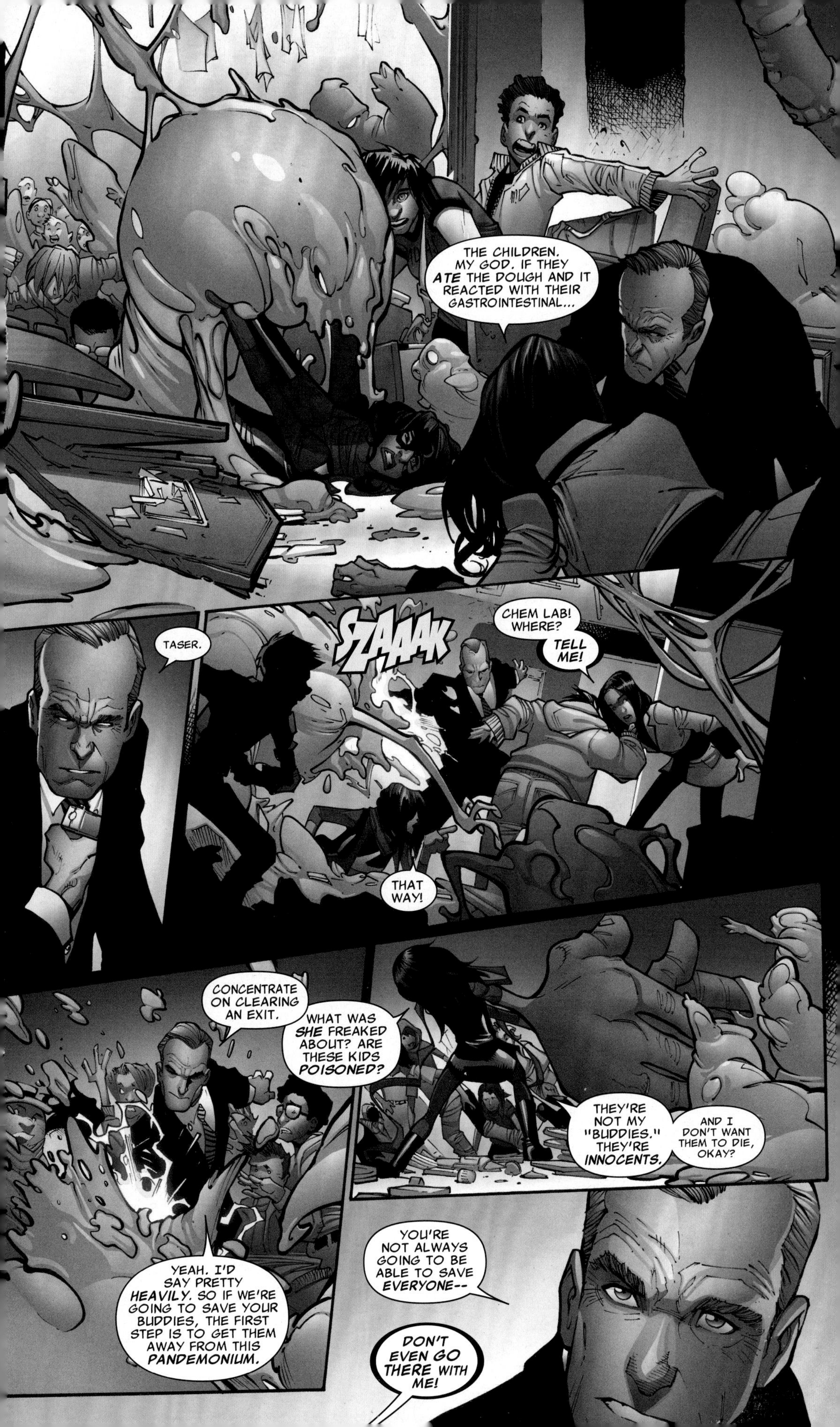
THE CHILDREN. MY GOD. IF THEY ATE THE DOUGH AND IT REACTED WITH THEIR GASTROINTESTINAL...
TASER.
SZAAAK
CHEM LAB! WHERE? TELL ME!
THAT WAY!
CONCENTRATE ON CLEARING AN EXIT.
WHAT WAS SHE FREAKED ABOUT? ARE THESE KIDS POISONED?
THEY'RE NOT MY "BUDDIES." THEY'RE INNOCENTS.
AND I DON'T WANT THEM TO DIE, OKAY?
YEAH. I'D SAY PRETTY HEAVILY. SO IF WE'RE GOING TO SAVE YOUR BUDDIES, THE FIRST STEP IS TO GET THEM AWAY FROM THIS PANDEMONIUM.
YOU'RE NOT ALWAYS GOING TO BE ABLE TO SAVE EVERYONE--
DON'T EVEN GO THERE WITH ME!

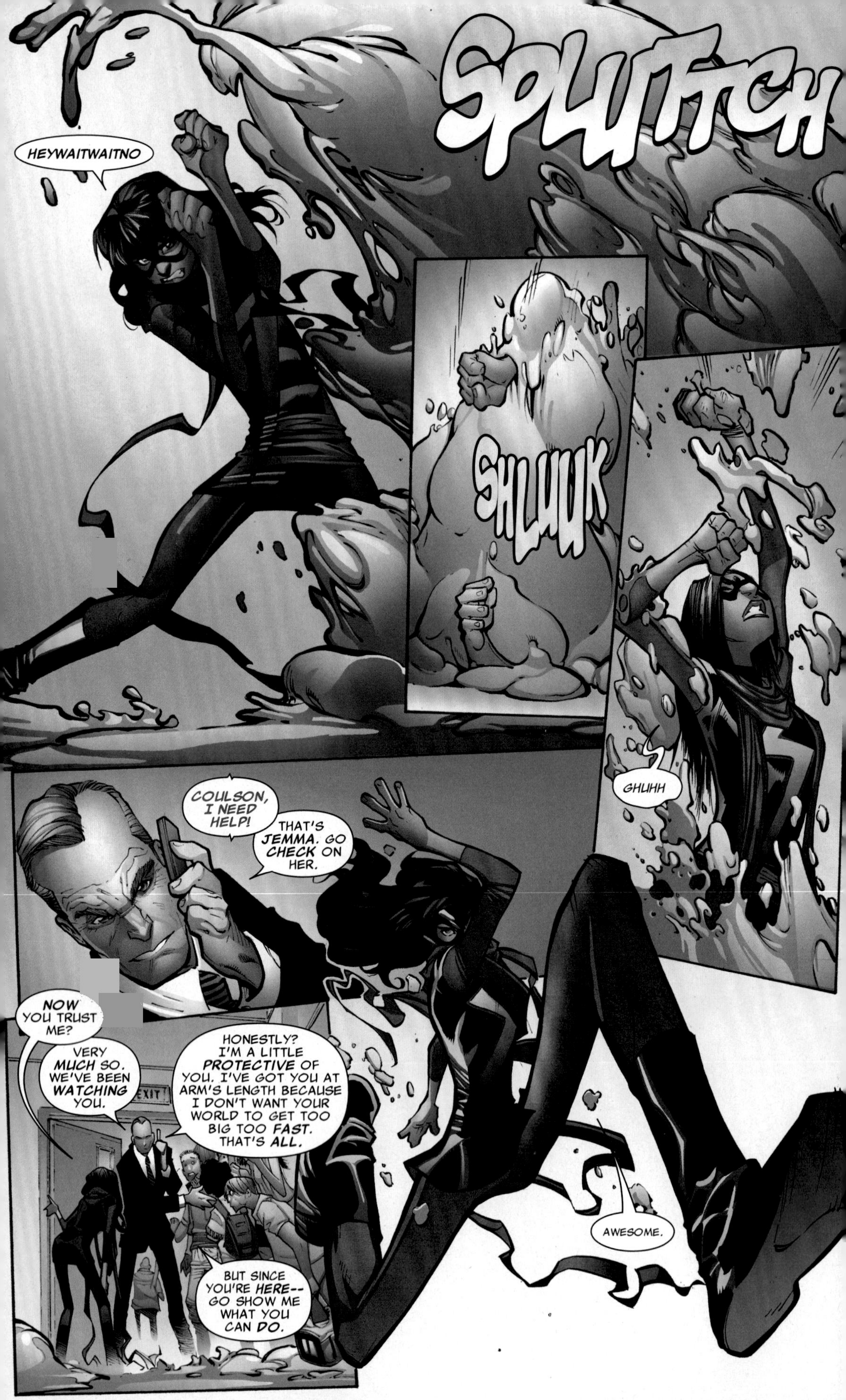
SPLUTCH
HEYWAITWAITNO
SHLUUK
GHUHH
COULSON, I NEED HELP!
THAT'S JEMMA. GO CHECK ON HER.
NOW YOU TRUST ME?
VERY MUCH SO. WE'VE BEEN WATCHING YOU.
EXIT
HONESTLY? I'M A LITTLE PROTECTIVE OF YOU. I'VE GOT YOU AT ARM'S LENGTH BECAUSE I DON'T WANT YOUR WORLD TO GET TOO BIG TOO FAST. THAT'S ALL.
BUT SINCE YOU'RE HERE--GO SHOW ME WHAT YOU CAN DO.
AWESOME.

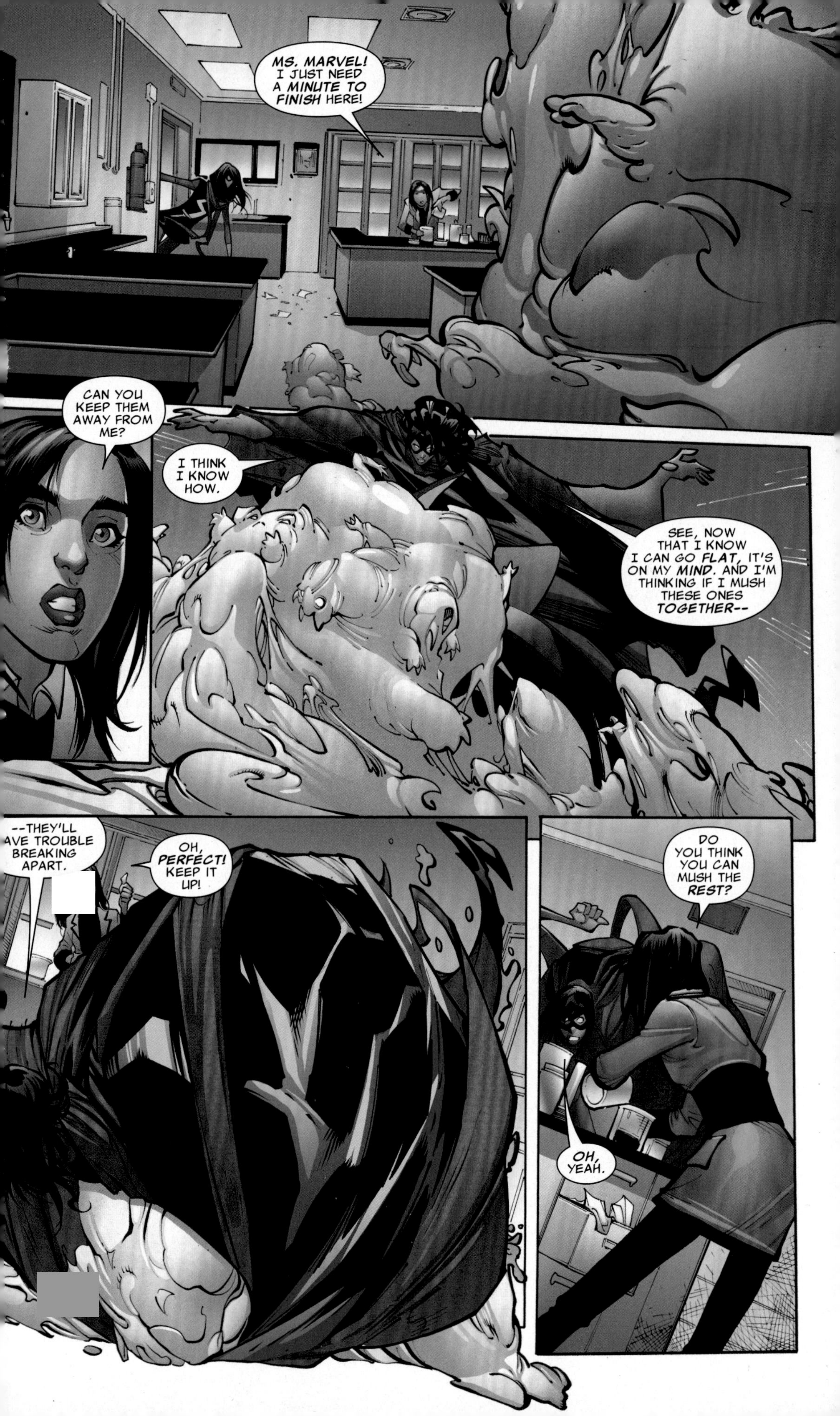
MS. MARVEL! I JUST NEED A MINUTE TO FINISH HERE!
CAN YOU KEEP THEM AWAY FROM ME?
I THINK I KNOW HOW.
SEE, NOW THAT I KNOW I CAN GO FLAT, IT'S ON MY MIND. AND I'M THINKING IF I MUSH THESE ONES TOGETHER--
--THEY'LL AVE TROUBLE BREAKING APART.
OH, PERFECT! KEEP IT UP!
DO YOU THINK YOU CAN MUSH THE REST?
OH, YEAH.

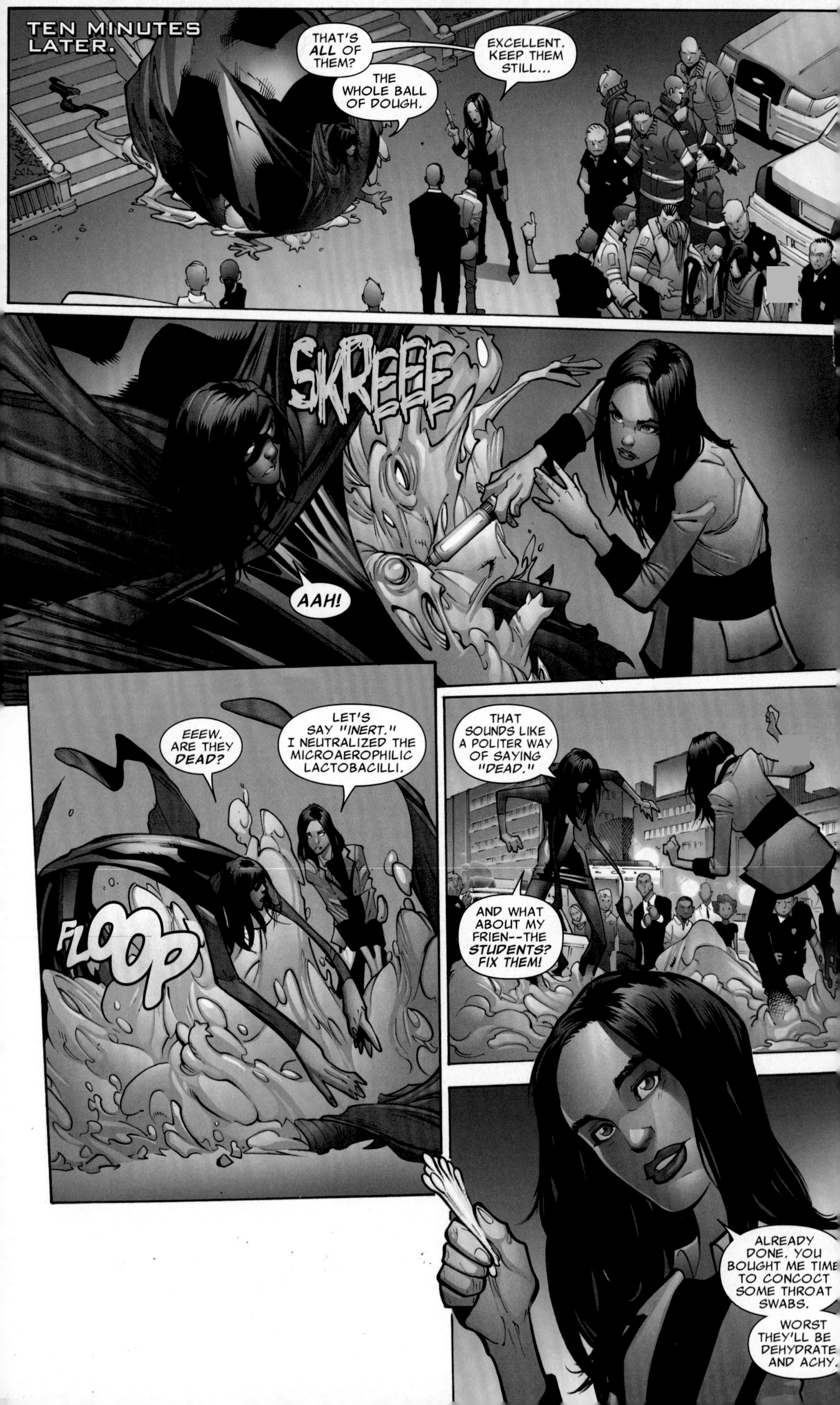
TEN MINUTES LATER.
THAT'S ALL OF THEM?
THE WHOLE BALL OF DOUGH.
EXCELLENT. KEEP THEM STILL...
SKREEE
AAH!
EEEW. ARE THEY DEAD?
LET'S SAY "INERT." I NEUTRALIZED THE MICROAEROPHILIC LACTOBACILLI.
FLOOP
THAT SOUNDS LIKE A POLITER WAY OF SAYING "DEAD."
AND WHAT ABOUT MY FRIEN--THE STUDENTS? FIX THEM!
ALREADY DONE. YOU BOUGHT ME TIME TO CONCOCT SOME THROAT SWABS.
WORST THEY'LL BE DEHYDRATE AND ACHY.

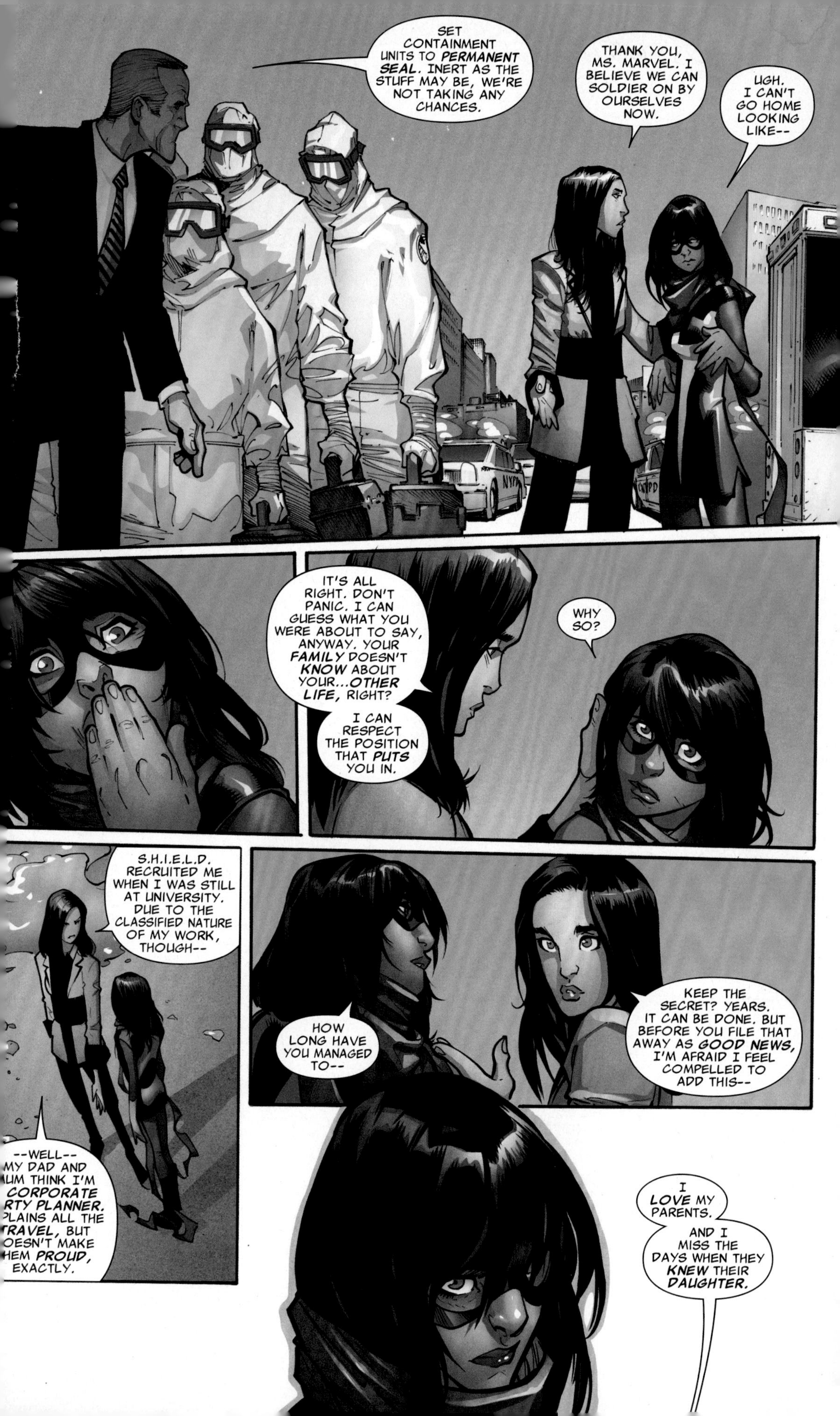
SET CONTAINMENT UNITS TO PERMANENT SEAL. INERT AS THE STUFF MAY BE, WE'RE NOT TAKING ANY CHANCES.
THANK YOU, MS. MARVEL. I BELIEVE WE CAN SOLDIER ON BY OURSELVES NOW.
UGH. I CAN'T GO HOME LOOKING LIKE--
NYPD
IT'S ALL RIGHT. DON'T PANIC. I CAN GUESS WHAT YOU WERE ABOUT TO SAY, ANYWAY. YOUR FAMILY DOESN'T KNOW ABOUT YOUR...OTHER LIFE, RIGHT?
I CAN RESPECT THE POSITION THAT PUTS YOU IN.
WHY SO?
S.H.I.E.L.D. RECRUITED ME WHEN I WAS STILL AT UNIVERSITY. DUE TO THE CLASSIFIED NATURE OF MY WORK, THOUGH--
--WELL-- MY DAD AND UM THINK I'M CORPORATE RTY PLANNER. PLAINS ALL THE TRAVEL, BUT OESN'T MAKE HEM PROUD, EXACTLY.
HOW LONG HAVE YOU MANAGED TO--
KEEP THE SECRET? YEARS. IT CAN BE DONE. BUT BEFORE YOU FILE THAT AWAY AS GOOD NEWS, I'M AFRAID I FEEL COMPELLED TO ADD THIS--
I LOVE MY PARENTS.
AND I MISS THE DAYS WHEN THEY KNEW THEIR DAUGHTER.

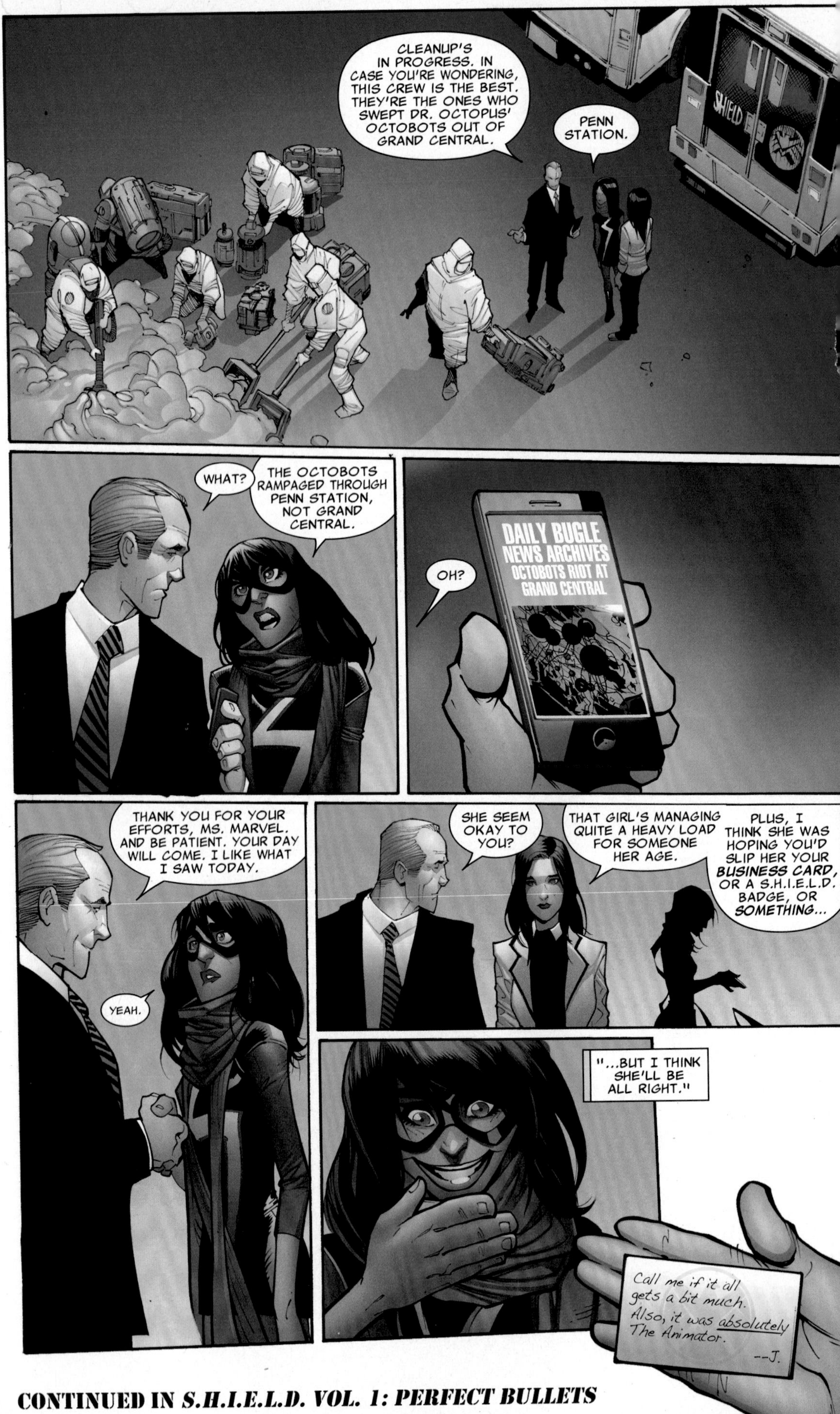
CLEANUP'S IN PROGRESS. IN CASE YOU'RE WONDERING, THIS CREW IS THE BEST. THEY'RE THE ONES WHO SWEPT DR. OCTOPUS' OCTOBOTS OUT OF GRAND CENTRAL.
PENN STATION.
SHIELD
WHAT?
THE OCTOBOTS RAMPAGED THROUGH PENN STATION, NOT GRAND CENTRAL.
DAILY BUGLE NEWS ARCHIVES
OCTOBOTS RIOT AT GRAND CENTRAL
OH?
THANK YOU FOR YOUR EFFORTS, MS. MARVEL. AND BE PATIENT. YOUR DAY WILL COME. I LIKE WHAT I SAW TODAY.
YEAH.
SHE SEEM OKAY TO YOU?
THAT GIRL'S MANAGING QUITE A HEAVY LOAD FOR SOMEONE HER AGE.
PLUS, I THINK SHE WAS HOPING YOU'D SLIP HER YOUR BUSINESS CARD, OR A S.H.I.E.L.D. BADGE, OR SOMETHING...
"...BUT I THINK SHE'LL BE ALL RIGHT."
Call me if it all gets a bit much. Also, it was absolutely The Animator.
--J.

CONTINUED IN *S.H.I.E.L.D. VOL. 1: PERFECT BULLETS*

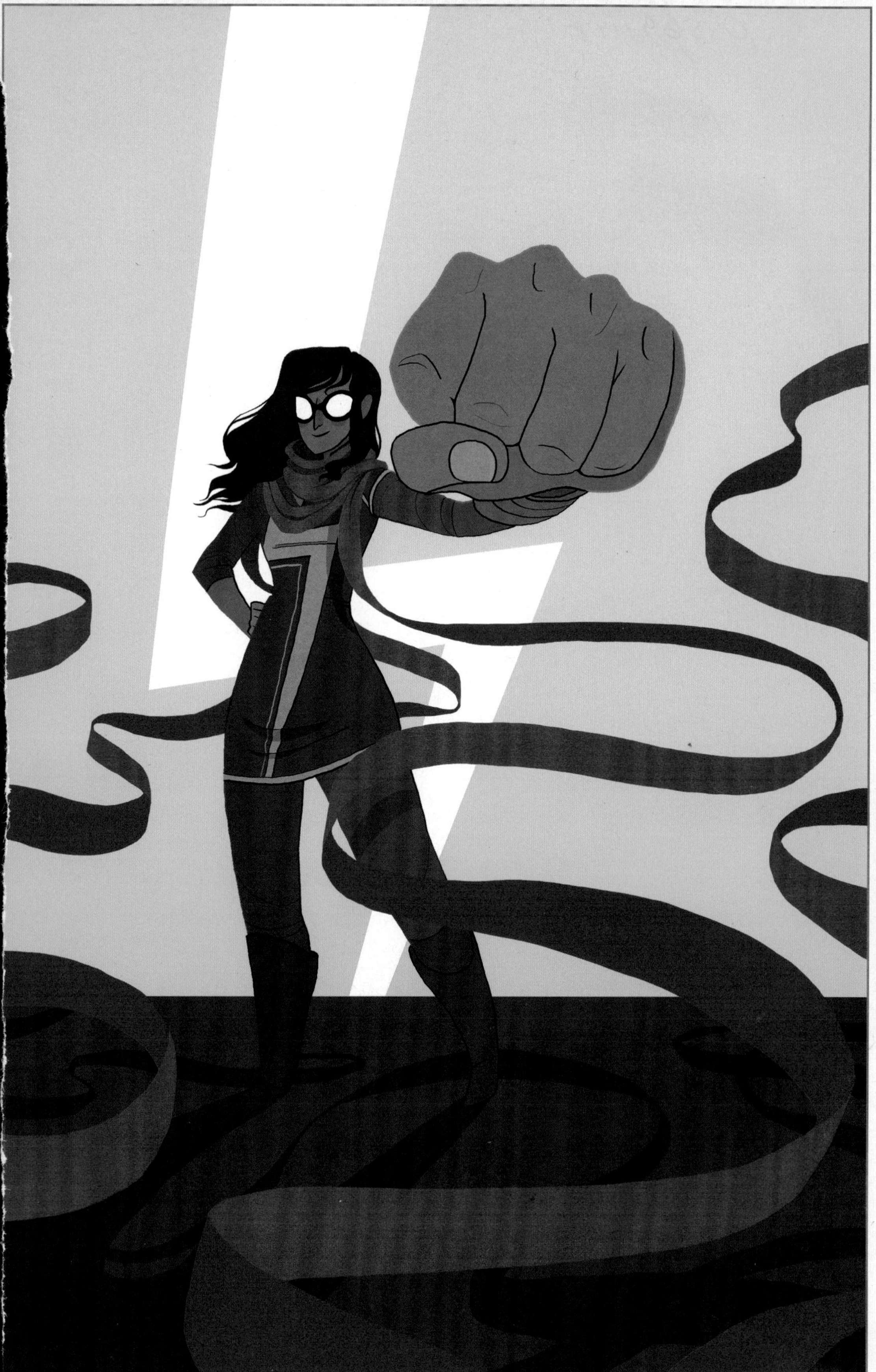

MS. MARVEL #13 WOMEN OF MARVEL VARIANT
BY NOELLE STEVENSON

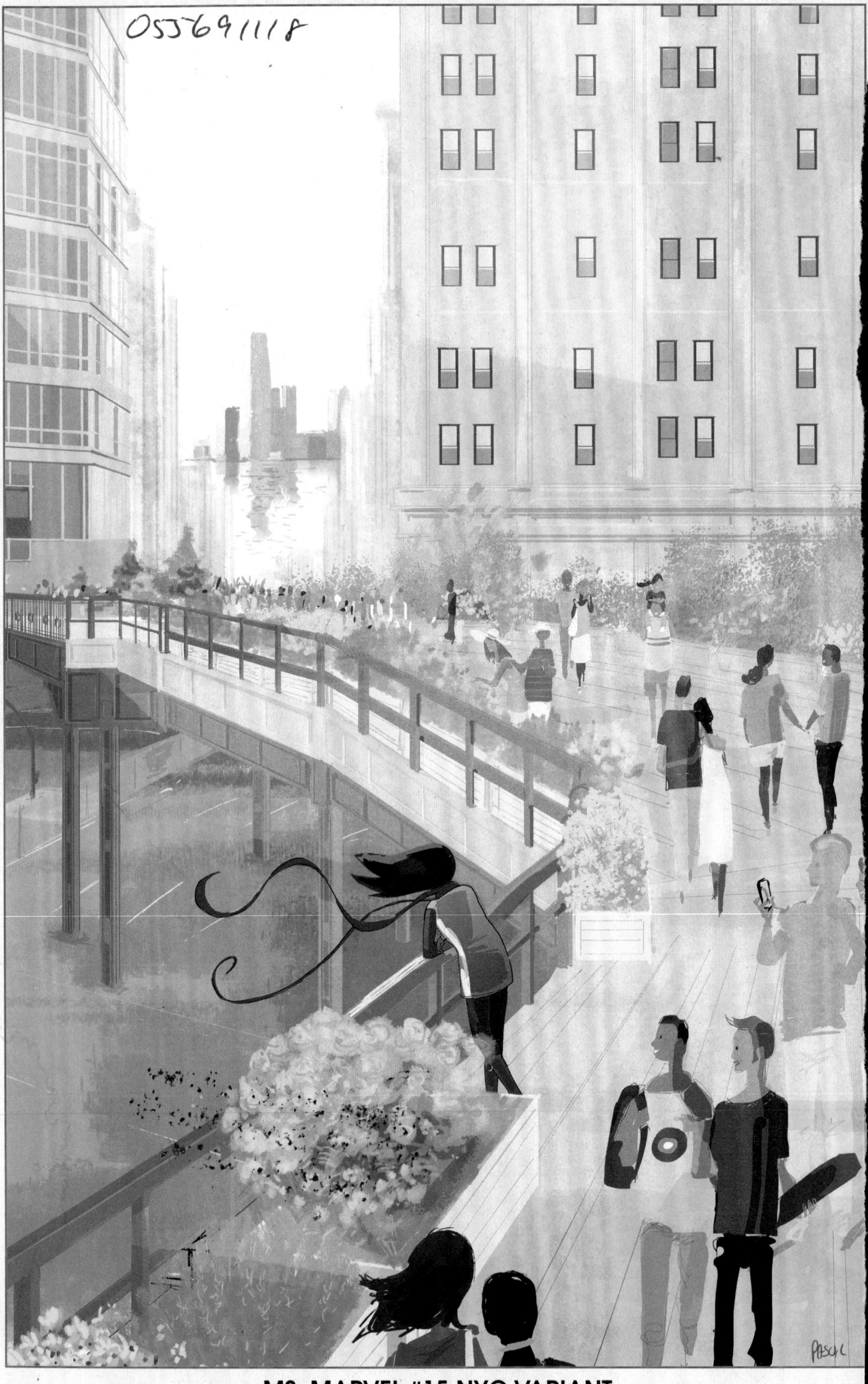
PASCAL

MS. MARVEL #15 NYC VARIANT

BY PASCAL CAMPION